Massage Therapist Student Handbook

A Custom Publication for Corinthian Colleges

Corinthian Colleges, Inc.

CCi
CORINTHIAN
COLLEGES, INC.

SAUNDERS
ELSEVIER

SAUNDERS
ELSEVIER

11830 Westline Industrial Drive
St. Louis, Missouri 63146

Notice

Neither the Publisher nor the Editors assume any responsibility for any loss or injury and/or damage to persons or property arising out of or related to any use of the material contained in this book. It is the responsibility of the treating practitioner, relying on independent expertise and knowledge of the patient, to determine the best treatment and method of application for the patient.

The Publisher

ISBN-13: 978-1-4160-3958-7
ISBN-10: 1-4160-3958-9

Managing Editor: Lynne Gery
Developmental Editor: Barbara Cicalese
Publishing Services Manager: Pat Joiner
Project Managers: Jennifer Clark and Gena Magouirk
Designer: Mark Oberkrom

Printed in the United States of America.

Last digit is the print number: 9 8 7 6 5 4

Credits

Editor and Project Manager
Melissa Wollin, MT, BS, Curriculum Manager, Health Sciences, Santa Ana, CA

Some material in this book is adapted from the following sources:

Career Development for Health Professionals, Chapters 1-3 and 9-11, 2nd edition, Lee Haroun, 2005, Saunders, Philadelphia.

Learning Strategies for Allied Health Students, Revised Edition, Chapters 4-8, Susan Marcus Palau and Marilyn Meltzer, 2007, Saunders, St. Louis.

Step-by-Step Medical Coding, Appendix D, 2005 Edition, Carol J. Buck, Saunders, Philadelphia.

Dental Assistant Student Handbook, Appendix B, Corinthian Colleges, Inc., 2005, Saunders, Philadelphia.

Essential Sciences for Therapeutic Massage, 2nd edition, Sandy Fritz and M. James Grosenbach, 2004, Mosby, St. Louis.

Fundamentals of Therapeutic Massage, 3rd edition, Sandy Fritz, 2004, Mosby, St. Louis.

Massage Therapy, 2nd edition, Susan G. Salvo, 2003, Saunders, Philadelphia.

Contents

PART I

About Corinthian Colleges, Inc. (CCi)

Corinthian Colleges, Inc. was founded in 1995 and completed an initial public offering in 1999. As of June 30, 2007, Corinthian Colleges, Inc. had approximately 8,950 employees in North America, including 3,674 full-time and part-time faculty members. As of June 30, 2007, Corinthian Colleges, Inc. operated 93 schools in 24 states, operated 17 schools in the province of Ontario, Canada, and served the large and growing segment of the population seeking to acquire career-oriented education. Through hard work, dedication, and vision, Corinthian Colleges, Inc. is managed by an experienced executive team with considerable industry, operations, marketing, financial, and regulatory knowledge.

The mission of Corinthian Colleges, Inc. is to help students prepare for new careers or to advance in their chosen careers. With more than 62,000 students, Corinthian Colleges, Inc. is one of the largest post-secondary educational companies in North America and Canada. Corinthian Colleges, Inc. offers short-term diploma programs and associate's, bachelor's, and master's degrees for occupations in demand. Corinthian Colleges, Inc. main program areas include healthcare, criminal justice, business, information technology, transportation technology and maintenance, and construction trades. In addition, Corinthian Colleges, Inc. offers online degree programs that include business, accounting, criminal justice, paralegal, and information technology.

GROWTH STRATEGY

Our growth strategy consists of the following components:

Enhance Growth and Existing Campuses

Integrated and Centralized Marketing Program. We employ an integrated marketing program that utilizes an extensive direct response advertising campaign delivered through television, the Internet, newspaper, and direct mail. A professional marketing staff at our campus support center coordinates marketing efforts with advertising agencies and utilizes our in-bound call center and our lead-tracking capability.

Curriculum Expansion and Development. We develop, refine, and acquire curricula based on market research and recommendations from our faculty, advisory board members, and our curriculum development team. We believe considerable opportunities exist for curriculum adoption and we expect to continue to acquire and develop new curricula and selectively adopt existing curricula into both existing and new locations. In fiscal 2007, we successfully adopted 58 programs into existing U.S. schools and 14 programs into existing Canadian schools.

Facilities Enhancement and Expansion. We remodel, expand, and relocate our existing colleges to ensure we have sufficient capacity to meet our expected enrollment demand, as well as to improve the location and appearance of our facilities. We expect to continue to systematically remodel and relocate selected colleges within their respective markets. Since 2003, 32 colleges have been relocated, and an additional 107 campuses have been either remodeled or enlarged. We believe modern attractive education environments enhance our students' learning experience. During fiscal 2007, we remodeled, relocated, or expanded

8 colleges. As of June 30, 2007, the total square footage of all our properties was approximately 4.8 million square feet.

OPERATING STRATEGY

Key elements of Corinthian Colleges, Inc. operating strategy include the following components:

Emphasize Student Outcomes. Corinthian Colleges, Inc. believes that positive student outcomes are a critical component of our long-term success. Accordingly, Corinthian Colleges, Inc. devotes substantial resources to maintaining and improving the retention and placement rates. Corinthian Colleges, Inc. has implemented a variety of student service programs, including orientation and tutoring, academic advising, ride-sharing, and referral programs, all of which are designed to improve student retention to assist our students in achieving their career goals. Utilization of a curriculum development team comprised of campus representatives, corporate program directors, and textbook publishers, which is assisted by the advisory board comprised of local business professionals, to help ensure that our curricula provide our students with the skills required by employers. Corinthian Colleges, Inc. has also maintain dedicated career services personnel at the schools that undertake extensive placement efforts, including identifying prospective employers, helping students prepare resumes, conducting practice interviews, establishing externship programs, and tracking students' placement success on a monthly basis.

Create a Supportive Learning Environment. Corinthian Colleges, Inc. views the students as customers and seeks to provide a supportive learning environment where student satisfaction is achieved. The wide variety of campuses offer flexible schedule of classes, providing our students with the opportunity to attend classes throughout the day, as well as nights and weekends. Schools operate year-round, permitting students to complete their course of study quickly. The campuses maintain reasonable class sizes and focus the efforts of our faculty on teaching students rather than research. Personal interaction between students and faculty is encouraged, and we offer several support programs, such as on-campus advising and tutoring, which are designed to help students successfully com-

plete their courses of study. Corinthian Colleges, Inc. also maintains a toll-free student hotline to address and help resolve student concerns.

CCI BRANDS

Corinthian Colleges changes lives by providing students the skills they need to pursue the careers they want. This is done through two distinct school brands. Each brand was developed to offer essential skills and training to students in a variety of practical fields.

Everest

Everest campuses offer diploma and/or degree programs in the health care, business, and computer technology career field. There are over 100 Everest campuses located across the United States and Canada. Popular programs include accounting, business administration, dental assisting, massage therapy, medical assisting, medical insurance billing and coding, paralegal, and pharmacy technician.

> *Everest includes the following:*
> Everest College
> Everest College of Business, Technology and
> Health Care (Canada)
> Everest Institute
> Everest University
> Everest University Online, a division of Everest
> University
> Everest College Online, a division of Everest
> College Phoenix

WyoTech

WyoTech is dedicated to college-level, career-oriented education in the automotive, diesel, motorcycle, watercraft, HVAC, electrician, and plumbing fields. The WyoTech campuses are located in: Blairsville, Pennsylvania; Daytona, Florida; Fremont, California; Laramie, Wyoming; Long Beach, California; and Sacramento, California.

Unlike traditional post-secondary institutions, we provide an education that is focused on the job-oriented needs of nontraditional students in a learning environment that fosters on-the-job success. We also go one step further by helping our graduates find the right jobs and, in the process, helping employers find the skilled workers they need.

Operational Structure

Operations at all Corinthian locations are coordinated through the executive vice president of operations, divisional presidents, regional vice presidents of operations, and regional vice presidents of admissions.

At the campus level, an academic dean or education director as well as admissions, placement, and finance directors assist a college president; the staff at corporate headquarters oversees the student body, individual campuses, and regional and divisional territories.

Integration Process. Acquired and new branch campuses have been successfully integrated into our operational structure since the original founding of the company. Prior to purchasing or opening a new campus, we develop intensive infrastructure and marketing plans to ensure a smooth transition, as well as optimize capital expenditures and marketing and acquisition investments.

ON-LINE EDUCATION

Online education, or education delivered via the Internet, has become an increasingly important component of the higher education market. The online programs are designed to prepare students for successful employment in the workplace. The courses emphasize real-world training that is tailored to meet the needs of potential employers. Corinthian Colleges offer online learning to two categories of students: those attending online classes exclusively and those attending a blend of traditional classroom and online courses. The majority of our students participating in online learning are now registered in exclusively online programs.

Corinthian Colleges, Inc. began enrolling exclusively online students through our Florida Metropolitan University (FMU) colleges in fiscal 2002. In the fourth quarter of fiscal 2005, we started to offer exclusively online degrees through our regionally accredited Everest College in Phoenix, Arizona. Online degree programs are offered in business, criminal justice, accounting, higher education management, criminal investigations, applied management, homeland security, computer information science, and medical insurance billing and coding. In total, 18 accredited degrees are available exclusively online at the master's, bachelor's, and associate's levels.

During fiscal 2007, Corinthian Colleges, Inc. experienced a significant increase in the number of students taking our online courses. Our online learning participation increased by approximately 28% to 107,111 course registrations in fiscal 2007. As of June 30, 2007, Corinthian Colleges, Inc. offered 259 online courses through 30 campuses serving approximately 8,015 exclusively online students.

MISSION STATEMENT

We create, acquire, and operate educational units that deliver quality instruction at a fair price, while maintaining full regulatory compliance and ensuring an appropriate financial return to investors.

PART II

Chapter 1

Your Career Starts Now

YOUR FIRST STEP ON THE ROAD TO SUCCESS

"Today is the first day of the rest of your life."

Congratulations! By choosing to study for a career in health care, you have taken the first step toward achieving a productive and satisfying future. You have made a significant **commitment** to yourself and your community. By enrolling in an educational program, you have demonstrated your ability to set your sights on the future, make important decisions, and follow through with action. You have proved you have the strong personal foundation on which you can build the skills and **habits** needed to ensure your success in school and in your career.

The purpose of this book is to help you succeed in this building process by sharing the knowledge and techniques that have helped other students achieve their goals. It is written with the hope that you will apply what you learn here to maximize your investment in education, secure the job that you want after graduation, and find satisfaction in your career as a competent and caring health care professional.

Connecting School and Career

The process of becoming a health care professional began the day you started classes. In addition to learning important technical skills, this process involves acquiring the **attitudes,** personal characteristics, and habits of a successful professional. What you think and do while in school will determine, to a great extent, the quality of the professional you will become. Students who demonstrate good work habits in school generally carry those same habits into the workplace. The opposite is

true, too. Students who practice poor conduct in school tend to struggle on the job. You are faced with a great opportunity to determine your future. Your career has indeed started now.

The organizational and study skills presented in the first three chapters of this book are designed to help you succeed in school. But they can also be applied to your professional and personal life. In fact, the term "study skills" is misleading, because these skills are not isolated sets of activities restricted to school situations. The skills you will learn have many applications on the job. Let's look at four skills that will be discussed more fully in future chapters. Each one can be applied to your studies, the job search process, and your future work in health care.

1. **Time Management.** For busy people, time is one of their most precious possessions. Juggling class attendance and study time with family responsibilities, work, and time for yourself involves **prioritizing** and careful planning. Your success in school will be heavily influenced by how well you organize your time.

   An effective job search typically requires you to devote time each day to identifying leads, making appointments, attending interviews, and completing follow-up activities. You must allocate adequate amounts of time for these efforts and organize your time to avoid delays that could cost you employment opportunities.

   Once on the job, effective use of time is critical in health care work. Many health care professionals are responsible not only for their own time, but also for planning other people's time. Medical assistants, for example, are often in charge of the physician's daily appointment scheduling, a task that can affect the profitability of the practice. Insurance coders and billers must submit claims on time to avoid rejections and financial losses. Nurses have patient care responsibilities during designated hours, and it is essential they plan a schedule that permits them to see every patient during their shift.

2. **Oral Communication.** Strong communication skills are essential to success. Expressing yourself clearly is important for giving presentations, as well as for asking and answering questions in class. It also contributes to your ability to establish and maintain satisfactory relationships with your instructors and classmates.

A critical part of the job search process is the interview, in which you combine your ability to think clearly and use verbal skills effectively. Feeling confident about expressing yourself will enable you to present your qualifications in a convincing way.

All jobs today require good communication skills. This is especially true in health care because many positions involve constant interaction with others, including patients, co-workers, supervisors, and the general public. Physical and occupational therapy assistants are examples of the many health professionals who provide extensive patient education. The effectiveness of their explanations of exercises and self-care techniques influences the rehabilitation progress of their clients.

3. **Taking Notes.** You may think of note-taking as being limited to use in lecture classes, but this skill is used extensively outside the classroom. During the job search, it will be important to accurately record information about openings, as well as interview appointment dates and times and directions for locating facilities. After interviews, you may want to make notes about the job requirements, additional information you need to send to the prospective employer, and other important facts to remember.

When you become employed, you will be expected to absorb a lot of new information about your facility's rules and procedures, the location of supplies and equipment, people's names, and many other details. You can use your note-taking skills to create a personal reference notebook, a resource that will increase your efficiency on the job. Note-taking is also an important health care job skill. Many professionals are responsible for interviewing patients and taking notes on special forms called patient histories. Another specialized form of medical note-taking is called charting.

Charting involves writing notes on patient medical records, which include information about symptoms, treatments, and medications prescribed. Both procedures affect patient care and require total accuracy. Medical records are legal documents and their quality depends on the professional's note-taking ability.

4. **Taking Tests.** You may think you have escaped the dreaded test once you leave school, but testing is not limited to the classroom. The truth is that life is full of tests. Job interviews are a form of test designed to assess your ability to present yourself and your qualifications. Many health care occupations, such as licensed practical nurse, radiologic technologist, and physical therapist, require you to pass a professional exam before you can work legally. Other occupations, such as medical assisting, have voluntary tests to obtain certification that improves your chances of getting a job.

Once on the job, you are in a sense, being tested every day. Although you may not think of your everyday tasks as tests, they are applications of what you have learned, and your ability to perform them correctly will be noted by your patients, coworkers, and supervisor. The annual employee performance evaluation may be considered a type of test in which your supervisor writes a report about your work and then meets with you to discuss it. Learning to perform "when it counts" is a valuable skill and represents the ultimate ability to take and successfully pass a test. The mother of an infant wants to know that the health care professional giving the injection has "passed the test" and is qualified to safely perform this task.

From these examples you can see that skills traditionally labeled personal or school skills have valuable applications during the job search and on the job. Throughout this book you will continue to see how "school skills" are also valuable job skills.

Maximizing Your Education

You are making a significant investment of time, effort, and money in your education. You can simply get by, doing only what is required to pass your classes, or you can fully benefit from this investment. A worthy personal goal is to do everything possible to become the best health care professional possible. Both you and your school have responsibilities to ensure that this happens.

Your Rights as a Student

"Making mistakes is inevitable. Not learning from them is inexcusable."

1. **Make Mistakes.** You may think this sounds a little strange. After all, aren't you supposed to do the best you can, earning the highest grades possible? Yes, but many students see grades as ends in themselves, rather than as signs of having mastered the skills needed in the future. Good grades do not guarantee mastery, nor do you receive grades for all the skills that will determine your future success.

   Many students want to know "what's on the test" so they can focus their efforts on learning only what they will be tested on. But think about it—can you possibly be tested on everything you will need to master to perform your job? If you were, all class time would have to be devoted to testing, leaving little or no time for learning! Studying only what you need to pass tests and earn grades may make you a "good student," but a good student is not necessarily a good health care professional.

   Compare your educational experience with learning to ride a bike. First, you use training wheels, go slowly, and tip over once in a while. Eventually you become a proficient cyclist, ready for the big race. School offers you a rehearsal for professional life, providing you with opportunities to learn from mistakes that would be unacceptable if you made them on the job. If you do not score 100% on an exam, it has still served you by allowing you to make mistakes and learn from them so you avoid making them on the job when the consequences are more serious. The health care worker may have made mistakes when practicing the use of a walker with a classmate. But she learned from them and is now able to use correct techniques to help her patients.

2. **Ask Questions.** You are attending school to benefit from the knowledge and experience of your instructors. Take advantage of this opportunity by being an active participant in your classes. Don't be an invisible student. Even if the textbooks and lectures are excellent, you may still need to ask for explanations, examples, and additional resources. If there is anything you don't understand, ask questions. Students aren't expected to understand everything the first time they hear or read it—maybe not even the second time. Consider this: there would be no need for you to attend school at all if you already knew the information presented in your program!

   Many adults are afraid of "looking stupid" and hesitate to admit they don't understand or are confused. However, failure to ask questions not only decreases the chances of maximizing your education, it prevents you from learning a critical health care skill—asking questions. Consider the serious consequences for professionals who are not sure of drug dosages or steps in a procedure but are afraid to ask their supervisors for direction. In these situations, risking the well-being of patients is indeed stupid, while asking questions demonstrates intelligence. Start learning now to be comfortable asking questions. If it is too difficult for you to speak up in class the first few times you have questions, start out by speaking with your instructor at the break, after class, or during office hours.

   You should not use questions, however, to substitute for reading your textbook or studying assigned material before each class meeting, because this results in the misuse of class time and is unfair to those students who are prepared. A related on-the-job example is employees who arrive late and unprepared for meetings, thus wasting their coworkers' time. Develop habits that show consideration for others and will contribute now to the efficiency of the classroom and later to the workplace.

3. **Take Advantage of School Resources.** Every school wants every student who enrolls to graduate, and considerable resources are spent on services to support this effort. Find out now what services are available to you, the hours they can be accessed, and whether appointments are necessary. Two of the most important services that all students should become familiar with are the library (or resource center) and career services (sometimes called job placement).

   If you are having personal problems or academic difficulties, ask whether your school provides counseling and/or tutoring. Some schools refer their students to outside agencies that offer assistance for difficulties such as dealing with domestic abuse and finding reliable child care. Asking for help when you need it can make the difference between dropping out or graduating and becoming successfully employed.

The school catalog is an often overlooked information resource that can help you succeed in school. Many students never take the time to read it and, as a result, are unaware of available resources. Even worse, they risk unknowingly breaking rules or missing important deadlines. Spend a few minutes becoming an informed student by reading the catalog and other printed information. On the job, you will likely be expected to read organizational handbooks and procedure manuals. Getting in the habit of reading informational literature is a good job skill.

Your Responsibilities as a Student

1. **Attend All Scheduled Learning Activities.** Health care educational programs feature a variety of learning opportunities including lectures, lab sessions, guest speakers, field trips, and hands-on experiences in health care facilities. Your instructor may also recommend additional activities outside of those organized by the school, such as watching a television documentary, attending a professional meeting, or visiting a medical supply company. These activities are designed to help you to understand and master all the knowledge and skills necessary for your future work, as well as providing exposure to your future work environment. You cannot afford to miss them. They are opportunities to develop the competencies essential for working in health care. Learning to perform essential tasks, such as the administration of injections, requires you to spend time and put forth effort under the guidance of your instructors. Now is the time for learning and making mistakes, not when you are faced with your first patient. Your ability to properly perform tasks that affect the well-being of others makes it essential that you fully participate in every learning activity offered in your program.

Employers routinely request information about a student's attendance record. Good attendance is considered a valuable job skill because health care services are driven by time requirements. The success of a private physician's practice depends heavily on efficient patient scheduling and service. Hospitals have daily responsibilities for performing hundreds of treatments, procedures, and surgeries that must be completed in a timely way. In both settings, effective care can be provided only if the staff is available to perform their work. Patients

who need help should not have to wait because someone didn't show up for work. Start now to develop the habit of consistent and punctual attendance.

2. **Apply Your Best Efforts to Learning.** As a student, you have the right to ask questions and make mistakes. At the same time, it is your responsibility to complete all reading, written, and lab assignments and to participate actively in class. Instructors cannot cover everything you are expected to know. Understanding and applying new information can be challenging, and the study techniques and suggestions for learning presented in the following chapters are intended to help you succeed as a student.

In performing your work as a health care professional, you will encounter new situations in which you will apply what you learned in school. To be successful, you must now focus on your studies, work hard, and be persistent. The willingness to do the "shoulds" when you would rather be doing the "wants" is a major determinant of student success. You will not always feel like studying after a day that may include classes, a few hours on the job, and family responsibilities. Being an adult student is not always easy. Keeping your long-term career goals clearly in mind will help you find the self-discipline to stick with it.

3. **Ask for Help When You Need It.** Instructors and administrators want to help their students succeed. Educators are interested in helping students complete their programs and graduate. At the same time, you must take responsibility for requesting assistance. Ignoring problems will not solve them; they usually only get worse. Don't wait until you are hopelessly lost in a class and cannot possibly be ready for the upcoming final exam before asking for help. Take charge of your learning and at the first sign of trouble, ask about tutoring, study groups, computer labs, and any other learning resources available through the school.

Remember that asking for help when you need it is a sign of strength, not weakness, and it can be one of the main actions that distinguish a graduate from a dropout.

The flip side of asking for help is being willing to give it. Offer your assistance to others in the school community. Volunteer to hand out papers for the instructor. Give a student who lives in your area a ride to school. Tutor a classmate who is struggling with a subject you find easy. (This doesn't mean sharing your work; it means helping the other person understand and learn.) You have chosen a profession that is based on giving service, and this is a habit you can start practicing now in all areas of your life. Students who give of themselves are the type of people who become indispensable employees.

Planning for Career Success

The time to start thinking about your first job in health care is now as you are starting your educational program. In the following pages, we will look at how you can use job search tools, such as a resume, to help guide you to a successful career.

And the Product Is ... You!

Marketing is a multi-step process that begins with an idea for a new product and ends with the sale of that product. Mastering this process is essential for the survival of any business. Successful marketing is similar to successfully starting a new career. You—the combination of your skills, characteristics, and talents—are the product. To make sure you have the skills and qualities needed by employers, you must prepare appropriately for the workplace and learn to present yourself effectively during the job search.

The marketing process can be organized into a five-part plan called the "Five Ps of Marketing":
1. **P**lanning
2. **P**roduction
3. **P**ackaging
4. **P**resentation
5. **P**romotion

You can use the 5 Ps to develop your own personal marketing plan now, as you begin your health care studies, to help ensure future career success. We will discuss the first P, Planning, in this chapter and the remaining four Ps in Chapter 10.

PLANNING: THE FIRST "P" OF MARKETING

"Give yourself a running start."

Studying the needs of customers is called market research, and its purpose is to find out what customers want. Your customers will include your future employers and patients. Waiting until the end of your educational program to think about getting a job is like creating a product without doing market

research. Designing and manufacturing a product that no one wants or needs doesn't make sense. Just like a business, you are investing time, effort, and money in the development of yourself as a product.

What Do Employers Want?

In recent years, employers in all industries have expressed concerns that entry-level workers are not adequately prepared for the modern workplace. Employers are looking for job candidates who are not only qualified technically, but who bring essential supporting skills such as the ability to communicate effectively, work cooperatively with others, accept responsibility, and solve problems. These skills are especially critical in the health care industry, because it is service-based and depends heavily on the quality of its personnel. This is even truer today as health care facilities strive to provide higher quality care at lower costs.

National Health Care Skill Standards. A project of special interest to future health care professionals is the National Health Care Skill Standards, a list of entry-level worker competencies. Box 1-1 contains examples that apply to all health care

---

Box 1-1   Examples of National Health Care Skill Standards and Accountability Criteria

Health Care Workers Will:
- Follow attendance policies of the employer or educational institution
- Adopt personal appearance and hygiene habits appropriate to the health care environment and industry expectations
- Understand accepted **ethical** practices with respect to cultural, social, and **ethnic** differences within the health care environment
- Encourage the practice of preventive health behaviors among their clients
- Communicate effectively, both verbally and in writing
- Demonstrate courtesy to others
- Practice personal integrity and honesty
- Maintain confidentiality
- Demonstrate professionalism when interacting with fellow students, coworkers, and the organization
- Act responsibly as a team member, completing assigned tasks in a timely and effective manner

occupations. You can see that they are not limited to technical skills, like taking a blood pressure, but include the ability to communicate, maintain good attendance, and demonstrate responsibility. Some employers report that these so-called "soft skills" are as important as technical skills when providing good health care.

Did you notice how many standards mention the ability to communicate well? The lack of effective communication skills among health care workers is reportedly the leading contributor to patient dissatisfaction and personnel problems in health care facilities. Your future success can be greatly enhanced by your ability to listen and to convey information effectively.

Professional Organizations. Many professional organizations that represent specific health care occupations have statements outlining the characteristics needed to work in their fields.

What Do Patients Want?

Patients want to receive competent care delivered with consideration and respect. When seeking health care, people are often at their most **vulnerable.** They fear what might be discovered during a diagnostic test or that they will experience pain during a necessary treatment. The **self-esteem** of patients can be threatened by a feeling of powerlessness that often accompanies illness and injury.

Many patients want to participate in making decisions about their care. They have the right, both ethically and legally, to be fully informed about their conditions, treatment options, and possible outcomes. Health care professionals must give clear explanations in everyday language and offer patients the opportunity to ask questions and receive honest answers. At the same time, patients want and have the legal right to confidentiality. As a health care professional, you must guard the privacy of your patients. Without the patient's permission, nothing can be discussed with anyone other than the health care team members directly involved with the patient's care, and all files and paperwork must be securely stored.

Changes in American society and the development of managed care organizations, designed to control medical costs, have brought special challenges for patients as well as for health care professionals. In the past, many people had the same physician throughout their lives. Doctor and patient belonged to the same community, and a sense of trust developed over the years. Patients today may see a different physician each time they visit their health care facility. They may face a serious illness or life-threatening situation in the care of a stranger, adding to the stress of an already difficult situation. Studies have shown that patients who belong to a caring, supportive community recover more successfully than patients who don't. Providing a supportive health care community can improve patient outcomes. As a health care professional, you can demonstrate a caring attitude that helps develop a bond of trust with patients by being attentive, listening carefully, and practicing empathy.

Health care professionals today face the challenge of working with patients from many different ethnic backgrounds, some of whom have beliefs about health care practices that differ from those of traditional Western medicine. Patients also come from many different economic and social groups. They may have lifestyles or personal beliefs with which you disagree. All patients have the right to be respected and to receive appropriate, high-level care, regardless of your personal opinions about them. Every patient deserves your best efforts.

Patients seek help in solving their health problems, but your responsibilities in meeting their needs go beyond performing a painless blood draw, giving effective breathing treatments, or sending out accurate bills for payment. You must be willing to combine a caring attitude with technical competence by treating each patient as worthy of your full attention.

The Patient Care Partnership. Health care organizations have formally recognized the rights of patients to receive proper care. The American Hospital Association has written a brochure for patients entitled "The Patient Care Partnership: Understand Expectations, Rights and Responsibilities" that many health care facilities nationwide use. These include, among others, the rights of patients to:

☐ be treated with compassion and respect
☐ receive information about the benefits and risks of treatments
☐ have their privacy protected
☐ participate in making decisions regarding their care, including the right to refuse treatment
☐ have their health goals and values taken into account as much as possible

What Do You Want?

"If you don't know where you're going, chances are you'll end up somewhere else."

In addition to exploring the needs of your customers, an important part of planning is to identify what you want. You must consider your own needs and desires as you create your professional self. The clearer you are about your career goals and expectations, the greater the chance you have of achieving them.

Beginning now to think about your specific career goals and workplace priorities will keep you alert to appropriate employment possibilities as you go through your educational program. Take every opportunity during your studies to observe, ask questions, and read about your field. Then compare your findings with your own interests. Many fields in health care today feature newly created positions and expanded responsibilities for traditional jobs. A wide variety of choices is available for new graduates. Being aware of these opportunities improves your chances of finding employment that matches your interests and preferences.

Developing a Philosophy of Work. Most of us spend a significant number of our waking hours on the job. How we spend that time determines, to a great degree, the quality of our lives. It makes sense, then, to think about what work means to you. Exploring your personal beliefs will help you increase the amount of satisfaction you get from your career. The following list contains a variety of reasons why people work:

☐ Survive financially
☐ Define self
☐ Gain self-respect
☐ Demonstrate competence
☐ Gain power
☐ Help others
☐ Learn
☐ Experience variety
☐ Contribute to the community
☐ Experience enjoyment
☐ Fill time

People are generally happiest and most productive when their work provides them with more than material rewards. Some people are motivated by continual challenges, others value consistency, and still others are content with either condition as long as their work allows them to help others.

Health care is a complex, ever-changing field that offers both opportunities and challenges for those who choose to work in it. Here are some of the major sources of satisfaction you can expect to experience.

1. **Meaningful Work.** Good health is a basic need for both human survival and happiness. Working in a field that promotes health gives you the opportunity to make meaningful contributions to the well-being of others. Whether you provide direct patient care or perform supporting activities, your work directly affects patients, and the quality of your work can truly make a difference in their lives. A career in health care has purpose and value.

2. **Opportunity to Serve.** People seek the services of health care professionals when they need help. They come with the hope you can help them solve their problems, and they entrust themselves to your care. You have opportunities to enter both the physical and emotional space of others, sharing close personal contact. People who are ill or injured are often afraid and anxious. You are in a position to influence their recovery.

3. **Career Stability.** The need for health care will always exist, even if job titles change over time. The reorganization taking place in today's health care delivery systems is causing continual shifts in the need for specific occupational positions. A decrease in the number of job openings for one position is often balanced by an increase in another. You may need to redefine your job in the future, but you will always have a solid knowledge base on which you can add the experience or training needed to qualify for new positions.

4. **Interesting Work Environment.** The world of health care is changing at a rapid rate, both scientifically and organizationally. Advances in our understanding of how the body works, along with discoveries about the causes and treatments of diseases, are reported almost weekly. Computers have increased our capacity to collect and organize information, as well as provided us with a sophisticated tool that is itself constantly being upgraded. Medical scientists are making discoveries at an astounding rate. You will witness advances in knowledge that extend and improve the quality of human life. The health care environment is never boring. There will be a steady stream of interesting information to learn, apply, and use.

5. **Opportunities for Advancement.** The health care field provides many opportunities for upward mobility if you are willing to continue learning and adding to your skills. Many jobs offer opportunities for on-the-job learning that enable you to increase your value to your patients and employer, as well as your eligibility for promotion. In addition, many occupational specialties in health care present the chance for **career laddering.** Career ladders are jobs within one occupational area requiring different amounts of knowledge and skills. The higher level positions almost always require further education and additional **certifications** or **licenses,** which are official approvals for working in a specific occupation. (You will learn more about these approvals in Chapter 10.)

Work Preferences. It is also a good idea to begin thinking about the kinds of tasks you like to do and the working conditions you prefer. A wide variety of work settings exists for health care professionals. Being clear about your own preferences will help you choose and prepare for the most appropriate types of positions in your career area.

Alignment with Employers. While it is important to try to meet your personal needs when seeking employment, you must also have realistic expectations. An essential activity in career planning is to compare your work preferences with the needs of potential employers to see how well they match. Students sometimes have unrealistic goals for the positions they hope to fill immediately following graduation. Recent graduates are qualified for entry-level positions. You can avoid frustration and disappointment if you understand the workplace and adjust your expectations. This way, you can maximize the benefits of your first work experiences in health care.

Formal training is only the beginning of your journey to developing competence as a health care professional. Your skills will continue to grow and be refined as you accumulate hands-on practice and everyday experience in the field. When starting a new career, it may be wise—even necessary—to trade your "perfect job" requirements for opportunities that lead to long-term career success. Consider looking for a first-time job that allows you to do the following:

1. Gain self-confidence
2. Work with a variety of people
3. Acquire additional knowledge
4. Increase your skill base
5. Explore specialties within your field of interest
6. Network with other professionals
7. Demonstrate your abilities

Your first employer is giving you the gift of his or her confidence in your abilities. You will be entrusted with serious responsibilities that may include patient welfare, accuracy and confidentiality of important records, and other matters that influence the reputation and success of the facility. You will have a chance to prove your value by learning as much as possible, finding ways to help your employer and coworkers, and contributing to the overall success of the organization. Entry-level jobs, performed well, can be the first important step leading to positions that meet all your hopes for a fulfilling career.

Alignment with Your Profession. Health care professions vary in the type of work performed. You need to be aware of the daily tasks and working conditions of the occupation you have chosen. For example, respiratory therapy and radiology require the technical aptitude to work with complex equipment. Occupational therapy requires the ability to apply oral communication skills to teach patients and their families. Health information technology and insurance coding require accuracy and attention to detail when creating, filling out, and organizing medical records and forms.

You may need to consider trade-offs to obtain a balance that offers maximum career satisfaction. For example, a recent nursing graduate who wants the excitement of a hospital emergency room and the convenience of a 9:00 a.m. to 5:00 p.m. weekday schedule may have a conflict. To avoid a mismatch between your expectations and the real world, learn as much as possible about the specific requirements of your future profession so you can rethink and reprioritize your requirements, if necessary.

Adjusting your short-term expectations doesn't mean giving up your long-term goals. In fact, purposeful planning now can help you arrive where you want to be in the future. If you discover that the specific type of job you want requires previous work experience, you can set short-term goals to serve as stepping stones to acquire that experience. Find out now what skills are emphasized in your target position and look for opportunities to learn as many of them as possible during your studies,

clinical experience, and first job. For example, Rosa wants to work as a back-office assistant with a plastic surgeon, helping the physician with outpatient procedures. Her research shows there are only a few plastic surgeons in her area and they prefer to hire assistants with previous work experience. Rosa decides to look for a job with a general practitioner or pediatrician who does minor surgery in the office. Her short-term goals are to gain experience with **sterile technique, standard precautions,** surgical assisting, and patient care. While in school, she asks her instructor to recommend references about plastic surgery and to allow her to spend extra practice time in the lab so she can reach a high level of competence with sterile technique, surgical instruments, wound care, and related topics.

Employees who are willing to meet the expectations of their employers are often rewarded with additional (and interesting!) responsibilities and promotions. Some employers even create new positions so they can use the talents of their employees. For new health care professionals who are well prepared and who contribute enthusiastically to the success of their employers, entry-level jobs can serve as launch pads for career success. You, too, may benefit by having new and interesting responsibilities added to your job description, receiving a promotion, or having a job created that brings you satisfaction. Serving the needs of others can provide you with opportunities to meet your own needs.

Chapter 2

Developing Your Personal Skills

SETTING UP YOUR MISSION CONTROL

Starting on a new career path is a lot like launching a spacecraft. Both students and astronauts are entering new worlds, and to be successful, their missions require careful planning and preparation. Final destinations must be clearly defined so progress can be continually monitored and adjusted as needed for the journey to stay on target.

A helpful activity when planning a career launch is writing a mission statement. Stephen Covey, the author of personal success books, suggests mission statements as a way to identify what is really important to you. Individual mission statements are based on personal values. Values are our beliefs about what is important in life. They are the result of the teachings of family, school, religion, and friends as well as our experiences in life. Values provide a foundation for making important life decisions, such as what we hope to contribute to the world, how we perform our work, and what we believe our obligations are to others and to ourselves.

A personal mission statement can help you choose an appropriate destination and then stay on track until you arrive. Many people, Covey points out, get sidetracked in life because they either lose sight of their basic values or fail to identify them clearly in the first place. Developing a mission statement as you begin your career can help you clarify and state what is important to you: your basic beliefs about how you want to live your life and what you want to accomplish. Mission statements are usually written out, but there is no set format. You might want to write yours as a list, a series of paragraphs, or even a letter addressed to yourself. If you prefer, you can create a poster or collage, with each picture illustrating a value.

Mission statements help you focus your attention on the purposes that guide your life and can serve as powerful motivators when you feel adrift or discouraged. For example, if you are committed to the well-being of your future patients, this value, rather than the need to pass a test, should guide your studying. Suppose you have an anatomy test tomorrow morning. It is 10:00 p.m. and you have just finished a day filled with classes, work, and family responsibilities. Studying the skeleton becomes more meaningful when placed in the context of your dedication to helping future patients. You are not simply memorizing a collection of bones—you are learning about the source of Mrs. Jones's painful arthritis, and the more you know and understand about the bones and joints, the more you will be able to help her.

Keep in mind throughout your program that your future patients will be directly affected by both what and how you are studying now, so you should be guided by your highest values. Here's another example: your mission statement includes the objective, "Provide high-quality care to all patients." You have an important exam for which you feel unprepared, and you are offered an opportunity to cheat. Cheating may take care of what you believe to be your most urgent need—getting a passing grade. But the consequences of this action—not learning the material and compromising your integrity—do not align with what should be your major goal of competently serving the needs of future patients. A well–thought-out mission statement functions as the control center that keeps guiding you in the right direction toward achieving what is most important to you.

Goals—Signposts on the Path to Success

"The purpose of goals is to motivate, not to paralyze."
—MAUREEN PFEIFER

Goals are based on your mission statement and serve as signposts, giving your life direction and measuring your progress on the road to success. You can use them to motivate yourself and mark your accomplishments.

Effective goals have the following characteristics:

☐ Based on your values and mission statement: The goals help you achieve what you believe to be important in life.

☐ Reasonable: You may have to work hard, but you can accomplish them.

☐ Measurable: You'll know when you have achieved them.

☐ Clearly stated and written: Writing goals greatly increases your chance of reaching them.

☐ Worth your time: They are related to your career success, personal growth, and so on.

Here are two examples of well-stated goals for a health care student:

1. Over the next 10 weeks, I will learn the definition, pronunciation, and spelling of 150 new medical terms.

2. Within the next month, I will attend one professional meeting and talk with at least two people I have not met before.

Making Goals Work for You

Many people fail to achieve what they want in life because they fail to set clear goals for themselves. The first step, then, to making goals work for you is to spend some time creating them. The next step is to put together an action plan in which you outline what you need to do to reach your goal. Include reasonable deadlines for completing each action. This is also the time to identify and locate any resources you will need to carry out your action plan. Examples of resources include people, materials, classes, equipment, and money. Greg, a medical transcription student, is taking a medical terminology course.

Make working on goals a part of your daily life. What can you do each day—even if it is something small—to move closer to achieving them? Long-term goals often get put aside in the scramble to meet everyday obligations, so it's a good idea to periodically review your goals to track your progress.

Long-Term Goals. Goals vary in the time and effort required to achieve them. Write your long-term goals first; then prepare short-term supporting goals. Link them together in a progressive series so each one supports the next. For example, Jaime's long-term career goal is to become successfully employed as an x-ray technician in a large city hospital. Here is his plan:

Long-Term Goal: Employment as an x-ray technician.

Supporting Goals: Graduate from an approved x-ray training program.

☐ Earn at least a B in all courses.

☐ Take a study skills course.

☐ Maintain perfect attendance for all classes.

☐ Complete all homework assignments on time.

☐ Receive a rating of at least "Above Average" on clinical experience.

☐ Pass the state licensing exam on the first try.

As we discussed in Chapter 1, you may have to set short-term employment goals as a means of achieving your long-term ideal job goal. In Jaime's case, he discovers that the large urban hospital where he wants to work hires only technicians who have at least 1 year of experience. Furthermore, they prefer technicians who are able to perform specialized x-rays not taught in most x-ray technology programs. So Jaime adjusts his goals as follows:

Long-Term Goal: Employment in x-ray department at Grand Memorial Hospital

Short-Term Goals: Receive a rating of "Excellent" on clinical experience.

☐ Improve communication skills.

☐ Work for at least 1 year in a facility that performs a variety of x-rays.

☐ Complete three specialized x-ray courses.

☐ Network with local professionals.

☐ Become active in the x-ray professional organization's local chapter.

Jaime knows his clinical experience will provide valuable opportunities to demonstrate his hands-on competence as a technician. This will serve him when he applies for his first job after graduation, as well as supplement his work experience when he applies at Grand Memorial. His action steps to achieve his short-term goals include arranging reliable transportation (his old car is no longer dependable) so he can always arrive at his clinical site on time. By planning ahead, setting goals, and identifying appropriate action steps, Jaime has greatly increased his chances of achieving what he really wants.

Success Tips for Achieving Your Goals

☐ Visualize yourself achieving your goals.
☐ Use affirmations.
☐ Work on goals even when you don't feel like it. (Especially then!)
☐ Don't give up!

It's All in the Attitude

"Man is not disturbed by the things that happened, but by the perception of things that happened."
—CONFUCIUS

Your attitude, the way you mentally look at things, can be your strongest ally or your worst enemy. It is more powerful than physical strength, more important than natural talents, and has helped people overcome seemingly impossible difficulties. Many survivors of concentration and prison camps, for example, attribute their survival to having a positive attitude. The best thing about attitude is that it does not depend on other people or circumstances. It is yours alone, one of the few things in life over which you have complete control.

We hear about positive and negative attitudes to describe how people interpret things. Is the weather partly sunny or partly cloudy? Is a difficult class an opportunity to grow intellectually or a nightmare? Dr. Philip Hwang, a popular professor at the University of San Diego, tells his students he prefers to interpret a popular offensive gesture as "half a peace sign." He chooses his reaction, and this is the key to the power of attitude: we all can choose how we react to any situation.

"Well," you may say, "that doesn't make sense. If someone insults me or I'm having a bad day, it's natural to get angry or feel frustrated." It does seem natural because we are in the habit of responding negatively to situations that are annoying or upsetting. But how does this benefit you? In most cases, nothing is gained except bad feelings. For example, if you develop a negative attitude about a class ("I'll never learn how the endocrine system works," or "She really can't expect us to perform 20 perfect venipunctures after 2 weeks!"), you are working against yourself. Your attitude, whether positive or negative, will not change the circumstances. Your negative attitude, however, can make it more difficult, or even impossible, for you to understand the endocrine system or master venipunctures. A negative attitude is distracting, drains your energy, and interferes with your ability

to concentrate. Choosing to approach life with a positive attitude releases you from the control of circumstances and frees you to focus fully on your priorities and actions that are in line with your mission and goals.

Tripped Up by Your Thoughts

"The only thing we have to fear is fear itself."
—FRANKLIN ROOSEVELT

What we expect is often what happens—we get or become what we think! In fact, negative expectations can be just as powerful as positive ones, sometimes even more powerful. This is because our mental images, whether positive or negative, create our reality. It is important to understand that doubts and worries can actually bring about the outcome you fear. For example, Melinda thinks her supervisor dislikes her, so she avoids him and reacts defensively whenever he makes suggestions about her work. As a result of Melinda's behavior, chances are good the supervisor will have a problem with her. Tripped up by her thoughts, Melinda ends up creating what she expects and fears.

The fact is, your attitude greatly influences your performance in school and your ability to secure and succeed in the job you want. Expect the best for yourself and you are likely to get it.

MAKE TIME WORK FOR YOU

"Plan your work and work your plan."

Your success in life depends, to a great degree, on how you manage your time. Learning to use it to your advantage requires planning and self-discipline, but the payoffs are well worth the effort. One fact of life is true for everyone: there will never be enough time for everything you want to do. There are ways, however, to use your time more effectively. Two key strategies are prioritizing and practicing efficiency. Prioritizing means deciding what is most important and spending enough time to make sure it gets done. Your goals should determine your priorities. What do you most want to accomplish? Are you spending enough time and energy on activities that will help achieve your goals? For example, if your goal is to graduate from a medical lab technician program with honors, are you spending the necessary time attending class, studying, and developing the work habits required of a lab technician? Or are phone conversations with friends and television viewing taking up a lot of your time?

Adults have many responsibilities, and adding the role of student often requires major adjustments. Determine which activities are critical to your success as a student and then focus on these. Some things may have to be postponed until you finish school and get your career underway. For example, washing the windows and waxing the car may have to wait. Attending classes and studying must take priority in your life.

Efficiency means planning and making the best use of time—getting the most done with the least effort. Examples of inefficiency include running to the grocery store to pick up a forgotten item, spending time looking for misplaced homework, and stopping for gas when you're already late for class rather than taking care of it the day before. It's easy to feel very busy and yet be inefficient. Pay attention to how you spend your time. A short break from studying to "rest your eyes" can stretch into an evening of lost hours in front of the television set.

Keeping a calendar is an important part of good time management. There are many types of calendars and planners, such as *Saunders Health Professional's Planner*. The new electronic planners ("palms") are handheld devices that work like small computers. They allow you to store lots of information, including your schedule, telephone numbers, and other reference information. Some even enable you to access the Internet. Paper planners also work very well and some people even prefer them over the electronic variety. The important thing is to select the best kind for you—one you will use. It should be convenient to carry with you and should have room to list several items for each date.

Collect all sources of important school and class dates: schedules, catalogs, and class syllabi. Mark important items on your calendar, including dates of quizzes and tests; due dates for assignments, projects, and library books; school holidays (for both you and your children); and deadlines for turning in required paperwork, such as financial aid and professional exam applications, and for paying fees. Add important personal dates: birthdays of family members and friends, deadlines for bills and taxes, doctors' appointments, and back-to-school nights for your children. If you work, note dates you need to remember: company potluck party, performance review, project deadlines.

Colored ink is a good way to mark events you don't want to miss, like the day your professional exam is given! Again, the important thing is to create a planning tool that works for you.

Success Tips for Managing Your Time

☐ Consider your priorities and goals when you plan your schedule and decide how to spend your time.

☐ Plan a weekly schedule. Take a few minutes every week to plan ahead. This allows you to coordinate your activities with family members, plan ahead for important days (to avoid trying to find just the right birthday present on the way to the party), combine errands to save time, and plan your study time to avoid last-minute cramming.

☐ Schedule study time every day. This is your top priority! Give yourself a chance to succeed. Arrange not to be disturbed and let friends and family members know that when you are at your desk, the time is yours.

☐ Schedule around your peak times. We all have individual body rhythms, specific times of the day when we feel most alert and energetic. Some people do their best work late at night. Others accomplish the most between 5:00 a.m. and 9:00 a.m. Class and work schedules cannot always accommodate your needs, but when you have a choice, do the most challenging tasks during your best hours.

☐ Do the hardest thing first. When you have a number of things to do or subjects to study, try tackling the most difficult (or boring or tedious) one first when you are freshest. Completing unpleasant tasks gives you a surge of energy by removing a source of worry and distraction from your mind and rewarding you with a sense of accomplishment.

☐ Be realistic about what you can accomplish and how much time tasks will take to complete. For example, thinking you can complete a research paper in one weekend can be a serious mistake because you may run into difficulties and end up with no time to spare. You will learn more about your work speed as you progress through your program. At the beginning, it is best to plan more time than you think you will need. On the other hand, take care not to spend more time than necessary on one project or assignment causing you to neglect all others.

☐ Prevent feeling overwhelmed by breaking work into small segments. (The thought of writing this book was overwhelming until the author broke it down into chapters, topics, and pages.) Plan deadlines for each segment and put them on your calendar. Ask for help and cooperation from family members and friends.

☐ Learn to say "no." Your schedule cannot always accommodate the requests of other people. It's difficult, but sometimes necessary, to turn down demands on our time such as an invitation to a party or request to help at the church rummage sale. An instructor who reviewed this book said the following response works very well: "I'm really sorry, but I won't be able to help. I wish you the best in finding someone who can."

Use down time to your advantage. There are many pockets of time that usually go to waste, such as when waiting for an appointment or using public transportation. Use this time to study flash cards, write lists, review class notes, brainstorm topics for a research paper, review the steps involved in a lab procedure, or summarize the major points of a class lecture. (The author did about half of the work toward her last college degree while sitting in airports and on airplanes!)

Defeating the Procrastination Demon

To **procrastinate** is to put off doing what needs to be done. Procrastinating can cause late assignments, failed tests, poor recommendations, and increased stress. Yet many of us fall victim to this self-defeating habit. Although it's natural to delay what we perceive to be difficult, tedious, or overwhelming, there are steps you can take to break the habit.

The first step is to identify the reason for your procrastination. What is holding you back? Are you afraid of failing? Do you believe you lack the ability to do what needs to be done? Does the task seem so unpleasant you cannot motivate yourself to start it? Is the project so large you feel overwhelmed and are the victim of "overload paralysis"? Once you have identified the reason, examine it carefully. Is it true you don't have the ability? Can the job be broken down into manageable portions? Can you match completing the task to a meaningful long-term goal?

The next step is setting a time to start, even if you simply work on planning what you are going to do. Accomplishing even a small amount can inspire you to keep going. Look for ways to break large projects into manageable pieces and plan deadlines for each. Develop a controlled sense of urgency (not panic!) to encourage yourself to meet self-imposed deadlines.

If you find yourself stuck, identify sources of help, such as your instructor, supervisor, or a friend. Perhaps you need additional materials or more information to get started. Try using affirmations such as, "I am capable of understanding how the nervous system functions. My presentation to the class will be interesting and well organized." Visualize yourself completing the work, concentrating on the satisfaction you will receive. Finally, focus on your future. Think about how completing the work will help you achieve your goals to graduate and get a good job.

Personal Organization: Getting It All Together

"A vital key to success is learning to work smarter, not harder."

The purpose of personal organization, like time management, is to make life easier. Organizational techniques build consistency and predictability into your daily routines, saving you time and energy. Surprise-filled adventures are great for vacation trips, but efficiency is a better way to ensure academic and career success. Hunting for your keys every morning and arriving late for class is a waste of your time and a sign of inconsideration for your instructor and classmates. On the job, lack of organization can reduce patient satisfaction. No one wants to wait while the medical assistant scurries about to gather the equipment needed for an eye irrigation or injection.

Organization, however, should never be an end in itself. It doesn't mean keeping a perfectly tidy house, with clothes arranged according to color and season. It does mean surveying your needs and developing ways to avoid unnecessary rushing, repetition, and waste.

Success Tips for Getting Organized

1. **Write Lists.** Most people today, especially students, have too many things on their minds to remember grocery lists, all the day's errands, who they promised to call, which lab supplies to take to class, and so on. Scraps of paper are easy to lose. Commercial organizers

and planners, both paper and electronic, give you a place to record phone numbers, addresses of stores, recommendations from friends, ideas you think of throughout the day, and so on.

2. **Carry a Big Bag.** A typical student's day may include classes, work, shopping, and errands such as returning a video. Start each day—either in the morning or the night before—by checking your calendar and to-do list to see what you need to take with you. If you go directly to class from work, pack your books, binder, uniform, and other necessary supplies. Take along a healthy snack to avoid having to raid the vending machines. Always carry your planner or calendar.

3. **Stock Up.** Running out of milk, shampoo, or diapers can lead to a frustrating waste of time and energy. Even worse is discovering at 11:30 p.m., while finishing a major assignment due in the morning, that your printer cartridge is empty and you don't have another. (The author knows that cartridges are well aware of deadlines and choose to dry up accordingly!) Keep important backup supplies on hand. A handy way to monitor these is to keep a shopping list on the refrigerator and instruct everyone in the household to list items as they run low. You can note needed study supplies on the same list.

4. **Give Things a Home.** Keeping what you need where you can find it can save countless hours of search time. It will also prevent redoing lost assignments or paying late fees on misplaced bills. If your study area is a dual-use area such as the kitchen table, try keeping your books and supplies in one place on a shelf or in a large box where everything can stay together. This way you can set up an "instant desk" when it is time to study. Organize your class notes and handouts by subject in a binder. Color-coded files work well for keeping ongoing projects and notes from previous classes in order.

5. **Keep Things in Repair.** Life is easier if you can depend on the car and other necessities. If money is tight, focus on keeping the essentials in working order and look for ways to economize elsewhere.

6. **Cluster Errands.** Modern life requires trips to the grocery store, the mall, the children's school, the post office—you name it, we go there! Save time and money by doing as much as possible on each trip. Look for shopping centers that have many services to avoid running all over town.

7. **Take Advantage of Technology.** If you are connected to the Internet, take advantage of opportunities to shop, pay bills, and perform other tasks online.

8. **Handle It Once.** If you find that mail, bills, announcements, and other paperwork accumulate in ever-growing piles, try processing each item as it comes in. Sort the mail quickly each day and do something with each piece: discard the junk, pay the bills (or file them together for payment once or twice a month), answer letters with a short note, read messages and announcements, and place magazines in a basket to be looked over when you have time. Handle other papers that come into the house—permission slips for the kids, announcements from work—the same way.

9. **Get It Over With.** Certain unpleasantries, like parking tickets and dental work, come into everyone's life. It's easy to spend time worrying about them. A good strategy is to get them over with as quickly as possible: pay the ticket or make an appointment with the dentist. Seek help if you need it, and do your best to take care of what needs to be done. Procrastinating and worrying can drain your energy and interfere with your concentration.

10. **Plan Backups.** Prearrange ways to handle emergencies: a ride to school if the car breaks down, child care to cover for a sick babysitter, a study buddy who will lend you notes if you miss a class. Backups are like insurance policies—you hope you won't need them, but if you do, they're good to have. And whenever possible, plan backups for your backups!

If getting organized seems like a waste of time, too much work, or just "not your style," consider the alternative: using even more time and energy in unproductive ways that result in frustration and inconvenience. You can start now to help yourself get it together at the same time you develop organizational skills that are valuable in all health care occupations.

Children in the House. Being a parent can present special challenges for students. Here are some ideas for balancing your responsibilities to your children and your studies:

1. If your children are old enough, work on homework together.

2. Have young children "help" you by drawing, coloring pictures, filling in sticker books, or performing other "desk work."
3. Exchange babysitting services with friends and family members, arranging to help them out when your study load is lightest.
4. Organize a study group of classmates who have children. Contribute to a babysitting fund, and hire someone to watch all the children while you study together.
5. Explain to your children why you are in school. Show them a picture of a health care professional, and tell them about your future job and how you will be helping people.
6. Ask your school if they have family days or picnics when children can see where their parents are spending so much of their time.
7. Try to turn your study time into a positive experience for the kids by saving their favorite videos, toys, and other activities for the times when you are busy.
8. Investigate activities such as day camps, sports teams, and craft classes. Some organizations, such as churches, offer reasonably priced activities.
9. Plan to spend some time with your children each day just doing something fun, even if only for a few minutes. Let them choose the activity.
10. Tell them how much you appreciate their cooperation.

WHAT IS THIS THING CALLED STRESS?

We hear a lot about stress these days. One friend says, "I'm so stressed over this exam." Another exclaims, "I just can't take any more of this stress." **Stress** refers to our physical and emotional reactions to life's events. These reactions can either help us or hurt us, depending on the circumstances. "Good stress" motivates us when we are called upon to perform beyond our usual comfort zone. For example, if you witness a car accident and stop to help the victims, your body probably experiences certain reactions: your heart rate speeds up, your blood pressure rises, and the blood vessels in your muscles and the pupils of your eyes dilate. These changes increase your energy, strength, and mental alertness so you can best deal with the situation.

You can draw upon these natural reactions to help you in important, although less dramatic,

situations such as taking a professional licensing exam, giving a speech in class, or planning your wedding. This is making use of good stress to maximize your performance. The excitement experienced when you pass the exam and start a new career or get married and begin a new life with the person you love is also a form of good stress.

Pressure and unresolved worries experienced over long periods of time can create "bad stress." When the physical responses to stress are repeated over and over, with no resolution or action taken, they can actually decrease your ability to cope with life's ups and downs. In a sense, your body wears itself out as it continually prepares you to handle situations that are never resolved. Signs of long-term stress include **insomnia,** headaches, digestive problems, muscle tension, fatigue, frequent illness, irritability, depression, poor concentration, excessive eating and drinking, and use of illegal substances. It's easy to see that these don't work in your favor and are likely to increase your stress level. It's possible to get caught in a vicious cycle of ever-increasing stress that leads to feelings of hopelessness. Your mental images become dictated by worry and pressure and may bring about, as previously discussed, the very thing you fear.

Sources of Stress

The first step in dealing with long-term stress is to identify its source. The following list contains some of the common sources of stress (stressors) for adult students:
☐ Financial difficulties
☐ Family problems: nonsupportive partner, abuse, children's behavior
☐ Poor organizational skills
☐ Inability to manage time; having too much to do
☐ Lack of self-confidence and poor self-esteem
☐ Feeling unsure about study skills and ability to learn
☐ Loneliness
☐ Health problems, pregnancy
☐ Believing that instructors are unfair or don't like them
☐ Poor relationships with **peers**
☐ Believing the assignments and tests are too difficult or not **relevant**
☐ Difficulty following school rules and requirements
The second step in handling stress is to examine the source to see whether it's based on fact or fiction. For example, if you worry about failing your courses because you are not "smart enough," this

may be based on a false belief about yourself. It is very likely you are intellectually competent. But believing you aren't can create stress that discourages you from even trying. After all, what's the point of making a significant effort if you're going to fail anyway? (The self-fulfilling prophecy at work!) A better approach is to seek guidance from your instructor or student services.

Finally, look for a practical solution. What are your options? Can you distance yourself from the stressor (for example, a negative friend who constantly asks why you are returning to school at your age)? Can you get help to resolve the problem (free financial counseling for budget and credit problems, tutoring in a difficult subject)? Can you empower yourself (math refresher course, speed reading tapes)? The important thing is to face the stressor and look for ways to take control. Convert bad stress into good stress by using it as a signal that you may have issues that can prevent you from achieving your goals and attaining the success you want and deserve. Then take action to deal with the issues.

Success Tips for Handling Stress. The very nature of being a student and working in health care brings a certain amount of ongoing stress that cannot be avoided entirely. Many of the practices that promote good health are excellent for relieving stress: exercise, adequate sleep, eating properly, and avoiding excess caffeine. Here are some other things you can try:

☐ **Practice Mentally.** If your stress is caused by an upcoming event such as a job interview, you can anticipate and mentally practice the event. Athletes use this technique to prepare for the big game. They "see" themselves performing the perfect tennis serve or making the foul shot. Employ your stress to motivate you to prepare in advance.

☐ **Use Time Management and Personal Organization Strategies.** Try the techniques suggested in this chapter to help you take control of your life. Decrease the conditions that have you feeling like you're racing downhill with no brakes.

☐ **Seek the Support of Others.** People do better when they have the support of others. Studies have shown that students who have just one other person who really cares whether they graduate are more likely to finish school than those who have no one. Seek the help of trusted

friends, family members, classmates, or school personnel for listening and sharing.

☐ **Perform Relaxation Exercises.** Meditation, yoga, deep breathing, and muscle relaxation can relieve physical discomfort and promote emotional well-being.

☐ **Engage in Physical Exercise.** Even a short walk can be a very effective stress reducer. Find something you enjoy doing and make a little time for it on a regular basis.

☐ **Adjust Your Attitude.** Focus on your goals, acknowledge all progress, and concentrate on the benefits you will receive.

☐ **Keep Your Sense of Humor.** Look at the humorous side of life and its events. Laugh therapy has been found to strengthen the immune system and positively affect health.

☐ **Use School and Community Resources.** Helpful information may be available from student services, your religious organization, or the local community center.

☐ **Make Use of This Book.** Chapter 3 contains many suggestions for developing effective study and life skills. Try them out and use the ones that work best for you.

LEARNING FOR LIFE

Learning means much more than getting by in school and remembering information long enough to pass tests. It means storing information mentally and mastering hands-on skills that you can retrieve and use when you need them on the job. Further, it means being able to apply what you have learned to solve problems and make informed decisions. For example, if you are learning about the circulatory system, you are not simply memorizing the parts of the heart and the path of blood through the body. You are acquiring information to help real patients with real problems. Your purpose for learning is far more important than simply studying to earn a grade. Your future patients will depend on your knowledge, and they deserve your best efforts to learn now.

How Do You Learn Best?

If you ever have trouble following your instructors' lectures or find that your class notes are a confusing jumble, you are not alone. It is possible that you learn better when instruction is presented visually or through hands-on experience.

Research has demonstrated that people learn in different ways, called **learning styles,** and that by identifying your own preferred learning styles you can be more successful in your studies. The three learning styles most commonly discussed are grouped by the senses used when acquiring and processing new information: auditory, visual, and kinesthetic (hands-on). Table 2-1 contains a description of each of these styles.

There are other learning preferences, in addition to the styles related to our senses. Table 2-2 contains six other approaches to learning.

None of us learns in just one way. And it is important to understand that there is not a "best way" to learn. Just as we have different personalities, we have different combinations of learning styles. The purpose of discovering your preferred learning styles is to help you study more effectively. Sandra, a nursing student, has found the following methods to work best for her:

1. Receive new information from a class lecture (auditory);
2. Review by studying notes alone (individual); and

3. Concentrate first on memorizing the important facts (deductive).

Developing Learning Strategies. Identifying your preferred ways of learning does not mean you will avoid the others. This would be impossible in a health care program that includes both theoretical and practical knowledge and skills. And individual instructors use a variety of approaches to teaching. Some will match your learning styles; others won't. For example, when teaching students how to take a blood pressure, the instructor might introduce the topic with a lecture (auditory), give a reading assignment (visual), demonstrate and describe the procedure (auditory and visual), assign a worksheet (individual), and have partners practice on each other (kinesthetic and interactive). In her lecture, she might list the individual steps first (inductive) or explain the purpose and significance of blood pressure before explaining how to take it (deductive). The good news is that you can learn in a variety of ways and benefit from your strongest methods while developing your weakest.

TABLE 2-1   Three Major Learning Styles

Learning Style	How Student Learns Best	Examples of Effective Learning Activities
Auditory	• Through *hearing.* Remembers information from lectures and discussions better than material read in textbook. • Prefers music to art and listening to reading. • Understands written material better when it is read aloud. • May spell better out loud than when writing. • Misses visual cues. • Prefers doing oral rather than written reports	Lectures, tapes, music, rhymes, speaking
Visual	• Through *seeing.* Remembers information presented in written or graphic form better than in lectures and discussions. Often needs people to repeat what they have said. • Takes notes when oral instructions are given. • Takes notes when oral instructions are given. • Prefers art to music and reading to listening. • Understands better when the speaker's face is seen. • Prefers doing written rather than oral reports.	Reading, pictures, diagrams, charts, graphs, maps, videos, films, chalkboard, overhead projections
Kinesthetic (hands-on)	• Through *doing.* Remembers information acquired through activities. • Reads better when moving lips and saying words silently or moving finger along the page. • Enjoys moving around while studying. • Likes to touch things, point, use fingers when counting or calculating. • Prefers doing a demonstration rather than an oral or written report.	Lab activities, skills practice, experiments, games, movement, building models

TABLE 2-2   More Approaches to Learning

INDUCTIVE VERSUS DEDUCTIVE	
Inductive	**Deductive**
Inductive learners prefer to learn facts before forming generalizations (the big picture). They prefer to first memorize dates, study individual events, and know the details. When learning about the circulatory system, for example, they would rather study the various parts of the system before learning how they all work together to circulate the blood.	Deductive learners want to see and understand the big picture, which they use as a framework for learning the details. When learning about cells, for example, they would want to know the purpose and function of the cell before learning the individual components.
LINEAR VERSUS GLOBAL	
Linear	**Global**
Linear thinkers learn best when material is organized in a logical sequence. They like to do things in order, building on material previously learned.	Global thinkers like to work with all the facts, regardless of the order. They are interested in relationships within the material.
INDIVIDUAL VERSUS INTERACTIVE	
Individual	**Interactive**
Individual-type learners prefer to work on learning tasks alone. They like to figure out all aspects of assignments on their own.	Interactive-type learners like to work with another student or in groups. They want to share their ideas and hear the ideas of others.

DOWN MEMORY LANE

Memorizing is not the same as learning, but it is an important component of the learning process. While you may be able to rely on your short-term memory to complete assignments and pass tests, it is the material stored in long-term memory that will serve you throughout your studies, when taking your professional exam, and afterward on the job. There are many ways to improve your memory and better retain the material you study.

The way to start is by making sure you understand the new material. Experiments have shown it is much more difficult to remember nonsense syllables or lists of unrelated numbers than material that has meaning. In other words, it is very difficult to remember what you don't understand in the first place. So ask questions in class, look up words you don't know, and read difficult passages several times.

Repeat, repeat, repeat. The very best way to retain new material is repetition over an extended period of time. In fact, the length of time information is remembered is often in direct proportion to the length of time over which it is learned. Review new material as soon as possible after you first encounter it and continue to review it on a regular basis, at least weekly.

Use strategies based on your learning styles. If you are an auditory learner, listen to or say new math formulas over and over. Visual learners can post the formulas on the bathroom mirror. And kinesthetic learners can try writing each new formula 10 times. Use your imagination. Studying does not necessarily mean working quietly at a desk. Create rhymes or funny images. Make up movements associated with each item you have to remember. One method, called "pegging," has you place imaginary pegs on walls around the house. On each one, "hang" a fact or idea you must remember. As you walk through the house each day, review the material on each peg.

Look for ways to relate new information to your own experience by connecting it to something you already know. When you study something new, start by making a list of what you know—or would like to know—about the topic.

Success Tips for Improving Your Memory

☐ **Relax.** Your ability to store and remember things does not work well when your body is tense and your mind is distracted with worry. Try doing a relaxation exercise before starting a study session.

☐ **Remove Distractions.** Studying for mastery requires concentration. Find a place where interruptions are limited and where you can use your chosen techniques. (For example, auditory learners who plan to use singing and tapping should probably not study in the school library!)

☐ **Break Up Your Study Sessions.** Most people can't concentrate fully for very long periods of time. The great thing about reviewing over time, rather than at the last minute, is you can take time for short breaks.

☐ **Overlearn.** Continue to review and repeat material you already know. This helps to firmly lock it into long-term memory.

☐ **Quiz Yourself.** Make up your own quizzes. Review one day and take the quiz several days later to evaluate your retention.

THE PERILS OF CRAMMING

Cramming is a well-known student activity consisting of frantic last-minute efforts, sometimes fortified with coffee and cigarettes, to finish assignments or prepare for tests. The major problem with cramming is that it serves only the immediate goal of meeting a school deadline. True learning rarely occurs. The conditions required for learning, such as the opportunity for repetition over time, are absent. Most of what is crammed is forgotten within a few days—or hours! Work in health care demands a higher level of competence than you are likely to achieve as a result of cramming. Do your future patients deserve your best efforts to learn or are the bits you may remember after a night of cramming good enough? This is an important consideration for students who claim that cramming works well for them because they can study only at the last minute when the deadline is close. This is true only if passing the test is their only goal.

Another problem with cramming is it leaves you with few options. If you are writing a paper the night before it is due and you discover that the information you have is inadequate (and the Internet is not available), you have no time to consult other sources. If you are studying for a test and realize there are several points you don't understand, it's too late to ask the instructor to explain them.

Finally, cramming adds more stress to an already busy life in which you are balancing your responsibilities as an adult with your role as a student. If it costs you a night's sleep, it can deplete your energy and interfere with your ability to concentrate. You end up creating a nonproductive cycle involving a continual game of catch-up and the danger of creating ongoing stress.

The reality is that things happen, you get behind, and you run out of time. Almost every student occasionally finds it necessary to cram. Here are some tips to make the best of a bad situation:

1. Don't beat yourself up and waste energy feeling guilty. You'll only distract your attention from what you have to do. Just make a mental note to avoid the need for future cramming.

2. Do a very quick visualization in which you see yourself accomplishing what you need to do in the time you have available.

3. Minimize all distractions. For example, see if you can find someone to watch the children.

4. Focus on the most important material. What is most likely to be emphasized on the test? What are the main requirements of the assignment?

5. Use the learning and memory techniques described in this section. Draw on your learning style to help you learn the necessary material.

6. Try to stay calm. Physical tension distracts from mental effort. Breathe deeply, stretch, and do a quick relaxation exercise.

MENTORS MAKE A DIFFERENCE

"People seldom improve when they have no other model but themselves to copy."
—OLIVER GOLDSMITH

A **mentor** is an advisor you choose for yourself, someone who has the experience and background to give you sound advice about your studies and career. This is a person you respect and see as a positive role model. Your chances of succeeding are greatly increased when someone you respect cares about your progress. This has been proved in both school and business settings. Where can you find such a person? It can be an instructor, school staff member, administrator, or someone who works in health care. You might find a graduate of your school who is working successfully. It is important to choose someone with whom you feel comfortable.

Once you have identified a person you would like to have as your mentor, ask for an appointment. Let him or her know you want to talk about mentoring. At the meeting, explain that you are pursuing a career in health care and would like this person to serve as your mentor and give you guidance. Ask how much time he or she has to meet with you. You should meet or talk with your mentor periodically to ask questions, stay motivated, and learn more about becoming a health care professional. Mentors who work in health care can give you information about the current state of your targeted occupation, suggest what you should emphasize in your studies, and introduce you to other health care professionals. If the first person you approach does not have the time or is not interested, don't be discouraged. Continue your search—it will be worth the effort!

LEARNING PRACTICAL SKILLS

Most jobs in health care involve a lot of hands-on activity, and the level of your performance is critical to your success on the job. Future health care professionals must master a variety of skills. Depending on your specific occupation, these skills range from filling out forms accurately to performing a urinalysis to taking an x-ray. Learning to apply the theory you learn in class to practical situations is one of the most important components of your education.

Some students enjoy learning practical skills, but don't take this part of their training as seriously as their **theory** courses. This is a serious mistake because hands-on practice builds a bridge between school and the world of work. There is a big difference between knowing about a procedure and being able to actually do it well. Actually performing a blood draw, for example, is much different from hearing about it. Practice sessions provide you with opportunities to take risks in a safe, monitored environment where you can learn from your experience—and from your mistakes.

At the same time, it is important to learn the theory and background information that support the procedures you will practice in the lab. For example, giving injections requires an understanding of the principles of infection control. Insurance coding requires knowledge of basic human anatomy terminology and medical diagnoses.

LEARNING IN THE LAB

Depending on your program of study, practice may include performing procedures, **role-playing,** working on the computer, and completing pencil-and-paper activities such as filling out insurance forms. You may solve problems, work with "patients," conduct tests, or do calculations.

Being Prepared for Lab Sessions

Advance preparation will help you benefit fully from lab sessions. Lab time is often limited, and the instructor will expect you to get started on the assigned activities without delay. The first step in being prepared is to read your textbook. Don't depend on your instructor's explanations or on being able to "figure it out." Reading gives you time to think through the steps and gives you a framework for lectures and demonstrations. Many health care textbooks present procedures in recipe or how-to format. Read through each step. Note all hints and cautions that contain important safety information for you and the patient.

In addition to reading your textbook, study the illustrations. Are the health care professionals wearing gloves? How are they positioned in relation to the patients and equipment? What do the equipment and instruments look like? How are they held? In which direction should movements be made? For example, in disinfecting a surgical site on the skin, it is important that cleansing be done in a circular motion, moving from the center toward the outside edges to avoid **contaminating** areas already disinfected. The effectiveness of a procedure is often based on details like these.

If your instructor demonstrates a procedure in class, focus on the steps or actions involved. Take notes only if doing so doesn't prevent you from watching and listening. If action is involved, mirror the instructor as closely as possible. For example, when watching a demonstration of the proper way to hold a syringe, use your highlighter or pen to copy the motion. The ability to observe carefully is, in itself, a valuable health care skill.

Don't hesitate to ask questions about any point you don't understand. Get as complete an understanding as possible before going to the lab to minimize mistakes and avoid wasting practice time.

Last—but very importantly!—pay special attention to learning and practicing safety rules. Many textbooks, as well as labs, use warning diagrams. Your future job may require you to operate expensive and potentially dangerous equipment and to handle chemical and biological hazards. The human immunodeficiency virus (HIV) and the hepatitis B virus can be spread through the mishandling of blood and certain body fluids. Proper disposal of contaminated items is regulated by law. All health care professionals must learn and follow the **standard (universal) precautions** developed by the U.S. Centers for Disease Control and Prevention.

Success Tips for Learning in the Lab

☐ Take along any study materials, reference books, supplies, or **protective equipment** needed to participate in the scheduled activities. Set them out the evening before if you have an early start the day of the lab.

☐ Work with "real patients." Treat the students you work with in lab as you would if you were on the job. Demonstrate courtesy and concern. (Remember: "Your career starts now.") If you are entering patient data on the computer or practicing patient scheduling, work as if the exercises involved real people who are depending on your ability to maintain accurate and efficient records and schedules.

☐ Aim for accuracy. All health care tasks depend on accuracy to ensure safe, high-level patient care. You will also be expected to follow various laws and regulations, both in the lab and on the job. In many procedures, "almost correct" is not good enough. Only perfection is acceptable. For example, a sterile field is a germ-free area prepared to prevent infection during procedures such as minor surgeries. It is either sterile or it is not. Brushing an ungloved hand against an object in the field may seem like a small error, but the field is no longer sterile. Work carefully in the lab. Never skip a step because this is "just practice" and these are not "real surgeries" or "real medications." When establishing your work habits, it is important that everything you do be done as realistically as possible.

☐ Respect your instructor's time but do ask questions as needed. If the instructor is busy observing or assisting other students, write down your questions so you won't forget them.

☐ Understand that there may be more than one correct way to perform a task. Your instructors, as well as future supervisors, may each have slightly different ways of performing a procedure. The important thing is that your technique follows accepted practice and is safe for both you and your patients.

☐ Keep up with your lab assignments. Many health care classes feature "check-off" sheets that the instructor uses to observe student performance of each required procedure. Health care procedures must be done in a certain way with many of the steps essential for the success of the procedure. When the procedure is completed satisfactorily, it is checked off on the sheet. Strive to complete these sheets in a timely way as you progress through each course.

Lab Follow-Up. Follow-up and review of lab sessions are important, just as they are for note taking and reading. You can do a number of things to help move what you learn in lab to your long-term memory.

1. Join or organize a study group to practice procedures and quiz each other on the rationale, safety concerns, and supporting theory.

2. Write out the steps of each procedure from memory. Include any safety concerns or rationale.

3. Make flash cards to help you remember important facts—rules and regulations, normal values (blood cell counts, body temperature), purpose of various lab tests, and so on.

4. Make charts, using color and illustrations to highlight important points about each procedure.

5. Recite the steps out loud or record them and review by listening to tapes.

6. Rehearse the steps for each procedure in your mind. Act them out. Develop mental checklists of the steps. Some students find it helpful to use mnemonics (techniques to help the memory). For example, RICE is a popular way to remember the immediate first aid treatment for sprains:
R = rest
I = ice
C = compression
E = elevation

Chapter 3

Developing Your People Skills

THE IMPORTANCE OF PEOPLE SKILLS

The previous chapter focused on you as an individual and the personal attitudes, habits, and skills that influence your academic and career success. In this chapter, we shift our focus to other people and how you relate to them. You can expect to work closely with many kinds of people in your career, and your ability to create and maintain mutually beneficial relationships will be an important factor in your job performance.

The quality and consistency of patient care are affected by how well health care professionals communicate among themselves and with patients and their families. Poor communication with patients contributes to the growing number of malpractice lawsuits. When patients feel they are listened to and understood, they are less likely to sue. This is true even if their treatment outcomes are negative.

At the same time, one of the most frequent complaints from employers today is that their employees lack good people skills. They don't know how to work well with others. More people fail on the job because of poor interpersonal skills than because they lack the necessary technical qualifications.

Good interpersonal skills are also important for academic success. Throughout your studies, you will have opportunities to learn from both your instructors and fellow students. Your ability to communicate effectively will influence how much and how well you learn. Activities such as working on teams, practicing hands-on skills with other students, and joining study groups are ways you can start now to practice working with others. Most of life's activities take place in relation to other people and improving the quality of these relationships can improve the overall quality of your life.

Respecting Others

"Be kind. Remember, everyone you meet is fighting a hard battle."
—THOMPSON

By choosing a career in health care, you have accepted the responsibility to serve others. Your duties may range from performing an uncomfortable medical procedure to explaining a complicated bill for an office visit. It will be your obligation to serve all patients or clients with an equal level of care and concern, regardless of their appearance, behavior, level of education, or economic status. Not everyone will look, act, or even smell as you would like. They will not all express appreciation for your efforts. People who feel sick may be irritable and cranky. The satisfaction you obtain from your work must be based on what you can give to others, not on what you receive from them.

Good health care practice is based on the principle that all human beings deserve to be treated with respect and dignity. The need to treat all patients equally and fairly has been recognized and endorsed by professional organizations such as the American Hospital Association (AHA). The AHA formalized this belief in "The Patient Care Partnership" mentioned in Chapter 1. Specifically, it states that patients have the right to "be treated with compassion and respect."

It is also important to demonstrate respect toward your supervisor and coworkers. The quality of work produced in any organization depends on the quality of the relationships among the people who work there, and good relationships are based on mutual respect.

Guidelines for Respectful Behavior
☐ **Be Courteous.** Many observers today have noted that as a society, we are moving away

from the practice of common courtesy. Many people fail to use expressions like "please" and "thank you." These are powerful words that improve the quality of both personal and professional relationships.

☐ **Maintain Professionalism.** As a student and on the job, it is important to display maturity and competence. Examples of inappropriate communication behaviors are chewing gum, arguing, swearing, and yelling.

☐ **Acknowledge the Other Person.** No one likes to be ignored. If you are busy working with someone else or talking on the telephone when a patient arrives, use eye contact and a quick nod to let the person know you are aware of his or her presence.

☐ **Don't Interrupt.** Avoid breaking in when another person is speaking. Some people need extra time to compose their thoughts or express themselves. Avoid the habit of finishing sentences for others. This frustrates the speaker, and your assumption about what they planned to say may be incorrect.

☐ **Show Interest.** Look at the other person when you are talking and listening. Show you are listening by nodding or using confirming sounds or phrases such as "uh, huh," "I understand," "okay," and so on. Don't turn your body toward the door as if to say, "Hurry up. I need to move on to something else."

☐ **Guard Privacy.** This is good practice in your personal life. In health care, patient privacy is protected by law. It is illegal to discuss patient information with anyone who is not working directly with the patient. Make a habit of never sharing anything told to you in confidence by family members, friends, or classmates. (Patients must even give written permission before information can be given to insurance companies, other health providers, and so on.)

☐ **Avoid Gossip.** Gossip can be a very serious problem in the workplace. It serves no useful purpose and can lead to hurt feelings, broken trust, and strained relationships. If it involves confidential patient matters, it can lead to a lawsuit.

☐ **Remain Calm.** It is important to behave and speak calmly when you are dealing with situations such as emergencies and angry patients. A calm demeanor both reassures others and enables you to focus on doing what can best help the situation.

Appreciating Diversity

"Commandment Number One of any truly civilized society is this: Let people be different."
—DAVID GRAYSON

The population of the United States is made up of people from all over the world. Immigration has increased dramatically in recent years, and Americans now more than ever represent a wide variety of races, religions, lifestyles, languages, and educational and economic levels. These variations are known as **diversity.**

Diversity also refers to differences not related to cultural background or race. These include age, sexual orientation, disabilities, and appearance. People who are different are sometimes ignored or treated inappropriately, sometimes even cruelly. This may not be done intentionally, so you must think about what you are doing and how it might be interpreted. For example, it is not uncommon for health care professionals to speak to younger relatives who accompany elderly patients as if the patients were not present. Other examples are using "baby talk" with the elderly or shouting at them if they are hard of hearing.

Our society can benefit from the contribution of people with different customs and ideas. By drawing from a variety of viewpoints, we increase our chances of solving the complex problems encountered in modern society. Learning from our differences can be beneficial. Many Americans, for example, find pain relief from the ancient Chinese practice of acupuncture, the insertion of very small needles into specific points on the body. Unfortunately, differences in values and beliefs about life can cause misunderstandings and even lead to violence. Learning to take advantage of the differences and to peacefully work out misunderstandings is one of the major challenges the world faces today.

Work in health care will give you opportunities to interact with people from many different backgrounds. Your personal actions and efforts to understand and serve others can contribute to a more harmonious society. The students in your school probably come from diverse backgrounds. If your own background is different from your classmates, you can serve as a source of information about your culture.

Promoting Understanding

When we learn about others, we also learn about ourselves and what it means to be human. You

Diversity on the Job

Everything we do is influenced by our cultural background. Knowing where some of these differences exist can help you to better understand the people you encounter at work. Words to live by that many of us take for granted, such as "It is important to always be on time," are not important to everyone. Making assumptions can result in misunderstandings. Let's look at an example. A patient has to wait 15 minutes before you can perform his lab test. In an effort to respect his time and not add to the delay, you keep conversation to a minimum and complete the procedure as quickly as possible. You believe you have been considerate. The patient, from a culture that does not consider time in the same way, is insulted. His interpretation of your behavior is that you obviously have more important things to do than work with him, so you are rushing along. The "right thing" in your eyes was the "wrong thing" in his. Of course, it is impossible to know and accommodate every cultural difference that you encounter. You can, however, be aware of what types of differences exist and strive to be sensitive to them. Ask questions if you are unsure about a person's feelings or understanding of a situation. Box 3-1 lists common areas of differences among cultures, which have a significant influence on how people live.

can enrich your life by embracing diversity and seeking opportunities to learn about different ways to view the world. Here are some suggestions to help people of all backgrounds better understand each other:

- **Put Fear Aside.** Many people are frightened by what they don't understand. Some are afraid that accepting certain differences among people will somehow result in negative changes in society. In fact, the contributions of people from different backgrounds have resulted in the economic success and political stability of the United States.
- **Listen to Other Points of View.** Seek opportunities to interact with people whose backgrounds are different from yours. Encourage them to express their ideas and opinions. Listen carefully to what they say.
- **Ask Questions.** Use questions to learn more, but not to challenge the other person. For example, instead of asking, "Why do you believe that?" you could say, "That sounds interesting. Could you tell me more about that?" Your goal

is to learn and understand, not to imply that the other person is wrong.
- **Avoid Stereotypes.** Don't make assumptions about people because of their age, race, gender, or other categories. Consider each person as an individual with a unique set of characteristics.
- **Don't Judge People by Their Appearance.** Outward appearances do not always represent who people are. To truly know people, you must talk with them and observe their actions. If you immediately dismiss them based on how they look, you may lose the opportunity to form a friendship or a beneficial working relationship.
- **Explore Different Cultures.** Many schools and communities sponsor activities that highlight the cultures represented in the local population. Check your local library and the Internet for other sources of information about the backgrounds of your classmates and future patients.
- **Learn about Other Value Systems.** People are defined by their values and beliefs about how they should live. Culture is much more than typical foods and daily customs. Develop a deeper level of knowledge and understanding through conversation and by learning about the religions and important beliefs of the people in your area.
- **Look for Commonalities.** As human beings, we share many of the same needs, concerns, and goals for our lives. Find out what you have in common with people who seem different.
- **Offer to Help Others.** Expand your attitude of caring by looking for ways to help others. For example, offer to help a classmate who has trouble with English.
- **Learn Another Language.** You may not have time now to study another language formally, but you can learn a few key phrases of any major cultural groups in your area. This can also increase your worth to an employer.

Experiencing Empathy

Empathy means attempting to see the world through the eyes of other people in order to understand their feelings and experiences. Putting yourself in the place of someone else is an important part of experiencing empathy. This is not always easy to do because we are all influenced by our own beliefs, values, and previous experiences. Being empathetic requires listening carefully to others without judging what you hear. You then

Box 3-1　Examples of Cultural Differences

Time	It is important to always be on time for meetings and appointments.
	Appointment times are just estimations of when they might take place.
	Time is valuable and should not be wasted.
	Time is not a resource over which we have control. It just is.
	Planning and using time productively is important.
	If something is important, it will eventually get done; there is no reason to rush.
	The present is more important than the future.
	The present should be used for planning and preparing for the future.
Personal Space	The distance comfortably maintained when people are talking ranges from a few inches (when you can feel the breath of the other person on your face) to over a foot away.
Age	Youth is valued. People should try to maintain a young appearance and lifestyle as long as possible (exercise, wrinkle creams, and hair dyes).
	Older people are valued for their wisdom and shown great respect.
	When elderly people are no longer able to care for themselves, it is appropriate to place them in nursing or retirement homes.
	Older people should live with and be cared for by family members until they die.
Touching	Shaking hands is okay for everyone.
	Only members of the same sex can shake hands with each other.
	Hugging is okay for everyone, even members of the same sex.
	Kissing is okay between women.
	When meeting a new person, only a slight bow is permitted, not touching.
Gender	A woman cannot be treated by a male physician.
	Women and men are equal.
	Men are dominant.
	Women act as the head of most families.
	Women have no economic or political power.
Eye Contact	Direct eye contact is a sign of sincerity, honesty, and interest in the other person.
	It is a sign of disrespect.
	Sustained eye contact communicates hostility and aggression or sexual interest.
Personal Control	Each person is in control of his or her own life.
	Luck, fate, or the will of God determines how things turn out.
Spiritual Practices	There is one God.
	God helps those who help themselves.
	God punishes those who sin.
	God answers all prayers.
	God may or may not exist.
	There is no God.
	Witchcraft and magic can both help and hurt us.
Definition of Success	Personal and professional achievement.
	Acquiring material possessions.
	Living a spiritual life.
	Achieving inner peace.
	Raising many children.
	Being a kind person and helping others.

Continued

Box 3-1   Examples of Cultural Differences—cont'd

Health Care Beliefs	Disease is caused by germs, environmental conditions, and personal habits such as smoking.
	Good health is a gift or reward from God.
	Illness is a punishment sent by God.
	Illness happens when the body's energy or humors get out of balance.
	Science has the best answers for preventing and curing disease.
	The body can heal itself naturally.
	Herbs are the best remedies.
	Only God can heal.
	Good health is a balance between the mind, body, and spirit.
	Individuals are responsible for their own health and healing.
Beliefs about Death and Dying	Death is a natural part of the life cycle.
	Death should be avoided at all costs.
	Dying is up to God.
	Death means the health care system has failed.
	Autopsies destroy the soul.
	Cremation frees the soul.
	Everything possible should be done to save life.
	People who are terminally ill or suffering should be assisted to die if this is their wish.
	Families should take care of the dying.
	Hospitals or other health care facilities should take care of the dying.

think about what you hear and, if necessary, ask for clarification or more information. What is the person trying to communicate or trying to hide? What clues are you getting from the person's body language? What is important to this person?

Health care professionals must have empathy with patients to understand their needs and learn how best to help them. Being empathetic sends the message, "You are important and worth my time and respect. I will make every effort to know who you are and what you need."

A key part of empathy is letting the other person know that you are trying to understand his or her experience. It is best, however, not to say that you know exactly how he or she feels. This sounds insincere because, in fact, it is impossible to know precisely how another person feels. In trying to be helpful, we may be tempted to share and compare our own stories—for example, saying, "Oh, I know just what you mean. The same thing happened to me ..." and then launching into a detailed explanation about what happened to us. This shifts the focus to us and away from the person who needs the attention.

Learning to experience empathy improves all interpersonal relationships, including those with friends, family members, classmates, instructors, coworkers, and supervisors. Your relationships can be more harmonious when you make an effort to see the views of others. Here are some ways to increase your practice of empathy at home and in school:

☐ When you talk with your classmates, listen carefully. How are their views different from yours? What experiences have they had that explain these differences?
☐ Are there students who exhibit poor behavior? Why do you think they behave in this way? What are some clues that might explain their actions?
☐ Why do family members sometimes "act out"?
☐ What kinds of experiences have shaped the opinions of your friends?

Oral Communication: Creating the People Connection

Many people believe they are good communicators because they are friendly and like to talk. But the ability to speak is only one part of effective communication. There are four other essential parts of effective communication: listening, thinking, requesting feedback, and using and interpreting **nonverbal communication** (body language, expressions, and gestures). Successful oral communication takes place when the receiver

Empathy on the Job

A medical office manager shared the following story: The receptionist, Grace, was a very efficient woman who treated all patients courteously. One of the patients, William, was a gay man with AIDS. Grace was courteous but stiffened visibly whenever he came for appointments. She had trouble accepting his lifestyle. One day William learned that Grace's son had been a missionary in Africa. On his next visit, William brought in a scrapbook that showed his experience working with missionaries in Africa. After that, Grace was warm and friendly to William. When asked why seeing the scrapbook had changed her behavior, she said that now she was able to see William as a person and not simply as a gay man with AIDS.

(listener) receives and understands the intended message of the speaker. We all know this is not always the case! Let's look at how you can increase the effectiveness of your communication.

Speaking. Speaking consists of creating and sending messages. The first step in creating a clear message is to determine your purpose. You need to know your communication goal.

Effective messages match the purpose of the speaker with the needs of the receiver. These needs are determined, in part, by the characteristics of the receiver.

Success Tips for Sending Effective Messages
☐ Choose a level of language that is appropriate for the receiver. If a person is heavily medicated, for example, use simple words and short sentences.
☐ Choose appropriate vocabulary. Using medical terminology is an effective way to be precise when speaking with coworkers, but it can be confusing for patients. They may hesitate to tell you they don't understand because they don't want to seem dumb.
☐ Avoid slang and nonstandard speech. These are often characteristic of certain age and social groups and can cause misunderstandings with people outside those groups. Speech that is appropriate among friends and at social gatherings may not be correct for school and work. For example, the current use of the word "goes" to mean "says" is understood by many young people but may be confusing to others.

☐ Speak clearly and at a moderate speed—not so quickly that you are difficult to understand or so slowly that the receiver's mind wanders. (We hear and comprehend many times faster than we speak.)
☐ Avoid speaking in a monotone. Speak naturally, but with expression in your voice. Make sure it is appropriate for your message. For example, speak with respect when asking questions in class, friendliness when greeting a new student, reassurance when calming fears, and firmness when giving instructions that affect patient safety.

Active Listening

"To listen well is as powerful a means of communication as to talk well."
—U.S. SUPREME COURT CHIEF JUSTICE JOHN MARSHALL

Active listening should not be confused with hearing. Listening requires effort, while hearing is more passive. To listen well, you must pay attention, focus on the speaker's words, and reflect on what you hear. Active listening demonstrates respect for the speaker. It is an essential skill for the health care professional because all patients want to work with someone who listens to them and makes every effort to understand their needs.

Think for a moment about your own listening skills. Do you sometimes catch your mind wandering and thinking about other things? Do you think about what you are going to say next? Do you argue mentally when you disagree? These habits can interfere with your attention and prevent you from hearing the speaker's message. Look over the following checklist of techniques designed to improve listening skills. Are there any you'd like to try?
☐ Prepare yourself mentally to listen by clearing your mind of other thoughts.
☐ Control the noise level of your environment as much as possible. Turn off the radio or television, look for a quiet place to talk, or move out of the busiest part of the office.
☐ Focus on the other person and concentrate on following what he or she is saying. Sometimes when we think we are listening, looking at the speaker, and perhaps even nodding in agreement, we are actually thinking about something else. Practice being aware of where your attention is directed.
☐ If you disagree with what you are hearing, try not to engage in mental arguments. Internal

self-talk interferes with your ability to listen. It is usually easy to understand people we agree with. It takes more effort to hear people we disagree with, but only by listening carefully can we begin to understand their point of view.

☐ Practice making quick mental notes about points you need to clarify. Work on being able to do this without losing track of what the person is saying.

☐ Focus on what is being said rather than how it is said. Move beyond the speaker's appearance, manners, language level, or even odor. Try not to let unpleasant factors about the person interfere with your ability to concentrate on what he or she has to say.

☐ Acknowledge the person even if you are taking notes or performing a test or procedure while he or she is talking. Look at the person from time to time and make eye contact.

Listening effectively is one of the most valuable skills you can develop for both personal and professional success. It can increase your learning, your effectiveness in helping others, and even your popularity. At the same time, it is a skill many people neglect because they assume they know how to listen. Working to improve your listening skills is one of the most important actions you can take to work well with others.

Feedback

Feedback is a communication technique used to check your understanding of what a speaker says. Even when you listen carefully, there may be times when what you hear is not what the speaker intended. We have all experienced the misunderstandings that occur when we assume we understand the speaker's message—and then learn that the intended message was quite different!

There are several methods for giving and requesting feedback. Here are three of the most common kinds of feedback:

1. **Paraphrasing.** This means saying what you heard in your own words so that the speaker can confirm or correct your statement.

2. **Reflecting.** This is similar to paraphrasing, but you repeat what the other person says using words as close as possible to his or her own words. This gives the person the opportunity to confirm or add additional information.

3. **Clarifying.** This involves asking the speaker to explain what he or she means.

Asking Questions

"No man really becomes a fool until he stops asking questions."
—CHARLES P. STEINMETZ

Scientific discoveries and technological advances are the result of people asking questions. What causes … ? What would happen if … ? How can we … ? Asking questions is a powerful tool for learning. You can increase your knowledge and understanding in school by asking questions. Yet many students sit through hours of classes and never ask a single question. Take advantage of your opportunities to learn and get ready to ask good questions in class. Here are some tips to help you get started:

☐ **Prepare Ahead for Class.** If you haven't read the assignment or completed the other homework, you won't have the background information on which to base a question.

☐ **Write Questions Down.** Suppose you did the reading and remember that there were several points you didn't understand. But you didn't write them down, and now you can't remember what they were! Don't let this happen to you. During lectures, write down questions as you think of them so that you can ask them at the appropriate time.

☐ **Don't Be Embarrassed.** No one wants to ask what they think is a dumb question. But if you already knew everything, you wouldn't be in school, right? Instructors welcome questions in class and are usually pleased when students take an interest in the subject. (Exception: You don't pay attention in class and/or don't read the assigned material and then ask lots of questions that force the instructor to repeat what he or she just finished saying.)

☐ **Ask Them Later.** If all the class time is taken up with the lecture or the instructor never gets around to your lab group, arrange a time to ask your questions later. Be willing to make the extra effort to get the information you need.

☐ **Be Brave.** Have you ever found yourself so confused in class you can't even phrase a question? This is exactly when you should ask a question. Try something like, "I'm lost here. Could we go back to … ?" Avoid waiting until you're so far behind you don't have a chance of catching up.

Types of Questions. There are four basic types of questions:

1. **Closed-ended.** Can be answered with a "yes" or "no" or in one or two words. They are used for getting specific facts.

2. **Open-ended.** Require a longer answer and request explanations, descriptions, examples, and other details.
3. **Probing.** Based on what the other person has already told you. The purpose is to acquire additional information.
4. **Leading.** Question is worded to provide a possible answer. These questions should be used with great care because they may encourage the other person to simply agree because he or she doesn't really understand the question or thinks you have provided the correct answer. Leading questions can be helpful with people who find it difficult to communicate because of injury, language barriers, shyness, or other problems that make communicating difficult.

Success Tips for Asking Effective Questions

☐ **Choose the Right Place.** Some important questions are personal, embarrassing, or potentially difficult to answer. A question for the instructor about a low grade you believe to be unfair is best asked in private, not during class. An interview with a patient with acquired immune deficiency syndrome (AIDS) should be conducted out of the hearing of others.

☐ **Choose the Right Time.** Asking your supervisor a question about your performance when he or she is ready to leave the office isn't fair to either of you.

☐ **Avoid Challenging or Judgmental Questions.** Your choice of words and tone of voice can communicate the negative message, "You are wrong, and I demand an explanation." For example, questions like, "Why did you do that?" or "What were you thinking?" may draw a defensive reaction or no response at all. A major goal of communication should be to encourage discussion so that issues can be resolved.

☐ **Know What Not to Ask.** There is a difference between showing interest in others and asking questions that are too personal and may offend. To show concern without prying, you can say something like, "You seem really upset. Is there some way I can help?" This allows the person to reveal as much information as is comfortable. If you must ask potentially embarrassing questions, explain why you are asking them and how the information will be used. Assure patients that anything they say will remain confidential, as required by law.

☐ **Know What's Legal.** Some questions, especially when asked in hiring situations, are illegal. These include asking about age, marital status, number of children, and other matters that are not related to job performance. (See Chapter 11 for more information.)

☐ **Allow Silence.** Some people need more time than others to think and prepare a response. Unless it is obvious they don't understand the question, don't feel that you must speak to fill the silence.

Nonverbal Communication

More than half of the content and meaning of our messages is communicated nonverbally through our movements, posture, gestures, and facial expressions. In fact, nonverbal communication is often more revealing than verbal communication because people are usually not aware they are doing it. That is, it is not completely under our control. For example, telling a friend that you are "fine" when you have a worried expression on your face sends a mixed message. The friend is more likely to believe your face than your words. Nonverbal communication can either emphasize or distort the content of verbal messages.

Use the following questions as a starting point for becoming more aware of your own nonverbal language.

1. Do you have nervous habits, such as jiggling your leg or playing with your hair, that distract from or distort your messages? These habits can give the impression that you would rather be somewhere else.
2. Is your general posture upright or slouching? Do you face the person you're talking with or partially turn away, as if looking for escape? Leaning slightly toward the other person communicates interest.
3. Do you assume an accepting body position? Crossing the arms, for example, can be a sign of being closed to what the other person is saying.
4. Do you use gestures to emphasize or add meaning to your words? Or are they routine habits that add nothing to your message? Gestures are especially helpful when used for demonstrations and to communicate with people who have limited ability to understand spoken language. Examples include very young children, non-English speakers, and the hearing impaired.
5. Does your face express interest or boredom? In class, do you usually face the instructor or

look out the window? When an activity is announced, do you roll your eyes and exchange pained looks with other students? Poor attitudes are easy to read and can negatively affect the quality of the class by putting the instructor on the defensive. Learning to control facial expressions is important because, as a health care professional, you will need to maintain expressions that convey caring and reassurance even in difficult situations.

6. Do you smile when it is appropriate? Does your face send the message "I'm glad to be here talking with you"?
7. Do you maintain appropriate eye contact? Failing to look at the other person while you are speaking tends to communicate a lack of sincerity, interest, or respect. (Exceptions to this include cultures that consider looking down to be a sign of respect.)

In addition to monitoring your own nonverbal communication, practice observing it in others. Learn to "listen between the lines." Do the speaker's words and actions match? Are there nonverbal signs of confusion, fear, or anger that you should take into account? Does your instructor give any nonverbal messages that communicate what is most important for you to learn?

Ask for clarification if verbal and nonverbal messages seem to conflict. Be willing to take the time and make the effort to get the true message. You can improve the interpersonal relationships in all areas of your life by combining an understanding of nonverbal communication with active listening and feedback.

Giving Presentations with Confidence

Many students find speaking in front of a group to be a frightening experience. This is a fear worth conquering, because the ability to speak with confidence can increase your opportunities to grow professionally and advance in your career. Proper preparation and a lot of practice can take the terror out of public speaking.

Preparing an oral presentation requires some of the same skills you use when writing, such as research and organization. It is said that an excellent way to learn something is to explain it to someone else. Try making oral presentations positive experiences by focusing on how you can learn from them.

Preparation. The six steps for preparing a speech are listed here and are similar for writing a paper:

Step One: Choose your topic early. It should be something you want to know more about or something you have strong feelings about. (Note: If you must speak on a topic with which you disagree, as sometimes happens with **debates** on controversial subjects, this is a chance to practice seeing other points of view and experiencing empathy.)

Step Two: Be clear about your purpose: inform, persuade, demonstrate, encourage people to take action, entertain.

Step Three: Find out about your audience. What is their background? How much do they know about the topic? What are their beliefs? What is their interest level?

Step Four: Identify what you need to find out and then do your research. Make sure you have accurate, up-to-date facts. Health care is constantly advancing and changing. Start now to develop the habit of verifying all information you use or distribute to others. In this sense, preparing for a speech is like preparing for a test: master the material you are going to present and feel confident about what you know.

Step Five: Organize your information. This includes mind maps, idea sheets, note cards, the brain dump, and questions.

Step Six: Divide your presentation into three parts:

Part One: The Introduction: "Tell the audience what you're going to tell them."
Engage your listeners with an interesting story or fact. Give them a reason to pay attention. Why is this topic important to them? What should they know about it? How does it relate to their lives? Approach your audience with the attitude that you have something to offer them. This helps put both you and them at ease.

Part Two: The Body: "Tell them."
This part takes up the most time. In it you explain and develop your ideas; give supporting facts, details, and examples; narrate events; and tell stories. This is the "meat" of your presentation.
Put the body of your speech together so it flows smoothly. For example, you might number your major points. Tell your audience how

many points there will be and then announce each one as you come to it:

"The kidneys have five important functions. The first is the regulation of fluid and electrolytes." (You then explain how they do this.)

"The second function is regulation of blood pressure." (More explanation.)

"The third is … " (etc.)

Part Three: Conclusion: "Tell them what you've told them."

Briefly review your major points, show how they tie together, and summarize why they are important. Tell the audience what action you want them to take or how they can use what you have told them.

It is especially important that oral presentations be put together in a logical, organized manner. With written material, readers can take their time and go back if they miss a point or don't understand something. Listeners don't have this advantage. You continue talking whether they are following what you're saying or not. You can lose them entirely if you jump from topic to topic, fail to support your ideas, or don't provide clear and complete explanations of the material.

Memory Joggers. It is usually a bad idea to read directly from your paper when giving an oral presentation. You may be tempted to look only at your paper instead of at the audience. Presentations that are read lack the warmth of human interaction and are less interesting for the audience. It is better to become familiar with your material and then use one of the following prompts to help you remember what you plan to say:

1. Note cards with key points.

A. *Advantages:* Small and easy to handle. Prevent you from reading directly from your paper. Encourage you to practice the speech beforehand and become familiar with the material.

B. *Watch Out For:* Having too many cards and getting them confused. Failing to number the cards and getting them out of order. Fiddling with them, which can distract the audience. Not including enough information on them and forgetting what you meant to say about each point.

2. Outline on full sheets of paper.

A. *Advantages:* Includes more information than note cards and may increase your confidence in remembering what you plan to say.

B. *Watch Out For:* Rattling the paper while you speak. Looking at the paper instead of the audience. Holding the paper with both hands and failing to use natural gestures while you speak.

3. Mind map with major topics and supporting points in graphic form.

A. *Advantages:* Easy to see major points at a glance. Especially helpful if you are a visual or global learner and don't need a lot of notes to remember what you plan to say.

B. *Watch Out For:* May be less room on the page to include detail, so be sure you know your material. Sometimes mind maps have words written at angles and are difficult to read quickly. Make sure you set it up in an easy-to-read format so that you don't get lost. Nonvisual learners are not likely to find mind maps helpful.

4. Key points written on overhead transparencies, on charts, or listed on the board. They can serve both as visual aids for the audience and as a guide for you.

A. *Advantages:* You and the audience are working together and sharing the experience of looking at the same materials. Listeners may become more involved if they are both listening and seeing. This technique also helps visual learners (the majority) follow your presentation. Take care, however, to explain each point, rather than simply reading them the list. The audience can do this for themselves!

B. *Watch Out For:* Poorly prepared visual aids that have too much information or lettering that is difficult for the audience to see. Equipment failures such as burned-out light bulbs or no extension cord (or discovering at the last minute that the projector is being used by another class!). Prior planning and consulting with the instructor are critical to prevent being tripped up during your presentation.

Practice

"The audience is not the enemy. Lack of preparation and practice is."

Give yourself the best chance possible to make a smooth presentation by practicing it a few times before doing it for real. Run through your presentation in front of a mirror, and then try it on friends and family members. Use the materials that will serve as your prompts to make sure they are clear and easy to follow. Time yourself to find out if you need to lengthen or shorten your presentation. Rehearsing in advance will give you the reassurance that comes from being familiar with your materials and knowing you have anticipated potential problems before you stand in front of an audience.

Should you memorize what you plan to say? Unless you are entering a formal speech contest or it is part of the assignment, this is usually not necessary or even a good idea. First, it is time consuming. Second, it can make you sound stiff and unnatural. Finally, and perhaps most important, if you forget a line or lose your place, it can be hard to get back on track. Rather than continuing to talk as you would with natural speech, you are in the uncomfortable position of trying to remember exactly where you are. The resulting long pause is very uncomfortable for both you and your audience.

Whenever possible, check the room where you'll be giving your presentation for details like the following:

☐ Is there a place to set down your cards or outline, or will you have to hold them as you speak? If you are short (like the author), can you see over the podium?

☐ Do you know how to operate the overhead projector? In which direction should the transparencies be placed? How do you adjust the image? Is the machine in working order? Are there extra bulbs available? Are the transparencies legible from the back row?

☐ Is there chalk or a pen available for the blackboard or white board? Will you have time to write out what you need? Is there an eraser?

☐ Is there a place to hang your charts, graphs, and other illustrations? Will you need tape, tacks, and so on?

☐ If you have models, samples, or other objects to show, is there a place to set them? Will the audience be able to see them? Will you pass them around?

Success Tips for Making an Oral Presentation

☐ Before you start to speak, take a breath, smile, and look at your audience. Even if you don't feel glad to be there, act as if you are. Try putting yourself and everyone else at ease.

☐ Look at the audience while you are speaking. Make eye contact with them. Look around the audience, not just in one direction. Catch the eyes of people who appear to be listening attentively and are "with you" to increase your feelings of support.

☐ Pause briefly if necessary. Some speakers even use pauses for dramatic effect. If you need a moment to gather your thoughts, stay calm. It is better to pause than to nervously ramble on or repeat filler words ("uh") that, if overused, are distracting. Pauses also give the audience time to reflect on what you have said.

☐ If you do lose your place or blank out a whole portion of your talk, stop and take a breath. Try not to panic. Acknowledge the audience with a smile or a nod (they may be as nervous as you are), and then concentrate on getting reorganized.

☐ Shift your focus from yourself to the audience. Remember that you have prepared well and have something of value to share. The audience needs this information, and you are being of service by sharing it with them.

☐ An old trick used by speakers is to imagine the audience in a funny situation: dressed in silly costumes, wearing big fake noses, standing on their heads—anything to change your perception of them as a threat.

☐ Consider organizing a buddy system. If you are already in a study group with classmates, that might do the trick. Practice your speeches with each other and offer constructive suggestions. Ask them to "cheer you on" by making eye contact when you are speaking, signaling when your time is almost up, and letting you know if you need to speak louder. Ask them to help you with handouts or visual aids. You will feel less alone.

Developing Your Teamwork Skills

If you are in a study group like the one suggested for giving speeches, you are already working on a team. Modern health care delivery relies on specialized professionals who work together. Look through the help wanted ads for health care jobs and you will see "team player" and "teamwork" mentioned in many of them. **Teamwork** refers to the efforts of individuals to coordinate their work to achieve common goals. High-quality patient care depends on how well people communicate and function as team members.

People do not always work together easily and naturally. Competition, rather than cooperation, is built into many aspects of our educational system. As a student, for example, you may be competing for grades, especially on tests that are scored on a curve. On the job, there can be competition for pay raises, bonuses, and recognition by the supervisor. But competition can get in the way of providing good care. The focus must always be on serving patients, not on fulfilling the individual needs of the health care workers. Teamwork is so important in health care that an entire section of the National Health Care Standards is devoted to teamwork criteria.

President John F. Kennedy is often quoted for his famous statement, "Ask not what your country can do for you, but what you can do for your country." Kennedy encouraged Americans to work together to reach goals ranging from establishing the Peace Corps to putting a man on the moon. Americans achieved both, proving that when people work together, they can accomplish amazing things.

You can begin practicing teamwork in school. Group activities assigned by instructors and lab sessions are excellent occasions to prepare for real work situations. Study groups provide opportunities to learn to cooperate. Many students report disliking group activities, saying they much prefer being responsible for their own work. If you feel this way, be aware that learning to work together and knowing how to encourage group members who fail to do their part are essential job skills. Welcoming opportunities to work with others while you are still in school is a good strategy for future career success.

Differences among Team Members. When team members support each other, work becomes a pleasant experience. On the other hand, teams in which members don't get along can slow down the work process and make life difficult for everyone. People have differences that can interfere with communication, cause hurt feelings, and disrupt the workflow. Understanding and taking advantage of these differences can help teams flourish rather than fight.

Just as we all have different learning styles, we also have different work styles. Identifying and taking advantage of the styles of each team member can help prevent misunderstandings and allow each one to make useful contributions. There are no right or wrong work styles. Ignoring styles, however, can decrease the effectiveness of the team and reduce the satisfaction of the people on it.

Here are some common approaches to work. As you read the list, check the ones that apply to you.

☐ Work methodically and complete one task or part of a task before moving on to the next.

☐ Work on several projects at the same time.

☐ Work alone and be responsible for your own work.

☐ Work with others in situations where cooperation determines the success of the project.

☐ Like working with details. Enjoy striving for accuracy and neatness.

☐ Think of ideas, but prefer to let someone else carry them out.

☐ Receive assignments with clear deadlines.

☐ Know exactly what is expected.

☐ Receive general instructions and a final due date. Figure out yourself how to get it done.

☐ Generate new ideas, products, and ways to work. Like to be creative.

☐ Receive a lot of guidance. Have someone check and approve your work as it progresses.

☐ Work with little supervision. Ask questions when you need help.

☐ Prefer quiet and order.

☐ Find noise and activity stimulating.

After reading this list, you can see how work styles are not only different, but even contradictory! It is not surprising that people sometimes find it difficult to work together. Attempting to understand the views and needs of your coworkers and supervisors is part of empathy, discussed earlier in this chapter. Applied in the workplace, empathy contributes to establishing good relations among staff members and creating a positive work environment.

Success Tips for Being an Effective Team Member

☐ **Understand the Ground Rules and Agreements.** These may not be formally stated or written down, but they are important for keeping communication open and preventing misunderstandings.

☐ **Be Clear about the Purpose and Goals of the Group.** Everyone should know what is to be accomplished. Have you been assigned a specific project? Or is the goal an ongoing effort related to your role as a student or an employee?

☐ **Do Your Part—and Then Some.** Follow through and complete any work you have been assigned or have volunteered to do. Let the group know if you run into problems. Ask for help. Someone may be willing to pick up the slack. Letting things go can result in serious consequences, such as affecting the group's grade, endangering patient safety, or costing the facility money.

☐ **Listen to What Others Have to Say.** What can you learn from them? What are their ideas about how to accomplish the work? What are their needs? What can they contribute?

☐ **Speak Up.** Share your ideas and opinions.

☐ **Take Advantage of Differences.** Maximize group efficiency by assigning tasks that are appropriate for each member.

Understanding Organizations

Organizations, such as schools and dental offices, have their own personalities, just as individual people do. These personalities are known as **organizational cultures,** and they include the goals, rules, expectations, and customs of the organization as a whole. Schools have cultures. For example, some are formal and emphasize respect for authority. Students are required to address their instructors by title and last name. Uniforms must be worn, and rules are strictly enforced. At other schools, the atmosphere is more casual, with students and instructors on a first-name basis. At some health care facilities, people eat lunch together, celebrate birthdays and holidays, and meet after work. At others, there is a clear distinction between work and social life. Some organizations stress orderliness, engage in detailed planning, and have clear work assignments. Others move at a fast pace, with informal job descriptions and planning done "on the run."

It is important to be aware of the culture you are in—or plan to enter—to see if it matches your preferences or if you can at least adapt to it. Sometimes we can learn from a culture that has values we would like to develop in ourselves. For example, if you have poor study habits and find yourself in a strict school, this can be a great opportunity to get the encouragement you need to develop new habits.

Understanding Your Instructors

We have discussed how people have different learning and working styles. Another factor that can influence your academic success is teaching and classroom management styles. Instructors are individuals who have their own ideas about education, teaching methods, and the proper roles of instructors and students. Understanding what is important to your instructors will help you benefit fully from your classes. You will use these same skills to identify the characteristics of your future supervisors so you can work with them more effectively.

Here are some common characteristics of instructors, along with suggestions for what you can learn from each:

1. **Strict.** Rules are emphasized. They are clearly explained, and there are consequences if they are broken.

   You Learn: Good habits for health care work situations in which rules must be followed to ensure patient and worker safety.

2. **Value Appearance.** Students must be neat, with clean, pressed uniforms and polished shoes. Points may be deducted from grades for infractions. Students who arrive out of uniform are sent home to change. (In a work environment, improperly dressed employees may also be asked to leave.)

   You Learn: To practice the habits of excellent hygiene that are critical in health care work. (Remember: Your professional career began when you started school.)

3. **Believe Students Should Be Responsible for Their Own Learning.** Instructors with this philosophy may allow you to go all term without ever mentioning that you haven't handed in all your homework assignments. You interpret this as meaning that it's not important and are shocked to receive a final grade of D or F. Never assume that no nagging means "not important." The same can happen at work. An employee may not be told about unsatisfactory work performance until the day of a formal evaluation or the initiation of a disciplinary process.

   You Learn: To take responsibility for yourself and what you must do. On the job, supervisors won't have time to remind you constantly about your tasks. It will be up to you to get them done.

4. **Believe They Must Monitor Students Closely.** Some instructors believe it is their responsibility to prompt students to complete their work. They give constant reminders, check their progress frequently, call students

who are absent, and generally provide "super-support." They are like those supervisors who are very organized and nurturing and are willing to tell employees what's to be done. They provide a lot of feedback.

You Learn: To work with frequent deadlines and a hands-on manager. How to meet deadlines and avoid falling behind in your work. Be careful, however, that you don't become dependent on continual help, because you can't always count on it being there for you.

5. **Value Order.** The classroom is neat and tidy, lectures follow a clear pattern, and class activities are well planned.

You Learn: To practice orderly habits when necessary. Although your home may be comfortably chaotic, order is necessary in many areas of the health care environment. Forms must be filled out in a very specific way, tests performed in a prescribed order of steps, and disinfecting procedures carried out precisely. Tidying up the classroom or lab before you leave is a good habit to develop and your instructor will certainly notice and appreciate your efforts.

6. **Value Creativity Over Order.** Classes may seem disorganized. Lectures are mixed with interesting stories and don't follow an orderly plan. Group activities and creativity are emphasized over doing things the instructor's way.

You Learn: To be creative and think for yourself, to work with classmates, and to practice the teamwork skills discussed in this chapter.

The teaching styles chosen by instructors are often reflections of their own learning styles or the way they remember being taught themselves. Instructors may rely on lectures to teach because they are auditory learners or because they believe that their role is to tell students what they know. You can take advantage of different teaching styles to help you improve your weak areas. For example, if an instructor uses a lot of group activities and you prefer to work alone, you now have an opportunity to increase your ability to work with others, something you might not choose to do if it weren't required.

If you have difficulty with an instructor, the first step in resolving the problem should be to speak privately with him or her. If you go straight to a school administrator, neither you nor the instructor has a chance to explore the problem and try to work out a solution. Furthermore, the administrator doesn't have personal knowledge of the situation. The problem has been moved away from its source. If speaking with the instructor fails to resolve the situation, inquire about the proper procedure to follow at your school. If you have problems with your supervisor at work, it is expected that you speak with that person first.

Most instructors decide to teach because they want to share what they have learned about their profession. They are motivated by concern for their students. This does not necessarily mean they strive to be liked by their students, because this is not the purpose of teaching. Their job is to train students to be excellent health care professionals. You may not like all your instructors, but given a chance, they all have something of value to share with you. And although you may not like all your supervisors, you can still find satisfaction in your work.

Dealing with Difficult People

People problems cannot be avoided entirely. There will be classmates who annoy you, who don't do their share of the work on a group project, or who take up a lot of class time with questions because they never read the assignments. Family members may criticize you because they are upset about the amount of time you spend studying. Friends may be jealous of your future career possibilities. Some of your future patients, clients, coworkers, and supervisors will be challenging, too. Learning to get along with difficult people helps make life more pleasant and productive.

In difficult situations, do your best to separate your role from you as a person. It is often your position with which the other person has a problem. For example, your family may be annoyed with your role as a student because of the time it takes away from them. Or a patient may take his anger out on you as a representative of the clinic with which he has a problem.

Empathy, which we discussed earlier in this chapter, can help. Listen carefully to the other person. Try to see the world from his or her point of view. What might explain the behavior? Might there be personal problems you don't know about? Is there a chance you have unintentionally done something to hurt his or her feelings? It can be helpful to acknowledge the other person's feelings without agreeing to feel the same way. For example, you might begin your discussion like this: "I can see why you feel that way, but ... " and then state your view. Recognizing the validity of the other person's feelings often decreases the negativity. Remain calm and courteous. Reacting negatively only makes the situation worse. (But this does not mean you have to take verbal or physical abuse. If this occurs, seek the assistance of your instructor, other school personnel, or your supervisor.)

Seek solutions to interpersonal problems by being honest and "up front." Tell the other person what you see as the problem and explain how it affects you. For example, with a lab partner who is never prepared to practice the assigned procedures, you might say, "I feel really frustrated when you continually come unprepared. I'm worried that I'm losing the chance to learn, and I can't afford to do that." Simply venting or arguing won't solve the problem; it may even make it worse. Work for a mutually acceptable agreement. Using the lab partner example, you could ask, "Can you agree to come to class prepared?" When there are serious consequences at stake, such as your grades or work performance, let the other person know what you plan to do if the situation is not resolved. Tell your lab partner, "If I can't depend on you to come prepared to work with me, I'll have to ask the instructor to let me change lab partners." As you attempt to find a solution, try to keep a positive attitude. Recall from our discussion about attitude in Chapter 2 that it doesn't make sense to give an unpleasant person the right to ruin your day. Do what you can to seek a positive solution and then move on.

We learn and develop professionally when we engage in all types of relationships, both positive and negative. Expressing kindness toward a troublesome classmate or giving an instructor the benefit of the doubt is a sign of maturity. It's easy to be professional when things are going well. True professionals can also deal effectively with challenging situations.

Dealing with Criticism

Criticism and constructive suggestions about your work present you with opportunities to learn. In school, you are paying for instruction that includes correction of your work. Your instructors would not be acting responsibly if they awarded inflated grades or withheld criticism to avoid hurting students' feelings. It would be unfair to allow students to perform work incorrectly, because this would only set them up for failure on the job where the consequences are more serious.

If you receive criticism that seems harsh, try to focus on the content and not on the way it is delivered. Not all instructors and supervisors are skilled at giving suggestions. If you don't understand what you did incorrectly, ask for clarification. It is your responsibility to learn as much as possible. Feelings must be put aside, if necessary, to ensure that you attain the skills necessary to be a competent health care professional.

Giving Constructive Criticism. The purpose of constructive criticism is to provide the person receiving the criticism with the means for improvement. It is based on the assumption that behavior can be changed for the better. It is important, when giving constructive criticism, to focus on the problem behavior rather than on the person. Suppose you have a coworker who frequently fails to return equipment to its designated storage space, causing you to waste time looking for needed items to do your work. State the problem behavior clearly: equipment is not being returned and this is affecting your efficiency. Avoid negative statements about the other person such as that she is inconsiderate, a poor coworker, disorganized, and so on. Judgmental statements about personal characteristics tend to put people on the defensive and make them less willing to examine their behavior and make positive changes.

Here are a few more suggestions for giving criticism that helps rather than hurts:

☐ Choose a private location to talk and allow enough time for the other person to respond and ask questions.
☐ Use empathy and show respect for the other person's feelings.
☐ Include positive statements along with the criticism.
☐ Be clear when explaining the problem. Give specific examples that illustrate the problem.

Neither giving nor receiving criticism is easy, but done well and taken in the spirit in which it is intended contributes to our learning and growth.

Prescription for Success 3–1
Getting to Know Yourself

The first step toward understanding others is knowing ourselves. Fill in the chart below with your own beliefs about each concept. You may use any of those listed in Box 3-1 or you can write your own.

Concept	My Beliefs
Time	_____
Personal Space	_____
Age	_____
Touching	_____
Gender	_____
Eye Contact	_____
Personal Control	_____
Spiritual Practices	_____
Definition of Success	_____
Health Care Beliefs	_____

Prescription for Success 3–2
Your Health Care Beliefs

1. What is your personal definition of "health"?

   _____

   _____

2. How much responsibility do you believe people should have for their own health?

   _____

   _____

3. What do you believe are the main causes of health problems?

   _____

   _____

4. What are the best ways to take care of health problems?

   _____

   _____

5. How do you think your own beliefs about health may influence your future work?

   _____

   _____

Prescription for Success 3–3
Rate Your Communication Skills

1. Do any areas need improvement?

   a. ____ Sending clear messages

   b. ____ Listening actively

   c. ____ Requesting feedback

   d. ____ Asking good questions

   e. ____ Understanding nonverbal communication

   f. ____ Demonstrating appropriate nonverbal communication

2. If so, what can you do to improve them?

   _____

   _____

3. What resources, including people, can help you improve your communication skills?

   _____

   _____

Chapter 4

Identifying the Three Levels of Understanding

READING WITH A PURPOSE

As students in the health care professions, you quickly discover the great amount of reading that you are required to complete. It is necessary that you accomplish these reading tasks as *efficiently* as possible. This means that you get as much understanding as you can during each of your study sessions. You cannot afford to waste time by performing at less than your best each time you sit at your desk and read. An excellent strategy that guarantees that each reading session will be successful is to read with a purpose. When you read with a purpose, you create a goal that you wish to accomplish each time you read. Having a goal to reach will keep you focused and involved in your reading. Your comprehension will be improved by reading with a purpose.

Introducing the Three Levels of Understanding

There is more than one way to understand what you are reading in your textbook. The goal or purpose you set for yourself as you read will determine the level of understanding required for comprehension of the reading material.

☐ The first level of understanding is called **literal understanding.** This level of understanding requires that you know what the subject of your reading is and the most important points being made about the subject. For example, when you need to learn important terms, names and functions of different parts of the body, or steps in a procedure from your textbook, you use literal understanding.

☐ The second level of understanding is called **interpretive understanding.** This level of understanding requires that you draw *conclusions* about what you are reading by examining the facts that are presented. For example, when you are reading to learn how to schedule patients according to the seriousness of their complaints, reading to learn how to decide on the proper medical insurance forms to fill out for a patient, or reading to learn how to examine stained smears for the presence of certain microorganisms, you use interpretive understanding.

☐ The third level of understanding is called **applied understanding.** This level of understanding requires that you see how ideas are similar so that you can use ideas from one situation in another related situation. For example, when you are asked to read a chapter about focusing the microscope and then you use one correctly in the laboratory or when you memorize from your text the proper handwashing technique and then use it when you handle patients, you use applied understanding.

Again, your goal or purpose for reading will determine which level of understanding you need to use when reading your textbook.

Let us now take a closer look at each of the different levels of understanding and see how each level suggests a strategy for improving reading comprehension.

Literal Understanding. When you read for literal understanding, you are reading for facts and information. You are trying to determine what the passage is saying in a basic, straightforward way. The strategy to use for literal understanding is to identify the topic and main idea of the selection you are reading. Finding the topic and main idea of a passage will give you a purpose for reading and will help you to concentrate on the essential points in the selection that you need to learn.

Identifying the Topic of a Passage

The topic is the key subject of the passage. To find the topic, you ask:

☐ What is this passage mostly about?

The answer will be the topic or subject of the passage and should be stated as briefly as possible.

Identifying the Main Idea

The main idea of a passage is what the passage is all about. The strategy to use to identify the main idea is to ask:

☐ What is the most important point being made about the topic?

The answer will be the main idea and should be stated in sentence form.

Example

Read the following excerpt from a health care textbook and pay attention to how the reader found the main idea by identifying the topic and then asking the question: What is the most important point being made about the topic?

Good business writing depends on clarity. If the basic element used to convey meaning–the sentence–is unclear, the entire message may be difficult to understand. Good sentence structure requires the application of all the rules of English grammar and the avoidance of certain particularly common errors.[1]

☐ What is this passage mostly about? Good writing = Topic.

☐ What is the most important point being made about good writing? Good writing depends on clear sentences = Main idea.

Notice that the first sentence in the paragraph, "Good business writing depends on clarity," contains the main idea of the selection. In this example the main idea was the first sentence. In other cases, however, the main idea may be in the last sentence, in the middle sentence, or in both the first and last sentences. In some instances, you may not be able to find a main idea sentence. In such cases, you will need to create your own main idea sentence. The strategy will be the same as you used for finding a given main idea sentence. You determine the topic and then ask the main idea question: What is the most important point being made about the topic? As long as you use this strategy, your answer should lead you to the main idea, regardless of where it is located. As long as you create and answer the main idea question, you should be able to make up your own main idea if one cannot be found in the passage.

Interpretive Understanding. When you read for interpretive understanding, you are reading to figure out something unstated in the passage. The strategy you use for interpretive understanding is to examine the facts or details in the passage and to use your own experience and background knowledge to draw a conclusion about the meaning of the passage. Drawing the correct conclusions about what you are reading will allow you to understand better what the writer really means and will allow you to function better in your workplace.

Details as Clues

When you use interpretive understanding, you need to go beyond the literal meaning of the passage and reason out in what direction the facts or details are leading. This requires that you infer or make a judgment about the meaning of the details. In other words, your responsibility when using interpretive understanding is to examine the details and use them as clues to help you form your own logical conclusions. In addition, you need to rely on information you have learned from your other classes and from your own life in order to come to the right explanation of the passage.

Applied Understanding. When you read for applied understanding, you are reading to learn ideas from your textbook so you can use these ideas in school or in the workplace. The strategies you will use for applied understanding include the strategies you use for literal and interpretive understanding.

☐ In order to apply information, you must first learn the facts. This will require that you learn

[1]From Diehl MO: Diehl and Fordney's Medical Transcription: Techniques and Procedures, ed 5, St. Louis, 2002, Saunders.

and remember ideas literally. Finding the topic and the main idea will help you focus on what is important.

☐ In order to apply information, you must be able to interpret what you are reading. This will require that you have some background knowledge of the subject and of the situation to which you will be applying the information.

☐ Finally, in order to apply information, you must use good judgment. You must be able to recognize the similarities and differences between the facts you read and the situations in which you will be applying these facts. You must be able to judge when and where it is appropriate and correct to apply these facts. This judgment requires that you know your facts and have experience.

REVIEWING THE LEARNING STRATEGIES

To Learn	Use This Strategy
Literal Understanding	Identify the topic of the passage by asking: What is this passage mostly about?
	Identify the main idea of the passage by asking: What is the most important point being made about the topic?
Interpretive Understanding	Examine the facts and details.
	Use your own experiences and background knowledge to draw conclusions.
Applied Understanding	Learn the facts for literal understanding.
	Use experience and background knowledge to interpret situation.
	Use your best judgment to determine when it is appropriate to apply facts to a new situation.

Chapter 5

Taking Notes

IMPORTANCE OF TAKING GOOD NOTES

Your success as a health care student depends almost entirely on how well you take notes from your textbooks and lectures. When it comes to preparing for tests, you must have textbook and lecture notes that adequately record the information you need to learn. Few people have the time to reread the vast amount of material from the textbook to prepare for a midterm or final examination. Few people have the ability to catch and remember every word spoken in a lecture. That is why it is important to have strategies for taking good notes from your books and lectures. You must learn to focus only on the information that is important. You do not want to waste your time recording and remembering facts that may not be necessary to learn. Knowing the strategies for taking good notes will not only save you time but will also enhance your test taking skills.

USING YOUR NOTES SUCCESSFULLY

Some students feel it is okay to take notes from their textbooks and lectures and then ignore them until test time. Other students, however, realize that to get good grades you must constantly review your notes. These students realize that textbook notes and lecture notes are interconnected. In order to get the best grades, they use the following strategies:

☐ Before lectures, take and review textbook notes on the subject of the lecture. This will build your background knowledge of the topic, and the lecture will be that much more understandable.
☐ After the lecture, review your textbook notes again. This will reinforce your learning of the information.
☐ Before test time, study both the lecture notes and the textbook notes until they are fully learned. This is good test preparation.

Time Management and Note Taking

An important aspect to good note taking is time management. This means allowing sufficient time for reading your textbooks and attending all lectures.

☐ Stay current. Do not fall behind in your textbook reading. You may be responsible for textbook information on exams and once you are behind, you may never be able to catch up. Maintain your scheduling calendars and keep pace with your reading assignments.
☐ Attend all lectures. Having to borrow someone else's notes is never as good as taking them yourself. If possible, ignore minor physical and emotional upsets and get into the habit of attending all your classes.
☐ Arrive early for your lectures. This will give you time to organize your notebook for good note taking. Also, you do not want to miss the beginning of the lecture. Many instructors introduce their main points at the very beginning of the class period, so this is something you may not want to skip.

Choosing Your Notebook

The first practical step for taking good textbook and lecture notes is buying and setting up your notebook. This will depend on personal preference. The main thing to keep in mind, however, is to organize your notebook so that each subject is kept separated from the other subjects. This may mean buying different 8 × 11 inch spiral notebooks for each subject or spiral notebooks that are divided into three to five sections. The advantage to using spiral notebooks is that they are lightweight and easy to carry. Also, you need to bring only the spiral notebook that is used for a particular daily class. The disadvantage to using a spiral notebook is that you may run out of paper. The manufacturer of these notebooks cannot anticipate how many pages you will actually need. You may find yourself having to buy more than one spiral notebook for each subject. This may prove bothersome and confusing.

An alternative to a spiral notebook is a hard cover loose-leaf binder. If this is your choice, be sure to buy the colorful dividers to keep each of your subjects separate. The advantage to using a loose-leaf binder is that you can control the number of pages for each subject section. If you use more paper in one class than in another, you can always insert more lined paper in that section. The disadvantage to using loose-leaf binders is that, depending on the type, they are not so *portable.* They may be heavy to carry and may not fit so well into your book bag or backpack. However, you can now purchase for each of your subjects an inexpensive lightweight loose-leaf notebook. Be aware, though, that there is always the possibility that the rings will not close right or will open at the wrong time, and that can mean disarranged or lost notes.

Whatever your preference in notebooks, remember that you must keep notes from each of your subjects separate and distinct from the other subjects. You may also want to consider using different notebooks for lecture notes and textbook notes. Again, the choice is yours.

Organizing Your Notepaper

Whether you are taking textbook or lecture notes, it is important to set up your notepaper in a way that will make your notes understandable when you read them days or weeks later. To organize your lecture notepaper, you must arrive in class a few minutes early to prepare your paper. To organize your textbook notes, plan to begin each study session with setting up your notepapers.

The first strategy to use in organizing your notepaper is numbering and putting the current date on top of each paper. This is important when it comes time to study for exams. By numbering and dating each page, you will know which notes are needed for a specific exam period. You will know

which notes to study. Also, if your notes should accidentally get loose, you will have a way of reorganizing them. Keeping your notes in numerical and *chronological* order is the best way of ensuring that your notes are well organized.

The next strategy for organizing your notepaper is to draw a line down the page, about an inch and a half from the red left-hand margin. When taking textbook or lecture notes, leave this space empty. Later you will write in this space if you need to add any information you missed, create headings, or jot down comments and observations you believe are necessary to finish your notes. Organizing your notepaper in this manner will ensure that your notes are complete and useful for test preparation.

Taking Notes from Your Textbook

As you probably realize by now, your time as a health care student is very precious. This means that you must use your limited amount of time sensibly. When it comes to reading assignments, you may feel overwhelmed because there is so much to read with so little time to do it in. When it comes to preparing for exams, you do not have the time to reread all the assigned chapters. Therefore you need strategies for taking good notes from your textbook for test preparation. Good textbook notes not only will save you time when you are getting ready for tests but will probably result in better test scores. The two strategies for taking textbook notes are:
☐ Highlighting
☐ Margin writing

Highlighting. Highlighting information in your textbook is probably the most popular way of *condensing* information in your textbook. To highlight important facts, you use a pen, pencil, or special highlighting marker and underline all the sentences you think are meaningful for learning the subject matter. The advantage to using the highlighting strategy is that it saves time. You do not have to rewrite information that is already written. Highlighting is quick and, when done properly, is probably the most efficient way of taking notes from a textbook. The disadvantage to highlighting is that most students tend to overdo it. You have no doubt seen a page in a textbook that is totally highlighted with a yellow marker. What is the point to highlighting every word on the page? The effectiveness of the highlighting strategy is that it is supposed to direct your eyes to only the most important words and ideas on the page. Therefore you must highlight only the most significant facts. To review this strategy:

☐ Look at the boldfaced headings on each page.
☐ Turn each boldfaced heading into a question.
☐ Highlight only those facts that answer the heading question.

Margin Writing. To **complement** your highlighting of the important points in your textbook, you may also want to consider writing in the margins of your textbook. Following is a list of suggested items that you may use for margin writing:

☐ *Headings:* You can divide lengthy passages into more manageable sections by creating your own headings. Write these headings between paragraphs or in the margin where you want to divide the passage.
☐ *Summaries:* You can summarize or condense lengthy passages into brief summaries by writing in the margins of your book. You will not be able to be wordy because of the limited space. Your margin summaries should cover only the most important information in the passage.
☐ *Symbols:* Using various symbols can be an easy way of emphasizing important facts from the textbook. Some useful symbols are "T" to show what details your instructor said will appear on tests; "B" to show what information in your textbook corresponds to information your instructor wrote on the board during a lecture; and "R" to designate those sections in the textbook that your teacher may have read aloud and discussed in class. Using symbols like these will help you connect important ideas from your lecture to the material in your textbook.

Instructors' Cues

Now that you have a system for taking lecture notes, you are left with the decision of determining what information is important to record. Fortunately, your instructor will willingly or unwillingly provide you with cues that should let you know what ideas are significant. By recognizing these cues, you will know what facts to write in your notes and possibly what facts to leave out. Following are the cues most instructors give to indicate meaningful material:

☐ Ideas Written on the Board: Make sure you copy any information the teacher writes on the board. As mentioned earlier, you may want

to indicate these facts with a "B" for board in your notes.
☐ Verbal Tips: You may be fortunate to have an instructor who will say, "this will be on the test" or "these are important ideas." Make sure you write these facts accurately and mark these notes with a "T" for test or an "I" for important.
☐ Numbering Ideas: Many teachers may introduce important points by numbering them. They do this by saying "first," "second," "third," etc. If your teacher goes to the trouble of numbering ideas, you should consider them important enough to copy in your notebook.
☐ Body Language: Some instructors will make their voices louder or gesture with their hands to indicate important ideas. Stay alert to these or other body signs that the teacher will use to suggest important ideas.

At the end of the lecture, resist the temptation to stop listening and gather your books. Many times the instructor will summarize the important points at the end of the lecture, so pay attention and stay put until the teacher finishes talking.

How Many Notes to Take

Many students are puzzled about how many notes they should be writing from their textbooks and lectures. The best strategy in this matter is to know the course requirements and let that help you determine how much to write. If the course deals with broad concepts, you probably will be held responsible for fewer or less detailed notes. If the course presents more factual information, you will need to write greater and more detailed notes.

The best way to determine the requirements of the course is to read the description in the course catalogue, talk with other students who have taken the course, or speak with the instructor directly. Getting this information while the semester is just beginning will help you determine how many notes you should be taking.

Faster Note Taking

Many people feel that they would be more successful students if they were able to take lecture notes more quickly. They express frustration at not being able to "catch" all the important points being taught in the classroom. They claim they would do better on tests if their notes were complete. By learning the strategies for faster note taking—streamlining your handwriting and abbreviating and using symbols—these students will improve the rate of their note taking and become better students.

Streamlining Your Handwriting. To take notes more quickly, it is sometimes necessary to make changes in your handwriting. Your note-taking rate will improve if you write in script rather than in print. When you write in script, one letter connects to the other so that the flow of your writing is faster. However, when you use script, make sure you eliminate any unnecessary strokes or curlicues. Your ability to use a plain streamlined script will greatly enhance your lecture note-taking skills.

Abbreviating and Using Symbols. Another strategy for faster note taking is to use abbreviations or symbols to replace common words. It is much quicker to write "&" for "and" or to spell "patient" "pat." You can use **conventional** abbreviations and symbols, or you can make up your own. If you make up your own, be sure you remember their meanings. It will do you little good if you use a symbol or abbreviation that you can't understand a few weeks later when you prepare for an exam.

Taping Your Lectures. Another strategy for ensuring well-written notes is to tape your lectures with a portable audiocassette recorder. However, before you attempt to do this, get your instructor's permission; some people feel uncomfortable when they know they are being taped. The advantages to taping your lectures are many. First, during your study period you can replay the tape and fill in any missing information. Second, listening to your lectures over and over again is a good strategy for test preparation. Third, you can listen to your lecture tape anytime—as you drive to classes, when you are commuting to school, or at your leisure at home. And, finally, you can have a friend tape a lecture for you if you cannot attend class.

Make sure that your recorder is easy to carry and battery operated. Always remember to carry extra batteries. Buy the long-running blank cassette tapes and sit up front, close to the instructor, so you can get a clear recording. You want your lecture tapes to be as distinct as possible.

Studying from Your Notes

After a lecture, as soon as you can, review your notes for completeness. This may mean listening to your tape or consulting with a fellow student.

Once you feel your notes are as thorough as possible, you should begin to learn these notes in a systematic manner. A wonderful strategy for learning notes is to use the heading method.

Creating Headings. Just as your textbook passages are divided by headings, so should your class notes be divided by headings. Decide where in your notes there is a topic change and, using a different color pen, put in a heading. To create the topic, ask yourself what this passage is mostly about. The answer will be the topic and will work well for a heading. Do this for all the pages in your notebook.

Once you have made headings for all the different topics in your notes, turn these headings into questions. When you are studying for an exam, focus on the information in your notes that will answer the heading question. Below is an example of how a student created headings and questions and highlighted only the important information that answered the heading question.

Example

☐ What is this passage mostly about?
☐ Influenza = Topic = Heading
☐ What is influenza = Heading question

*Influenza virus A produces the most serious form of influenza, with **symptoms of fever, chills, headache, myalgia, sore throat, and cough.** The **onset of symptoms** is approximately 1 **to 4 days after contact** with infected respiratory secretions. **Infected people shed the virus for 24 hours before the onset of symptoms and for 3 to 4 days during the course of the disease.** Death associated with this virus is usually the result of primary influenza pneumonia or a secondary bacterial pneumonia. The influenza viruses that are the cause of epidemics and nosocomial outbreaks change from season to season, and a new vaccine is manufactured each year.[1]*

Other Strategies for Studying Your Notes

You may believe that preparing for an exam means reading and rereading your notes. However, you may have had the experience of sitting at your desk, hour after hour, and "spacing out" when you should have been focusing on your textbook

[1]From Flynn JC: Procedures in Phlebotomy, ed 3, St. Louis, 2005, Saunders.

or lecture notes. You probably discovered at test time that all you accomplished was wasting time. Successful students are those who have discovered that more active strategies are necessary for quality test preparation. This means more active note-learning strategies.

An excellent strategy for using your notes to prepare for a test is to create quizzes. At the end of an evening's studying, and before you close the books, make up a quiz covering that day's materials. At the beginning of your next homework session, take the quiz and see how well you have done. Another good studying strategy is to make up a chart of all the information you need to learn. Make a second chart, omitting most of the information except for some guiding facts and try to fill in the chart without looking at the original. Also use your tape recorder and play back the lecture when you are washing dishes or sorting socks. Finally, make flash cards of the important vocabulary words. Print the word on one side of an index card and its definition on the other side. During your study time, look at the word and try to recall the definition. Or, for more variety, look at the definition and try to remember the word. Being creative about taking and studying textbook and lecture notes will go a long way toward making you a more successful student.

REVIEWING THE LEARNING STRATEGIES

To Learn	Use This Strategy
Successful Use of Notes	Time management
	Careful choice of notebook
	Notepaper organizing
Note Taking from Textbook	Highlighting
	Margin writing
Note Taking from Lectures	Indenting
	Interpreting instructor's cues
Length of Notes	Learning requirements of course
Faster Note Taking	Streamlining handwriting
	Abbreviating and using symbols
	Taping lectures
Note Studying	Creating headings
	Creating questions
	Making quizzes
	Making charts
	Listening to lecture tapes
	Making flash cards

Chapter 6

Improving Test Scores

HOW TO IMPROVE YOUR TEST SCORES

The purpose of tests is evaluation. Tests allow you, the student, and your instructor to find out what you have learned and what you still need to learn.

Of course, students worry about test grades. Doing well on tests is every student's goal. You can learn strategies to improve your grades. However, these strategies have to be applied long before the date of the exam.

Strategy 1: Plan Ahead

Your instructor will assign test dates in advance. Apply your time-management skills. Find out the assignments you need to study for the exam. Make sure that you know which information from your readings, lectures, or labs will be on the test. Then use your monthly, weekly, and daily calendars to schedule enough study time for your exam.

Many students in the health fields are juggling school with busy work and family schedules. Finding time to study can be a problem. Therefore organization is essential. Use your calendars to plan your study time. Stick to your schedule. Don't procrastinate! Avoiding your work today means doing a double assignment the next day.

Cramming, trying to prepare for an exam at the last minute, is not a successful strategy. Cramming increases anxiety. This nervousness often interferes with your test performance.

Do you understand how to plan ahead to schedule enough time to study for tests?
Yes _____ No _____

Strategy 2: Keep Up with Assignments

Assignments should be done on a regular basis. Keep up with all the reading on your class syllabus. Don't fall behind.

Be an active reader. As you read your assignments, remember to be an active reader. Preview the reading material. Ask questions. Write summaries and outlines. Learn the new vocabulary that helps you to understand the ideas in each chapter. Pay attention to illustrations and formulas.

Do you remember to use your active reading strategies when reading home assignments?
Yes _____ No _____

Use active listening and effective note-taking strategies. Be prepared for each class session. Don't skip classes. Regular attendance is necessary if you are to understand a sequence of information. In the health fields, details are important. Take accurate notes. Apply active listening strategies. Pay attention to all main ideas and details highlighted in each lecture or lab. Ask questions if you don't understand the material presented. Summarize or outline the material presented in class.

Do you concentrate during class lectures?
Yes _____ No _____
Do your class notes help you study for tests?
Yes _____ No _____

Strategy 3: Study and Learn Material

Even if you have attended every class and read every assignment, you still have to study before every test.
☐ Review all class notes, summaries, outlines, and underlined material from your textbooks periodically throughout the course. Don't cram!

- ☐ Organize information into categories. It will be easier for you to remember organized material.
- ☐ Review vocabulary. Definitions are important in helping you learn information in the health fields. In fact, it is helpful to keep a notebook of the words and definitions that are highlighted in each chapter. Some students prefer keeping words and definitions on 3 × 5 inch index cards. Learn these definitions before the test.
- ☐ Pay attention to illustrations and formulas. Make sure that you understand how these pictures and numbers relate to the ideas in the chapter.
- ☐ Use mnemonics, a technique for improving the memory, to help you learn formulas, definitions, or ideas in the text. Mnemonic devices are easily remembered words, sentences, or rhymes that help you to remember more difficult information. Mnemonic devices work by association and help you to remember information that is difficult to organize. Some common mnemonic devices are:

Rhymes
i before e except after c
or when sounding like a
as in neighbor and weigh

Acronyms - a word made from the initial letter of the parts of the information to be remembered.

HOMES - to remember the five Great Lakes
H—Huron
O—Ontario
M—Michigan
E—Erie
S—Superior
Try to create mnemonic devices to help you remember information.
Do you find mnemonics a helpful memory tool?
Yes _____   No _____

- ☐ Don't accept not understanding. Don't give up. Monitor your learning. When you don't understand information, try another approach to learning. Make sure that your study schedule allows you time to ask your instructor or other students to explain difficult ideas to you **before** the test.
- ☐ Find out how you learn best. Do you remember information by listening, reading, writing, or discussing the material? Do you find a combination of these methods most effective for learning? Use the learning style that works best for you.

- ☐ Design practice tests. Ask your instructor if the test questions will be objective, essay, or both. Answer the questions at the end of each chapter in your textbook.
- ☐ Check your answers. Then make up a practice test. Close your book and answer your own test questions. Correct your test. What do you know? What do you still have to learn? Students find that questions on their practice tests often turn up on the actual exam.

List those techniques that you think will help you to study and learn information.

Strategy 4: Take the Test Successfully

Learning how to take a test can improve your test scores. Whether your test is objective or essay, use these *strategies:*
- ☐ Read the test directions carefully before you answer any questions.
- ☐ Understand the grading system. Spend extra time on questions that are worth more points.
- ☐ Keep track of time.
- ☐ Answer the questions that you are sure of first. Then go back to questions that are more difficult for you.
- ☐ Answer the questions asked.
- ☐ Save time at the end to review your test and make any corrections or additions.
- ☐ Write clearly.

Taking Objective Tests. Objective tests are those with multiple-choice, short-answer, matching, or true-false questions. To do well on objective tests, you should learn how to answer four types of questions: multiple-choice, short-answer, matching, and true-false.

Learning How to Answer Multiple-Choice Questions

When you answer multiple-choice questions, you select one answer from several choices. The following strategies will help you learn how to select the correct answer.
- ☐ Statements that contain words like *always, every, never,* and *all* are usually too broad. They are often incorrect.
- ☐ If two choices have the same meaning, they are both incorrect. Therefore, you eliminate both these choices when you select your answer.
- ☐ Be aware of directional words such as *but, except,* and *however.* They signal opposite meanings.

- [ ] To answer multiple-choice questions, you need to know how to:
  - ○ Find the main ideas
  - ○ Find and remember details that support the main idea
  - ○ Draw conclusions
  - ○ Learn vocabulary meanings through context

Learning How to Answer Short-Answer Questions

Short-answer questions ask you to fill in the blank. When you decide on an answer, check to see that your answer fits into the sentence in both meaning and grammar.

Learning How to Answer Matching Questions

When answering matching questions, link answers from one column to explanations in another column. Keep track of the answers you have already used. In this way you monitor your progress. Matching questions are often used to link words with definitions or to connect cause-effect relationships.

Learning How to Answer True-False Questions

When answering the true-false questions,
- [ ] Pay attention to the part of the question that makes it either true or false.
- [ ] Pay close attention to detail before you choose your answer.
- [ ] Remember that the whole statement has to be correct for the answer choice to be true.
- [ ] If part of the statement is incorrect, the answer is false.

Taking Essay Tests. In an essay test, students are expected to state the main ideas and to support those general statements with details. Also, students should be able to draw conclusions from ideas presented. Clear, simple, organized writing, as well as content, often counts toward your grade.

Before Writing Your Answer:

- [ ] Read the entire test carefully.
- [ ] Pay close attention to the directions.
- [ ] Look at the point value of each question. You should spend more time on a question worth 30 points than on one worth 10 points.
- [ ] Read the questions carefully.
- [ ] Understand the question. Are you asked to list, explain, classify, contrast, or sequence information?
- [ ] Allow time for reading questions, thinking about, and organizing your answers.
- [ ] Arrange your thoughts. Write an outline.

While Writing Your Answer:

- [ ] State the main idea in a clear topic sentence.
- [ ] Support main ideas with relevant details.

After Writing Your Answer:

- [ ] Read all your answers.
- [ ] Check to see that you have answered the questions that were asked.
- [ ] Make sure that you have answered all parts of each question.
- [ ] Make necessary changes in content, mechanics, and organization.
- [ ] Use an editing checklist to help you revise your essay.

  Following is an example of an editing checklist:

	Yes	No
Content		
Are the ideas developed?	_____	_____
Is the presentation logical?	_____	_____
Are the examples appropriate?	_____	_____
Mechanics		
Did you check your choice of words?	_____	_____
Did you improve the sentence structure?	_____	_____
Did you make sure your use of punctuation is correct?	_____	_____
Organization		
Does your essay contain an introduction?	_____	_____
Does your essay contain a body with supporting evidence?	_____	_____
Does your essay contain a conclusion?	_____	_____

Strategy 5: Evaluate Test Results

Once your test paper is returned, don't just look at your score and throw away the paper. Look at what you know. Look at what you still need to learn. Go back to your notes and text to correct all errors. If you still need help, schedule a conference with your study partner, study group, and/or your instructor. Save all test papers. Use these tests to review for your final exam.

REVIEWING STRATEGIES FOR IMPROVING TEST SCORES

To Learn	Use This Strategy
To Plan Ahead	Apply time management skills.
To Keep Up with Assignments	Be an active reader. Use active listening and effective note-taking strategies.
To Study and Learn the Material	Review class notes and text, summaries and outlines, and underlined material. Organize information into categories. Review vocabulary. Pay attention to illustrations and formulas. Use mnemonics to improve your memory. Monitor your learning. Discover your best study method. Design practice tests.
To Take the Test Successfully	Learn strategies for taking objective tests. Learn strategies for taking essay tests.
To Evaluate Test Results	Look at what you know. Look at what you still need to learn.

Chapter 7

Writing Strategies

INTRODUCTION

Writing the first *draft* is when you, the writer, put all your ideas on paper. Remember, your first draft is not your finished *product.* Once you learn that writing is a process and that your first draft is not the end product, you will not have to worry about making the first draft perfect. This realization should take away your feelings of anxiety when you have a writing assignment. Remember that the writing process breaks the task of writing into manageable steps.

Getting Started

Sometimes, students find it difficult to get started on the first draft. Begin your first draft while all the ideas are fresh in your mind and you can get all these thoughts on paper. Start your first draft when you have realistically set up enough time to finish. It's best to work on your first draft uninterrupted. Don't attempt to initiate this step of the writing process if you know that in five or ten minutes you'll have to leave for a class or your job. Don't stop your work to answer phone calls or watch television. Find a place to work where you can write freely, away from distractions and interruptions. Realizing that you are not expected to write a perfect first draft should give you the *confidence* to get started.

Look over your writing plan. You've selected your **subject, purpose, form,** and **audience.** Expand this plan by developing your main ideas into sentences and paragraphs. Write freely. Remember, you'll have time to make your changes in the next step in the writing process, *revision.*

Getting the Main Ideas on Paper

Did you write all your main ideas on your subject? Did you include all of the details that you collected? Did you choose to eliminate information or did you just forget to include it? Look back to your first step in the writing process. Reread your writing plan and your collection of details. Check your first draft against your prewriting strategies. See if there is anything you need to add to your first draft.

Organizing Your Thinking

While you are writing a first draft, it is helpful to try to organize your thinking. Think again about your purpose for writing. Do you want to describe, explain, persuade, or narrate?

Try to write freely while you organize your information according to purpose. When you are describing, use adjectives which arouse the senses. Will a reader be able to see, hear, feel, taste, or smell when reading your writing? When you choose to explain something, you can give reasons and results. Hopefully, your readers will be able to *detect* a cause-effect relationship. If you compare or contrast things in your explanation, are you telling what something is like by letting the reader know how it is the same as or different from something else? You might choose to explain information by breaking it down into parts or by letting the reader know how something works. When you are writing to persuade, your purpose is to convince. Do you slant your writing? *Slanted* writing is writing that is deliberately chosen to sway a reader's opinion. Strong words are used to direct the reader to agree with the writer's opinion. When you are writing to narrate, you are telling a story. You might be telling about an experience you had or about an event that influenced you.

When you are narrating a story, pay close attention to your <u>sequence</u> of events because logical order is important if a reader is to follow and understand your writing.

WRITING AND REVIEWING THE FIRST DRAFT

To Learn	Use This Strategy
To Get Started	Follow your writing plan and collection of details
To Get Your Main Ideas on Paper	Check your writing plan and collection of details
To Organize Your Thinking	Organize your writing according to your purpose: describe, explain, persuade, or narrate
To Include All the Parts	Think about a beginning, middle, and ending as you write
To Finish the First Draft	Check that you have included all your main ideas by asking and answering the 5W (who, what, when, where, and why) questions

THE NEXT STEP

After you have developed your writing plan and completed your first draft you are ready for the next step in the writing process. Remember, your first draft is not your final draft. You have to go through the steps of revising, editing, and proofreading before you have a final version of your paper.

Revising is the changes you make to improve your first draft. You will want to look at the main ideas and make some additions or cut some unnecessary details. You might want to change the order of your information. It helps to follow a plan when you are revising. Otherwise, you might not make all the needed improvements to your final draft.

Following a Plan for Revising

You should follow this plan when you are revising your writing:

☐ Read the first draft several times.
☐ Think about the changes needed to improve your first draft. For example, ask yourself if you've included all the important ideas. Are any important details missing? Check to see if these ideas are clear, complete, and in the right order.
☐ Try to improve your writing by evaluating your own work. Look for the parts you want to keep. Look for the parts that need to be changed. You can use a revising checklist to help you evaluate your work and decide what changes need to be made to improve your first draft.

Using a Revising Checklist
The following checklist should help you to decide what to change as you revise your first draft. Ask yourself:

Did I...	Yes	No
follow my writing plan?	_____	_____
clearly express my main idea?	_____	_____
support the main idea with enough details?	_____	_____
organize the details according to my purpose?	_____	_____
write a clear beginning, middle, and ending?	_____	_____
write the ideas in the correct order?	_____	_____
include unnecessary details?	_____	_____
repeat ideas?	_____	_____
fulfill my purpose in writing?	_____	_____

Did I...	Yes	No
follow my writing plan?	Yes, except more specific details are needed to fit the form of a report.	
clearly express my main idea?		No, main point should be more directly stated.
support the main idea with enough details?		No, more specific details were needed to make the report complete.
organize the details according to my purpose?	Yes, reasons were given to support conclusion.	
write a clear beginning, middle, and ending?		No, middle needs to be more specific. Ending could be stronger.
write the ideas in the correct order?	Yes	
include unnecessary details?		No
repeat ideas?		No
fulfill my purpose in writing?		No, conclusion has to be rewritten to fulfill purpose.

Answering the questions on the revising checklist will help you to examine the strengths and weaknesses of the first draft. You will now decide how to change your first draft to make it better.

Example

Let's take a look at a student's first draft on the subject of child abuse:

Child abuse is a danger to children that results in harmful injury and even death. As health care providers, we have to be aware of the symptoms of child abuse. When we examine children who are repeatedly bruised, or accident prone, we should be suspicious. Neglecting to report cases when children are repeatedly being treated for broken bones could lead to greater injury. Child abuse affects children of all ages and crosses all economic groups. If we do not act on our suspicions because we want to protect the parents, the children will be endangered.

To see how the student answered the questions on the revising checklist, see the box above.

Using a Computer to Help with Revising. Many students use the computer from the first step in the writing process—planning—until they hand in their final draft. Other students prefer to do their planning and first drafts on paper and then type their work on the computer to do the revising and editing that is needed before turning in the final draft.

Word processing programs help you use the computer to add ideas and move sentences and even whole pages around. Using a word processor makes revising less **tedious.** Writing becomes less of a chore and more exciting. Students actually enjoy moving their ideas around. It's fun to see the changes as they appear on the computer screen. Editing is also easier with the computer. Computer programs have spell checks that scan for spelling errors and grammar checks that point out mechanical problems with sentences.

Using a computer will make it much easier for you to make the changes needed to improve your writing.

Following a Plan for Editing and Proofreading

When you have finished revising the ideas in your paper, you are ready for another step in the writing process, editing and proofreading. During editing and proofreading, you make your final changes. You carefully check your writing for errors in spelling and mechanics. You should follow this plan for editing and proofreading your writing: Check:
- [ ] sentences to determine whether they are smooth or **choppy.**
- [ ] for errors in spelling, punctuation, and grammar.
- [ ] your choice of words.
- [ ] the **presentation** of your finished copy.
- [ ] your paper one last time to make sure that you have corrected any mistakes.

Did I...	Yes	No
write clear and complete sentences?	_____	_____
use sentence variety?	_____	_____
write sentences of different lengths?	_____	_____
capitalize and punctuate correctly?	_____	_____
choose vivid, specific words?	_____	_____
check for repetition of words?	_____	_____
check for subject-verb agreement?	_____	_____
check for pronoun agreement?	_____	_____
check for verb tense?	_____	_____
check spelling errors?	_____	_____

Using a Checklist for Editing and Proofreading. The following checklist should help you to edit and proofread your writing. Ask yourself:

The questions on this editing and proofreading checklist will help you to make the final corrections needed to improve your writing.

Learning Some Basic Symbols for Proofreading. You can use proofreading symbols to help you mark up your revised paper so that you can make the final changes. Learning these symbols will also help you to understand your instructor's corrections of your writing.

Some common proofreading symbols are:

agr agreement
cap capitalization
frag sentence fragment
gram grammar
nc not clear
¶ paragraph
p punctuation
R repetitions
sp misspelled word
RO run-on sentence
TS topic sentence
u usage
wc word choice

PREPARING THE PRESENTATION

The presentation, or appearance, of your paper is a critical part of the writing process. Whether you write or type your paper, your work should be neat, well spaced, and easy to read. In writing, one cannot separate form from content. A finished paper with a good presentation is an essential part of the writing process.

AVOID TROUBLE SPOTS IN WRITING

When you are proofreading your paper, keep in mind certain areas in which students make errors. If you are aware of these problem areas in writing, you can correct your mistakes before you hand in your final paper.

Spelling. You can avoid making spelling mistakes by learning and applying a few spelling rules.

Some Common Spelling Rules

☐ Words ending in "y": When you write the plurals of words that end in *y,* change *y* to *i* and add *es.* If the word ends in *ey,* just add *s.*
  baby, babies; turkey, turkeys
☐ Consonant ending: When you add an ending like *ed* or *ing* to a one-syllable word with a short vowel, the final consonant is usually doubled.
  hop, hopping; tip, tipped
☐ "i" Before "e": *I* before *e* except after *c* or when rhyming with *say* as in *neighbor* and *weigh.*
  belief, conceit, sleigh
☐ Silent "e": If a word ends with a silent *e,* drop the *e* before adding an ending that begins with a vowel. Do not drop the *e* when the ending begins with a consonant.
  hope, hoping, hopeful

Commonly Misspelled Words. You should learn the following words that students often misspell:

Absence	Accurate
Absent	Across
Accept	Advise
Accident	Already
Accommodate	Analyze

Apologize

Attendance

Belief

Benefit

Benefited

Business

Characteristic

Committee

Competition

Convenience

Cooperate

Criticism

Decision

Dependent

Dilemma

Disease

Dissatisfied

Dying

Embarrassed

Environment

Excellence

Exercise

Exhaust

Extremely

Feasible

Foreign

Fragile

Friend

Fulfill

Government

Grievance

Guarantee

Guardian

Handicapped

Handkerchief

Harass

Hazardous

Height

Helpful

Hospital

Illegal

Immigrant

Independent

Intelligence

Interfere

Itinerary

Jeopardize

Judgment

Knowledge

Laboratory

Leisure

Maintenance

Medicine

Necessary

Neighborhood

Neither

Nuclear

Occasion

Occur

Omitted

Operate

Opinion

Pamphlet

Persuade

Physical

Physically

Preferred

Prejudice

Professor

Pronunciation

Psychology

Qualitative

Questionnaire

Receipt

Recognize

Recommend

Recurrence

Reference

Remember

Responsibilities

Safety

Schedule

Secretary

Separate

Significant

Suggest

Supervisory

Sympathize

Tedious

Temperature

Temporarily

Tendency

Tomorrow

Tragedy

Transferred

Traveling

Ultimately

Unconscious

Unfortunately

Unnecessary

Vehicle

Violence

Voluntary

Waive

Weigh

Welfare

Witnessed

Yield

Zeros

Words Often Confused. Read over the following commonly misused words. This list should help you find the right words to use in your writing.

accept to receive
except other than

allowed permitted
aloud with a speaking voice

already previously
all ready completely ready

capital the seat of government
        chief
        accumulated wealth
capitol a building that usually houses some part
  of government

choose to select
chose selected

council a group called together for certain tasks
counsel advise
        to give advice

desert a dry region
        to leave
dessert the final course of a meal

it's the contraction meaning "it is"
its the possessive form of "it"

loose free from restrictions
lose to misplace
    to fail to win

principal a school administrator
            most important
principle a rule

stationary a fixed position
stationery writing paper

than compares two things
then tells when

Parts of Speech	Use	Examples
noun	names	pen, Lewis
pronoun	taking the place of a noun	them, us, herself
adjective	describes a noun or pronoun	red, tallest
verb	action, linking, helping	watched, is, has been writing
adverb	describes a verb, an adjective, or another adverb	slowly, better
preposition	relates a noun or pronoun to another word; begins a phrase	among, around, on
conjunction	joins words	and, but, or
interjection	shows strong feeling	Ouch!

their possessive form of they
there indicates place or direction
they're a contraction meaning "they are"

to indicates direction
too also
    very
two the number "2"

who's the contraction meaning "who is"
whose the possessive form of "who"

you're the contraction meaning "you are"
your the possessive form of "you"

Sentence Errors. A sentence is made up of a subject and verb and expresses a complete thought. Check for sentence errors. Some common errors are sentence fragments and run-on sentences.

A fragment is a group of words that does not make a complete sentence.

Example: Thinks he can win.

This fragment is missing a subject. You can correct this fragment by adding a subject.

Corrected Sentence: My brother thinks he can win.

A run-on sentence is when two sentences are joined without punctuation or a connecting word.

Example: I thought he would never leave he just kept talking.

Corrected Sentence: I thought he would never leave. He just kept talking.

Parts of Speech. Learning the parts of speech will help you to know how to use words correctly in a sentence. Read over the chart above to learn how to use the parts of speech.

Agreement

Pronouns

Pronouns must agree in person and number with the words they replace.

Example: John told *Sonya* and *Mary* to meet him at work.

With Pronoun: He told *them* to meet him at work.

Example: Sylvia instructed *the employees* on how to operate *the computer.*

With Pronoun: She instructed *them* on how to operate *it.*

Subjects and Verbs

Subjects and verbs should agree in number. If the subject is singular, the verb should be singular. If the subject is plural, the verb should be plural. In the following examples the subject is in italic type and the verb is in boldface type.

Example: *Mindy and Helen* **were** absent.

Example: *Either of the doctors* **is** qualified to perform the surgery.

The following words take a singular verb:

Anyone	Everybody	Someone
Anybody	Everyone	
Each	Neither	
Either	One	

Capitalization. Capitalize:
- ☐ The first word of a sentence
- ☐ Proper nouns and adjectives

Example: *Celena* traveled to *England* and enjoyed touring the *English* countryside.

Punctuation. Read the following chart to learn how to use punctuation correctly.

.	Period	End of sentence that is a statement, command, or request
		After abbreviated title or initial
?	Question mark	End of sentence that asks a question
!	Exclamation mark	End of sentence that shows emotion
,	Comma	Items in a series
		In dates, addresses, and numbers
		After introductory expressions
		Around nonessential material
		To set off interruptions
		In direct address
'	Apostrophe	To form the possessive of singular and plural nouns
		In contractions
;	Semicolon	Between two closely related independent clauses unless they are joined by the connecting words (and, but, nor, yet, or, for, so)
:	Colon	After a complete statement when a list or long quotation follows
–	Dash	To show a change of thought or emphasis
" "	Quotation marks	Around the exact words of a speaker
		The name of a short story, poem, essay, or TV program

REVIEWING AND REWRITING THE FINAL DRAFT

To Learn	Use This Strategy
Make necessary changes to your first draft	Follow a plan for revising
Decide what changes are necessary	Use a revising checklist
Make additional changes	Reread your revision
Make revising easier	Use a word-processing program
Make the needed changes in spelling and mechanics	Use an editing and proofreading checklist
Mark your paper so you will remember to make all your changes to prepare your final draft	Use proofreading symbols
Prepare the final presentation	Remember that form cannot be separated from content
Avoid trouble spots in your writing	Review some basic rules and do practice exercises in spelling, sentences, parts of speech, agreement, capitalization, and punctuation

Chapter 8

Math Strategies

MULTIPLICATION

Multiplication is the fast way of adding similar numbers over and over again. You can recognize a multiplication problem when you see the × sign. To do multiplication problems well, you must memorize the multiplication tables. As an example, the multiplication table for 3 looks like the following:

$0 \times 3 = 0$
$1 \times 3 = 3$
$2 \times 3 = 6$
$3 \times 3 = 9$
$4 \times 3 = 12$
$5 \times 3 = 15$
$6 \times 3 = 18$
$7 \times 3 = 21$
$8 \times 3 = 24$
$9 \times 3 = 27$
$10 \times 3 = 30$
$11 \times 3 = 33$
$12 \times 3 = 36$

You can create similar multiplication tables for any number. However, there is a better strategy for learning the multiplication tables—making and learning the multiplication chart (Table 8-1).

The method for using this chart is as follows:

□ You are asked to figure out how many ounces of medicine Ms. Grande takes per week. You know that she takes 3 ounces a day.
□ In your mind you see the problem as $7 \times 3 = ?$, where 7 stands for the number of days in a week and 3 stands for the number of ounces of medicine Ms. Grande takes per day.
□ In the top shaded row, put your right finger on the number 7.
□ In the shaded column to the left, put your left finger on the number 3.

□ Slowly move your right finger down and your left finger to the right until they meet. The number at which both fingers meet is the correct answer.
□ "21 oz." is the answer to this problem.

Although a multiplication chart is very handy, it does not substitute for learning the tables by heart. Memorizing the multiplication tables until you know them as well as your name will make your personal and student life easier. To help you learn the tables, try making flash cards or find a computer program that will make the learning task enjoyable.

DIVISION

Like multiplication, you use division to solve many common, daily arithmetic problems. You can write division problems two ways:

$10 \div 2 = 5$

In this example the number 10 is divided by 2. In other words, you always divide the number after the sign into the number that goes before the sign. The second way to write division problems looks like this:

$$2\overline{)10}^{5}$$

In this example, you divide the number that is inside the box by the number that is outside the box. If you have learned your multiplication tables well, you will have an easier time with division. You may have noticed in the first example that if you read the problem from right to left, it reads like a multiplication problem. Consider the following:

□ Mr. Sheldon, a medical secretary, is asked to split a $3000 bonus among the three employees working in Dr. Joseph's office.

TABLE 8-1 Multiplication Chart

×	1	2	3	4	5	6	7	8	9	10	11	12
1	1	2	3	4	5	6	7	8	9	10	11	12
2	2	4	6	8	10	12	14	16	18	20	22	24
3	3	6	9	12	15	18	21	24	27	30	33	36
4	4	8	12	16	20	24	28	32	36	40	44	48
5	5	10	15	20	25	30	35	40	45	50	55	60
6	6	12	18	24	30	36	42	48	54	60	66	72
7	7	14	21	28	35	42	49	56	63	70	77	84
8	8	16	24	32	40	48	56	64	72	80	88	96
9	9	18	27	36	45	54	63	72	81	90	99	108
10	10	20	30	40	50	60	70	80	90	100	110	120
11	11	22	33	44	55	66	77	88	99	110	121	132
12	12	24	36	48	60	72	84	96	108	120	132	144

☐ Mr. Sheldon knows that $1000 \times 3 = 3000$.
☐ He reverses the procedure and divides 3000 by 3.
☐ Each employee will get $1000.

If you learn the multiplication tables thoroughly, you will be able to do more complicated multiplication and division problems.

Exercise 8-1

Directions: Spend some time learning the multiplication chart (Table 8-1). Then fill in the chart below. You may want to memorize one table at a time and then fill in the chart as you learn that table. Remember that learning the multiplication tables by heart will help you with both multiplication and division problems.

FRACTIONS

Fractions represent parts of a whole. You go to school 5 days out of 7 days. When this is written as a fraction, it looks like this:

$$\frac{5}{7}$$

In this example the number 5 on top is called the **numerator.** The numerator tells you how many parts of the whole. The number 7 on the bottom is called the **denominator.** The denominator tells you how many parts make up the whole.

This example of a fraction is called a **proper fraction.** In a proper fraction the numerator is smaller than the denominator, and the fraction has a value less than 1.

×	1	2	3	4	5	6	7	8	9	10	11	12
1												
2												
3												
4												
5												
6												
7												
8												
9												
10												
11												
12												

Consider this next fraction:

$$\frac{4}{2}$$

This is an example of an **improper fraction.** When the numerator is larger than the denominator, you have an improper fraction.

Sometimes you may see a whole number written with a fraction next to it. It will look like this:

$$13\frac{6}{12}$$

This is called a **mixed number.**

Reducing to the Lowest Term. Sometimes when working with fractions it is necessary to reduce them to their lowest terms. This means dividing the numerator and the denominator by the same number until you cannot go any further. Study the following problem:

$$\frac{50}{100}$$

□ What number is needed to divide both the 50 and 100 so that the answer comes out evenly?
□ Try 25: 50 divided by 25 is 2; 100 divided by 25 is 4. The answer so far looks like this:

$$\frac{2}{4}$$

□ Is it still possible to reduce this fraction? Is there still another number that can be divided equally into both the 2 and the 4?
  ○ Try 2: 2 goes into 2 once; 2 goes into 4 twice. The answer now is:

$$\frac{1}{2}$$

The lowest term for $\frac{50}{100}$ is $\frac{1}{2}$.

Raising to a Higher Term. Similarly, any fraction can be changed to a higher term by multiplying both the numerator and the denominator by the same number.

$$\frac{9}{18} = \frac{27}{54}$$

$9 \times 3 = 27$ and $18 \times 3 = 54$

Adding and Subtracting Fractions. To add and subtract with fractions that have the same denominator, you add or subtract only the numerator and copy the **common** denominator to finish the problem.

$$\frac{5}{11} + \frac{3}{11} = \frac{8}{11}$$

$$\frac{9}{64} - \frac{1}{64} = \frac{8}{64}$$

However, if the denominators are different, you need to find the lowest common denominator. The lowest common denominator is the smallest number that can be divided evenly by the denominators of all the fractions. For example:

$$\frac{2}{3}; \frac{5}{6}; \frac{3}{9}$$

□ Think of the smallest number that can be divided evenly by 3, 6, 9:

$3 \times 6 = 18$
$6 \times 3 = 18$
$9 \times 2 = 18$

Or

$18 \div 3 = 6$
$18 \div 6 = 3$
$18 \div 9 = 2$

18 is the lowest common denominator. The fractions now look like this:

$$\frac{2}{18}$$

$$\frac{5}{18}$$

$$\frac{3}{18}$$

□ To finish, you must take one more important step. Whatever you do to the denominator you must do to the numerator.
□ In the first fraction, you multiplied 3 by 6 to get the lowest common denominator of 18. Now you must do the same to the numerator 2. $2 \times 6 = 12$. The fraction is now:

$$\frac{12}{18}$$

□ In the second fraction you multiplied the denominator 6 by 3 to get the lowest common denominator of 18. Now you must do the same to the numerator 5. $5 \times 3 = 15$. The fraction is now:

$$\frac{15}{18}$$

☐ In the third fraction you multiplied the denominator 9 by 2 to get the lowest common denominator of 18. Now you must do the same to the numerator 3. $3 \times 2 = 6$. The fraction is now:

$$\frac{6}{18}$$

The fractions now look like this:

$$\frac{12}{18}$$

$$\frac{15}{18}$$

$$\frac{6}{18}$$

☐ These fractions are now ready to be added or subtracted.

Multiplying Fractions. To multiply fractions you simply multiply the numerators and then the denominators.

For example:

$$\frac{4}{7} \times \frac{10}{10} = \frac{40}{70}$$

If you are working with mixed numbers, it is important to change them into improper fractions before multiplying or dividing. Look at the following:

$$2\frac{4}{8}$$

☐ To change this mixed number into an improper fraction, first multiply the denominator by the whole number.

$$8 \times 2 = 16$$

☐ Next add the numerator of 4 to the 16.

$$16 + 4 = 20$$

☐ Finally copy the original denominator so the fraction now looks like this:

$$\frac{20}{8}$$

☐ The mixed number has now been changed to an improper fraction.

Dividing Fractions. To divide fractions, you do the following two steps:

$$\frac{4}{16} \div \frac{5}{15}$$

First you <u>reverse</u> the second fraction. In other words, the 15 becomes the numerator and the 5 becomes the denominator.

$$\frac{15}{5}$$

Then you change the division sign to a multiplication sign and multiply the numerators and then the denominators to get the answer.

$$\frac{4}{16} \times \frac{15}{5} = \frac{60}{80} = \frac{3}{4}$$

Sometimes, if the numbers are large, you may want to reduce them in a multiplication or division problem. Remember to work on a <u>diagonal</u> across the signs.

$$\frac{10}{20} \times \frac{5}{40} \times \frac{1}{10} =$$

$$\frac{\cancel{10}}{\cancel{20}} \times \frac{\cancel{5}}{40} \times \frac{1}{\cancel{10}} = \frac{1}{4} \times \frac{1}{40} \times \frac{1}{1} =$$

$$\frac{1}{4} \times \frac{1}{40} \times 1 = \frac{1}{160}$$

Exercise 8-2

Directions: Do the following fraction problems. Pay careful attention to the signs so that you perform the correct function. Remember to find the lowest common denominators if necessary and change any mixed numbers to improper fractions.

1. Reduce $\frac{12}{48}$:

2. Determine the missing numerator: $\frac{2}{3} = \frac{?}{36}$

3. Change to an improper fraction: $9\frac{2}{14} =$

4. $\frac{9}{11} - \frac{7}{11} =$

5. $\frac{4}{28} + \frac{9}{28} + \frac{14}{28} =$

6. $\frac{1}{3} \times \frac{1}{2} =$

7. $\dfrac{1}{3} \div \dfrac{1}{2} =$

8. $\dfrac{5}{14} \times \dfrac{7}{25} =$

9. $4\dfrac{8}{10} \div \dfrac{4}{5} =$

10. $2\dfrac{2}{4} \times 1\dfrac{5}{20} =$

DECIMALS

Decimal numbers are similar to fractions. They both describe parts of a whole number. However, there are two differences between decimals and fractions. The first difference is that denominators of decimals can be only 10, 100, 1000, etc. The second difference is that a decimal point or period is used to separate the whole number from the fraction. In the following example, note the difference between decimals and fractions of the same number.

$$\frac{2}{10} = 0.2$$

$$\frac{80}{100} = 0.80$$

$$\frac{425}{1000} = 0.425$$

$$\frac{734}{10000} = .0734$$

The way you read a decimal is determined by how many numbers are to the right of the decimal point. The first example, 0.2, is read "two tenths." The second example, 0.80, is read "eighty hundredths." The third example, 0.425, is read "four hundred twenty-five thousandths." And the last example, .0734 is read "seven hundred thirty-four thousandths."

Adding and Subtracting Decimals. When you add or subtract decimals, it is necessary to write the problem so that all the decimal points are lined up in a straight row. Then add or subtract decimal numbers the same way you would add or subtract whole numbers.

```
 4.258      90.58
 9.636      82.21
13.89       48.37
```

If you are adding or subtracting decimals, use zeros to fill in the places without a number after you align the decimal points.

```
 21.55     21.55      9.4707      9.4707
+62.20    +62.20     -4.2600     -4.2600
           83.75                  5.2107
```

Multiplying Decimals. When you multiply decimal numbers, multiply the same way you would with whole numbers. Then count all the numbers to the right of the decimal point in both rows of numbers in the problem. Put the decimal point that number of places in the answer.

```
0.798  (3 numbers to right of decimal point)
× 6.4  (1 number to right of decimal point)
5.1072 (4 numbers to right of decimal point)
```

Dividing Decimals. Dividing decimal numbers is similar to dividing whole numbers. If the number outside the box is a whole number, place the decimal point in the answer in the same decimal place as the number inside the box.

$$4\overline{)0.8} \quad = 0.2$$

If the number outside the box is a decimal, change this decimal number to a whole number by moving the decimal point to the right of the last number. Use a **caret** (^) to show the new place of the decimal. If the number inside the box is also a decimal number, the decimal point (following whole numbers) must be moved the same number of places as you did with the outside number. Also use a caret to show you have moved the decimal point. If necessary add zeros to get the same number of decimal places.

$$.400\overline{)80.000} \quad = 200.$$

Notice that the decimal point in the answer is placed exactly over the new position of the decimal point of the number inside the box.

Changing Decimals to Fractions. To change a decimal to a fraction, write the numbers in the decimal as the numerator and write the name of the decimal (tenths, hundredths, thousandths, etc.) as the denominator. Reduce the fraction if necessary.

$$0.50 = \frac{50}{100} = \frac{1}{2}$$

Changing Fractions to Decimals. To change a fraction to a decimal, divide the numerator by the denominator. The dividing line of a fraction means "divided by." To divide the numerator by the denominator, it will be necessary to add a decimal point and one or more zeros to the numerator. Carry the decimal point up to the answer.

$$\frac{1}{2} \quad 2)\overline{1.0}^{\,0.5}$$

Exercise 8-3

Directions: Solve the following decimal problems.
Add the following decimals:
a. 5.439 + 7.63 + 1.257 =
b. 0.428 + 0.029 + 8.35 =
Subtract the following decimals:
c. 21.719 − 5.83 =
d. 103.8 − 62.45 =
Multiply the following decimals:
e. 943.27 × 0.5 =
f. 1.3294 × 0.566 =
Divide the following decimals:
g. 70 ÷ 0.25 =
h. 160 ÷ 0.40 =
Change the following decimals to fractions. Reduce the fraction if necessary.
i. 0.020   0.8   0.45
Change the following fractions to decimals:
j. $\frac{4}{5}$ $\frac{6}{80}$ $\frac{50}{250}$

PERCENTAGES

Percentage numbers, like fractions and decimals, represent a part of the whole. The percentage represents hundredths and is indicated by the percent sign (%). Thus 47 hundredths can be written as

$$\frac{47}{100}, 0.47, \text{ or } 47\%$$

When doing percentage problems, you should change the percentage number to either a fraction or a decimal number and then solve the problem. Table 8-2 is a **conversion** chart of some of the more common percentages.

Changing Percentages to Fractions. To change a percentage to a fraction, use the number in the percentage as the numerator and put 100

TABLE 8-2   Converting Percentages to Fractions and Decimals

Percent		Fraction		Decimal
25%	=	$\frac{1}{4}$	=	0.25
50%	=	$\frac{1}{2}$	=	0.5
75%	=	$\frac{3}{4}$	=	0.75
12.5%	=	$\frac{1}{8}$	=	0.125
37.5%	=	$\frac{3}{8}$	=	0.375
62.5%	=	$\frac{5}{8}$	=	0.625
87.5%	=	$\frac{7}{8}$	=	0.875
$33\frac{1}{3}\%$	=	$\frac{1}{3}$	=	$0.33\frac{1}{3}$
$66\frac{2}{3}\%$	=	$\frac{2}{3}$	=	$0.66\frac{2}{3}$
20%	=	$\frac{1}{5}$	=	0.2
40%	=	$\frac{2}{5}$	=	0.4
60%	=	$\frac{3}{5}$	=	0.6
80%	=	$\frac{4}{5}$	=	0.8
10%	=	$\frac{1}{10}$	=	0.1
30%	=	$\frac{3}{10}$	=	0.3
70%	=	$\frac{7}{10}$	=	0.7
90%	=	$\frac{9}{10}$	=	0.9
$16\frac{2}{3}\%$	=	$\frac{1}{6}$	=	$0.16\frac{2}{3}$
$83\frac{1}{3}\%$	=	$\frac{5}{6}$	=	$0.83\frac{1}{3}$

as the denominator. Reduce the fraction if necessary.

$$35\% = \frac{35}{100} = \frac{7}{20}$$

Changing Fractions to Percentages. The easiest way to change a fraction to a percentage is to change the fraction to a decimal number first.

$$\frac{3}{75} = 75\overline{)3.00}^{\,0.04}$$

$$0.04 = \frac{4}{100} = 4\%$$

Changing Percentages to Decimals. To change a percentage number to a decimal number, erase the percent sign and move the decimal point two places to the left.

$$51\% = 0.51$$

Changing Decimals to Percentages. To change decimal numbers to percentage numbers, move the decimal point two places to the right and write in the percent sign.

$$0.76 = 76\%$$

Doing Problems with Percentages. To find a percentage of a whole number, change the percentage to a fraction or a decimal and then multiply by the whole number.

What is 25% of 500?

$$25\% = \frac{25}{100}$$

$$\frac{25}{100} \times 500 = 125$$

or

What is 8.5% of 250?
8.5% = 0.085
0.085 × 250 = 21.25

To find what percentage one number is of another number, turn the numbers in the problem into a fraction and change the fraction to a percentage.

5 is what percentage of 50?

$$\frac{5}{50} = \frac{1}{10}$$

$$\frac{1}{10} = 0.1 = 10\%$$

To find the whole number when a percentage is given, divide the whole number by the percentage. Change the percentage to a fraction.

10% of what number is 100?

$$10\% = \frac{1}{10}$$

$$100 \div \frac{1}{10} = \frac{100}{10} = \frac{10}{1} \times \frac{10}{1} = 1000$$

Exercise 8-4

Directions: Fill in the following chart. Check your work with the conversion chart in Table 8-2. Then solve problems 11 through 15.

	Percent	Fraction	Decimal
1.	50%		
2.			0.125
3.		$\frac{1}{6}$	
4.			0.7
5.	60%		
6.		$\frac{2}{5}$	
7.			$0.66\frac{2}{3}$
8.		$\frac{3}{8}$	
9.	80%		
10.		$\frac{1}{4}$	

11. What is 8% of 75?
12. 18 is what percent of 16?
13. 40% of what number is 48?
14. 27 is what percent of 72?
15. 6.25% of 300 =

RATIOS

A ratio is a **comparison** of two numbers using division. A ratio can be written in three ways:

1. 16 to 32

2. $\frac{16}{32} = \frac{1}{2}$

3. 16:32

Regardless of how you write the ratio, you would read it as "16 to 32." Read the following and find out how you would solve a ratio problem.

☐ Of Chloe's 28 teeth, 4 have crowns on them. Determine the ratio of crowned teeth to uncrowned teeth.

- ☐ Use the 4 crowned teeth as the numerator and the total number of teeth as the denominator and reduce the fraction.

$$\frac{4}{28} = \frac{1}{7}$$

- ☐ $\frac{1}{7}$ of Chloe's teeth are crowned.

Exercise 8-5

Directions: Solve the following ratio problems. Choose any of the ways to express your answer. If necessary, reduce fractions to their lowest terms.

1. At the veterinary school there are 10 instructors for 400 students. What is the ratio of instructors to students?
2. Out of 25 typed pages, the medical typist had to redo 5 of them because of errors. What is the ratio of redone pages to correct pages?
3. The laboratory assistant discovered that 6 of the 54 microscopes needed repairs. What is the ratio of working microscopes to broken ones?
4. Of the 228 graduates of the medical assistant program, 19 found jobs immediately after graduation. What is the ratio of working graduates to nonworking graduates?
5. Prudence cleaned 15 of the rat cages out of a total of 50. What is the ratio of clean cages to dirty ones?

PROPORTIONS

A proportion is a statement that two ratios are equal. A proportion can be written in three ways:

1. 1 to 2 = 5 to 10
2. $\frac{1}{2} = \frac{5}{10}$
3. 1:2 = 5:10

All three of these proportions are read as "1 is to 2 as 5 is to 10." Below is what a typical proportion problem would look like. Determine the missing number in the following proportion:

$$\frac{?}{10} = \frac{3}{30}$$

To find the missing number, figure out what number you would multiply 10 by to get 30. The answer is 3. Earlier in this chapter you were told that whatever number you use to multiply in the

denominator you must use for that numerator. So what number multiplied by 3 would equal 3? The answer is 1. The proportion equation now looks like this:

$$\frac{?}{10} = \frac{3}{30}$$

$$\frac{1}{10} = \frac{3}{30}$$

Exercise 8-6

Directions: Write each of the following statements as a proportion.

1. 4 is to 12 as 1 is to 3.
2. 16 is to 40 as 2 is to 5.
3. 35 is to 30 as 7 is to 6.
4. 108 is to 24 as 9 is to 2.
5. 77 is to 99 as 7 is to 9.

Exercise 8-7

Directions: Solve the following problems by finding the value of the unknown number (?). Remember that the number that was used to determine the denominator should also be used to determine the numerator.

1. $\dfrac{?}{16} = \dfrac{4}{8}$

2. $\dfrac{5}{1} = \dfrac{35}{?}$

3. $\dfrac{45}{?} = \dfrac{5}{9}$

4. $\dfrac{?}{7} = \dfrac{18}{42}$

5. $\dfrac{7}{12} = \dfrac{?}{108}$

6. $\dfrac{40}{?} = \dfrac{4}{12}$

7. $\dfrac{18}{35} = \dfrac{108}{?}$

8. $\dfrac{51}{25} = \dfrac{?}{1000}$

9. $\dfrac{?}{76} = \dfrac{66}{228}$

10. $\dfrac{62}{909} = \dfrac{?}{1818}$

REVIEWING THE LEARNING STRATEGIES

To Learn	Use This Strategy
Multiplication and Division	Memorize the multiplication chart
Fractions	Learn to recognize the numerator, denominator, proper and improper fractions, mixed numbers, lowest terms, and the common denominator
Decimals	Learn about place holding, reading decimal numbers, changing fractions to decimal numbers, and changing decimal numbers to fractions
Percentages	Learn about reading percentages and changing percentages to decimals or fractions
Ratios	Learn the definition of *ratio* and how to read and write ratios
Proportions	Learn the definition of *proportion* and how to read and write proportions

THE METRIC SYSTEM

The metric system is a system of measurements. Another system of measurements is called the English system. The United States is one of the very few countries that use the English system of measuring. Most of the world, including the health fields, use the metric system of measuring. Therefore, it is very important to be familiar with the metric system. Table 8-3 shows how measurements in the English system and the metric system are equivalent. Since some of the equivalent numbers can be long and complicated decimal numbers, they have been rounded off.

Exercise 8-8

Directions: Study Table 8-3. Then answer the following questions.

Change the following liters to quarts:
1. 3 liters
2. 18 liters

Change the following square centimeters to square inches:
3. 9 square centimeters
4. 10 square centimeters

Change the following kilometers to miles:
5. 4 kilometers
6. 30 kilometers

Change the following yards to meters:
7. 7 yards
8. 45 yards

Change the following pounds to kilograms:
9. 18 pounds
10. 50 pounds

To change from the metric system to the English system, multiply the amount of the metric measure by its equivalent in the English system. For example, to change 5 kilometers to miles, multiply 5 kilometers by 0.62 miles.

$5 \times 0.62 = 3.1$ miles

To change from the English system to the metric system, multiply the amount of the English measure by its equivalent in the metric system. For example, to change 2 inches to centimeters, multiply 2 inches by 2.54 centimeters.

$2 \times 2.54 = 5.08$ centimeters

TABLE 8-3   Metric System and English System Conversion Chart

Metric Lengths	English Lengths
1 meter =	39.37 inches
1 meter =	3.28 feet
1 meter =	1.09 yards
1 centimeter =	0.4 inch
1 millimeter =	0.04 inch
1 kilometer =	0.62 mile

English Lengths	Metric Lengths
1 inch =	25.4 millimeters
1 inch =	2.54 centimeters
1 inch =	0.0254 meter
1 foot =	0.3 meter
1 yard =	0.91 meter
1 mile =	1.61 kilometers

Metric Liquid Measure	English Liquid Measure
1 liter =	1.06 quarts

English Liquid Measure	Metric Liquid Measure
1 quart =	0.95 liter

Metric Measures of Weight	English Measures of Weight
1 gram =	0.04 ounce
1 kilogram =	2.2 pounds
1 metric ton =	2204.62 pounds

English Measures of Weight	Metric Measures of Weight
1 ounce =	28.35 grams
1 pound =	0.45 kilogram
1 short ton (2000 pounds) =	0.91 metric ton

Metric Measures of Area	English Measures of Area
1 square centimeter =	0.155 square inch
1 square meter =	10.76 square feet
1 square meter =	1.2 square yards
1 square kilometer =	0.39 square mile

English Measures of Area	Metric Measures of Area
1 square inch =	6.45 square centimeters
1 square foot =	0.09 square meter
1 square yard =	0.84 square meter
1 square mile =	2.59 square kilometers

Chapter 9

Beginning the Job Search

THE SEARCH IS ON

"Employment is nature's physician, and is essential to human happiness."
—GALEN

Congratulations! All the studying, assignments, labs, and clinical experience are about to pay off. You are ready to focus on the job search and on reaching your goal of working in the health care field. Completing your education and graduating represent important personal achievements. Your attitude played a large part in your success. In the same way, attitude will play an important role in helping you obtain the right job.

The Big A: Attitude

"Remember that your own resolution to succeed is more important than any one thing."
—ABRAHAM LINCOLN

Attitude is the single most important factor in determining whether a student finds a job. In Chapter 2 we discussed how we can control our attitudes and noted that any situation can be approached either positively or negatively. For example, some people are nervous and fearful about looking for a job. They worry about lacking the qualifications needed by employers and see each interview as a chance to be rejected. A more positive approach is to look at the process from the employers' point of view. Think about it: health care facilities cannot function without good employees. Employers must fill positions with well-trained individuals who can help them serve their patients. You are a recently trained person ready to fill one of these positions.

Knowing what skills and competencies you have is the first step in presenting yourself successfully as the person who fits an employer's needs. Students sometimes don't realize just how much they have learned. They tend to underestimate their abilities and the amount of practice they have had in applying their skills. Being aware of your accomplishments will build your self-confidence and help you present yourself positively at interviews. Take some time now to review what you have learned and to give yourself credit for what you have to offer.

Focus Your Search

"To find out what one is fitted to do, and to secure an opportunity to do, is the key to happiness."
—JOHN DEWEY

Knowing where to market yourself is the next step in carrying out a successful job search. This means identifying the type of job and facility in which you would prefer to work. As you worked through your educational program, you may have changed your work preferences.

It is sometimes necessary to set short-term goals to achieve long-term career success. When seeking an entry-level position, you'll do better if you are open to a variety of possibilities. School career services personnel report seeing students lose good opportunities by setting limits that are too restrictive. For example, some students don't want to have long commutes. But passing up a good position at an excellent facility by refusing to consider jobs just outside your immediate area may not be a good career move. Driving an extra 10 minutes may, in the long run, be worth the inconvenience.

Calculate Your Needs

An important part of preparing for the job search is to determine the salary you will need to support yourself and your family. While many occupations have salaries set within a certain range, knowing how much you need to live on will help you identify appropriate positions.

Making a Commitment to the Job Search

"You can't try to do things; you simply must do them."
—RAY BRADBURY

Obtaining a job has been compared to actually working at a job. It can take a lot of time and effort. You must dedicate a portion of each day to your search and be on call to follow up quickly on leads. Employment professionals recommend that job seekers spend between 20 and 40 hours per week on job search efforts. In this and the following chapters, you will learn about the many activities necessary to conduct a successful search, such as:

- ☐ Preparing skills inventories and examples
- ☐ Networking
- ☐ Finding leads
- ☐ Conducting searches on the Internet
- ☐ Writing and revising your resume
- ☐ Assembling your portfolio
- ☐ Writing letters
- ☐ Contacting references
- ☐ Creating a **reference sheet**
- ☐ Preparing for and attending interviews
- ☐ Writing thank-you notes

Failure to spend adequate time on these activities is one of the major reasons that people fail to get hired. You can apply many of the time-management tools and techniques suggested in Chapter 2 to your job search.

Time Management Tips for Your Job Search

- ☐ **Prioritize.** The job search should be your main focus. Dedicate sufficient time and attention to achieving this goal. Looking for a job is your job. Determine which search activities are most productive and spend the majority of your time on them.
- ☐ **Keep a Calendar.** Missing—or even being late for—an interview is a sure way to lose a job even before you are hired. Take care to note all appointments and follow-up activities accurately, and check your calendar daily. If you haven't developed a calendar system yet, now is the time to start.
- ☐ **Plan a Weekly Schedule.** Decide what needs to be done each week, and create a to-do list to

serve as a guide to keep you on track. It's easy to reach the end of the week and discover you've accomplished only half of what needed to be done.

- ☐ **Plan Ahead.** This is very important. Suppose that one morning you are notified that a hospital where you want to work is scheduling interviews for later the same day. You don't want to miss out because you haven't completed your resume or don't have a clean shirt to wear. Being prepared leads to being hired. Make sure your car is in good running order.
- ☐ **Plan for the Unplanned.** The unexpected tends to strike at the worst possible moment. Keep an extra printer cartridge on hand. Have extra copies of your resume printed. Leave early for interviews in case you get lost. (Better yet, take a dry run a day or two in advance to learn the route. Check out alternate routes in case of traffic.)

Setting Up Job Search Central

Create a personalized employment headquarters by designating a space for job search activities. Save time and prevent the loss of important information by gathering your resources and supplies in one location.

Dialing for Jobs

The telephone provides a vital link with potential employers and job lead sources. The telephone can be one of the job seeker's best friends. It can also be a barrier if not used properly. Employers form an impression of you based on your telephone manners, so be sure they hear you at your best. The following suggestions for making calls will apply to your telephone habits on the job as well as during the search to get a job:

1. Be prepared with pen and paper for taking notes.
2. Prepare what you plan to say ahead of time, and be as brief as possible without rushing and speaking too quickly.
3. Be courteous, never pushy. If the receptionist cannot connect you to the person you wish to speak with, leave a clear message and ask for a good time to call back.
4. Speak clearly and distinctly. Don't mumble or use slang or nonstandard speech that the listener may not understand.
5. When making appointments or gathering important information, listen carefully and repeat (use feedback) to make sure that you have the

correct date and time, address, suite or office number, and so on.

6. Always thank the other party and end the call graciously.

It is important that your school, potential employers, and other contacts be able to reach you in a timely way. Be sure the telephone number you distribute is accurate and includes your area code. If you have an answering machine, call your number to make sure it is working properly. The outgoing message should be simple and professional. Avoid the use of music, jokes, and clever remarks, such as "You know what this is and you know what to do." (This also applies to your e-mail address. If it's too cute or strange, it may send the wrong message to any potential employer who sees it.) Instruct everyone who might answer the telephone about proper telephone manners and how to write down a message. Every contact represents you, and employers don't have time to deal with rude adults or untrained children. If you are away from the telephone during office hours and don't have an answering machine, give out an alternate number where someone reliable can take messages for you. Don't lose out on jobs because you can't be contacted.

Communicating by Fax

An increasing number of employment ads read "Fax resume to...." If you don't own a **fax machine** or a computer that has fax capability, find a print, postal, or business supply store that provides this service. Some schools will fax student resumes to potential employers. When sending documents by fax, the print on the original should be clear and dark for maximum quality transmission. Be sure there is at least a one-inch margin on all sides so nothing gets cut off.

When faxed resumes are requested, it is best to follow the employer's instructions. Mailed resumes may arrive too late to be considered. Demonstrate that you are resourceful and can follow instructions. If you don't hear from the employer in a couple of days, call to make sure your resume was received.

Setting up a Support System

Your job search will be easier and more pleasant if you have people available who care about your success and are willing to help you. They can provide technical support or offer friendly encouragement. Could you use some help with any of the following tasks?

☐ Proofreading your resume and other written materials (more than one person should proofread)
☐ Role-playing with you to practice interviewing
☐ Discussing postinterview evaluations. (Postinterview evaluations are covered in Chapter 11.)
☐ Acting as a cheerleader
☐ Helping you to keep things in perspective and not get discouraged

You may want to work with just one other person who is qualified to help you in many areas. Or you might enlist the help of several "specialists." Be sure the people you choose are qualified to spot spelling and grammatical errors and are comfortable giving you constructive feedback. They should know when you need a push and when you need a hug. Consider drawing from friends, family members, classmates, school personnel, and health care professionals. If you have a mentor, this person might be an excellent choice.

Most people are happy to support your efforts to secure employment. Take care to keep your support system intact. Be considerate of everyone's time, be prepared for meetings with them, and show appreciation for their help.

The career services department at your school provides specific help and support to students as they conduct their job search. Find out what services are provided. In addition, some schools and communities have job clubs or support groups for people seeking employment. Consider using these to supplement your support system. They can offer additional viewpoints, encouragement, and helpful suggestions.

Understanding the Job Market

Employment conditions vary from one geographic location to the next. And economic conditions change over time. Think about the following factors when planning your job search strategies:

☐ Local employment customs
☐ Current economic conditions
☐ Current employment rate
☐ Trends in health care delivery
☐ Medical advances
☐ Changing government regulations

Local customs vary in what is considered acceptable dress for the workplace. In some parts of the country, health care providers dress casually, with males sporting long hair and even wearing an earring. In other areas, anyone who showed up for work looking like this would be sent home to change—or worse, sent home for good!

Local and national economic conditions affect the job seeker. When the economy is strong and unemployment is low, job seekers have the advantage. When the economy slows down, competition heats up and it becomes more difficult to find a position. Some health care occupations are suffering shortages and this will make finding a job easier for qualified candidates.

Health care occupations are also affected by state and federal laws. The demand for certain occupations is influenced by the reimbursement (payment for services) policies of both government and private insurance carriers. Knowing what's happening in your local area as well as being aware of national trends are important when planning both your initial job search and your long-term career strategy. Your local newspaper is a good source of information. Look in the business section for articles about the economy and local employment trends. Health care trends and major facilities are often featured. For example, a new state law that increased the required nurse-to-patient ratios in California hospitals was reported in the newspaper. The predicted result was (and is for the next few years, at least) a shortage of registered nurses to meet employer needs. This information is valuable for the recent nurse graduate or a student who is considering nursing as a career. Articles about major health care employers can give you an edge when choosing where you want to work. Knowing about the facility where you are applying enables you to present yourself at interviews as a candidate who has taken the time to learn about the employer.

Many newspapers publish a special weekly or monthly section dedicated to employment. These are good sources of information. They contain articles about resume writing, lists of local agencies that assist job seekers, and announcements of job fairs. News magazines such as *Newsweek, Time,* and *US News and World Report* also contain many articles about health care topics. The Internet also provides access to a wide variety of topics from literally millions of sources. For example, the Bureau of Labor Statistics maintains a web site with reports on employment trends and the national labor market.

Locating Job Leads

Many ways exist to find job leads, ranging from talking with people you know to searching the Internet. You can increase your chances of finding the job you really want by using a variety of lead sources. Don't limit yourself to the one or two methods you find easiest or most comfortable to use. People who work in sales know that it usually takes many calls to make a sale. In the same way, the more sources you use in your job search, the greater your chances of finding the right job for you. Employment experts recommend that no more than 25% of your time be spent on any one job search method.

When the economy is slow and there are few job openings, networking and developing personal contacts can be the most effective methods for finding a job. It's possible you won't find the "perfect job" under these conditions. Looking for an opportunity to gain experience may be the best strategy. When the economy is booming or there is a shortage of qualified workers in your field, you are likely to have a larger selection of opportunities. Under these conditions, you may find that responding to newspaper ads and directly contacting potential employers are very effective methods. It is a sure thing that you will experience all types of job markets during your career. The economy and employment levels run in cycles, and you must be prepared to deal with changing conditions.

Career Services at Your School. The staff at your school wants you to succeed. The goal of health care educators is to train future workers, and a sign of their professional achievement is when a graduate becomes satisfactorily employed. Schools have special personnel who are trained to help students find jobs. These people work to develop relationships with local employers. Your school may be contacted about job openings before they are even advertised. This is because it is expensive for employers to place help-wanted ads in the newspapers. It is also time consuming to review resumes, set up appointments, and interview large numbers of applicants. The success of a health care facility depends on the quality of its employees, so it is important that they find and hire the right people. Considerable time, expense, and doubt can be avoided if employers know they can count on local schools to provide qualified candidates. How can you be among those who are recommended by your school?

☐ Get to know the career services staff. Introduce yourself early in your program. Don't wait until you are beginning the job search. Seek their advice about how you can best prepare ahead for successful employment.

☐ Treat school staff with the same courtesy and respect you would an employer. They cannot risk the school's reputation with employers by recommending students who are rude or uncooperative.

☐ Maintain an excellent attendance record. Schools report that this is the question asked by nearly every employer about students. It ranks far above inquiries about grades. (Even great skills are no help to anyone if you aren't there to use them!)

☐ Participate fully in any career development classes or workshops that are offered. Attend every session and complete all assignments. Conduct yourself in practice interviews as if they were the real thing.

☐ Follow up on any leads you are given, even if you don't think the job is for you. Attend all interviews scheduled for you. Failure to do so embarrasses the school and may result in the employer refusing to consider candidates from your school in the future. Take advantage of all opportunities to meet potential employers. You will get valuable confidence-building interview practice. Even if the job isn't the one for you, the employer may know about one that is.

☐ Keep the school informed about how to contact you. If you move and career services can't find you, they can't help you.

☐ Let the school know when you are hired. Many agencies that regulate and accredit schools require annual reports to monitor graduation and job placement rates. These act as school report cards and are important for schools to stay in good standing. If the staff has taken the time to help you, return the favor by giving them the information they need to complete their reports.

Networking. Many people learn about job openings and become employed through personal contacts. It is recommended that you start early to meet people in the health care field. Professional organizations were suggested as an excellent source of contacts. In addition to providing you with useful information about your occupational area, they can be a source of job leads and referrals. If you have already met people through professional networking, let them know that you are launching your job search. Don't be shy about asking for their advice about where you might apply, as well as about the job search in general. People who are successful in their careers are generally happy to help newcomers. Do show consideration for their time, and send a thank-you note when they put forth effort on your behalf. It is critical that you follow up on any leads given to you by professional contacts. Failure to do so is not only rude; it may result in the withdrawal of their support.

In addition to professional contacts, general networking can be an effective way to get the word out about your search efforts. The author once learned about a job opening for a school director—a position she got and enjoyed for a number of years—from a friend who had seen the ad in the newspaper. Let the people in your life know you are seeking employment. By telling 10 people who each know 10 other people, you create a network of 100 people who know you are looking for a job. Of these 100, it is likely that a few work in health care. And most people use health care services. There is a chance that someone will know someone or something that can help you. Keep in touch with your classmates. Once they have jobs, they may be willing to pass on your name to their employers. When speaking with others about your career goals, present yourself positively and express enthusiasm about your field. People want to feel confident about passing your name along.

Employment Ads. The help-wanted section of the newspaper is one of the oldest and most traditional methods of locating openings. Many job search experts caution that ads are a waste of time because they suffer from overexposure. So many people see the same ad that employers may receive dozens—or even hundreds—of responses. This makes it difficult for a single resume to get attention. The truth is that ads can be a good source of job leads, but they should not be your only source. If you live in a growing area with many job openings, ads can be an excellent place to look. Even if there is competition, someone will be hired and it might be you! Writing a cover letter and mailing or faxing a resume is worth the time and expense it takes. Every action you take increases your chance of finding the right job.

The Sunday edition of the newspaper usually has the largest number of employment ads. When reviewing them, look under every category that might contain jobs for which you are prepared. For example, while "nursing assistants" are likely to appear in the "nursing" section, they may also be listed under "medical" or "health care." If your training has prepared you for a variety of positions, be sure to check all possible job titles. For example, graduates of health information programs may be qualified for the following positions: coding specialist, health information technician, managed-care specialist, medical records coordinator or supervisor, and patient records technician. New job titles are constantly being created to describe the many activities performed in the modern health care facility. The skill inventories you created earlier in this chapter will help you identify all the jobs for which you might apply. Don't be discouraged if you find only a few ads—or none—for your occupation. This may actually mean that there is such a shortage of applicants that employers have given up placing expensive ads.

In addition to the newspaper, many professional journals contain employment ads. These can be especially useful if you are willing to move to another area.

When you respond to an ad, point out how you meet the employer's needs. You can do this in the cover letter, which will be discussed more fully in Chapter 10. For now, let's look at a couple of sample ads and see how to encourage the employer to read your resume and call you for an interview. Even very short ads contain information you can use.

There is not one best way to write an effective response to an ad. Highlight your qualifications with a format that best suits the content of the ad. It isn't necessary—or even desirable—to repeat what's in your resume. A few quick highlights about how you meet the requirements mentioned in the ad are sufficient (see Prescription for Success 9-4).

Your Clinical Site.

Students who perform well during their clinical experience are sometimes offered jobs at the site. Some employers even create new positions for graduates who impress them with their attitude and skills. Although it is not appropriate to ask your clinical site for employment before completing your training there, you should work as if this were your goal. Even if the site is unable to offer you a position, your clinical supervisor can serve as a valuable reference and may recommend you to another employer.

Career and Job Fairs.

Some schools, community agencies, and large health care facilities organize activities to connect job recruiters and job seekers. In a single day, you can meet dozens of potential employers. You can gather information, ask questions, and submit your resume. Check your local newspaper for events in your area. You can also see upcoming career fairs across the nation on web sites such as CareerFair.com.

Here are suggestions for taking full advantage of job fairs:

☐ Dress as you would for an interview. If the event takes place at school and you will go directly from class in uniform, be sure it is clean and pressed.

☐ Prepare a list of questions in advance. It's easier to think of them beforehand than to remember them all in a noisy room. Good questions to ask include:

1. What types of jobs does your facility offer?
2. How can I get more information?
3. What are the most important qualifications you look for when hiring employees?
4. Can you give me a written job description?
5. What is the application procedure?
6. Who do I contact to set up an interview?

☐ Take copies of your resume. Carry them in a large envelope or folder to keep them clean and neat.

☐ Smile, make eye contact, and introduce yourself to recruiters. Thank them for any information they give you. Leave graciously by telling them it was nice meeting them, you appreciate their help, and you look forward to speaking with them again.

☐ Take something in which you can collect brochures, job announcements, and business cards. A small notebook is helpful for taking notes.

☐ As soon as possible after the fair, organize what you collected and use your job lead log pages to record the people you met and what you learned. Prepare a list of follow-up activities, such as people to call and resumes to send.

Employer Information Meetings and Telephone Job Lines.

Some large facilities that do a lot of hiring have public meetings at which they explain their employment needs and application process.

Contact personnel departments, watch the local newspaper, and visit employer Internet sites to find announcements. You may not have a chance to meet personally with the hiring staff, but it is still important that you make a professional impression by dressing and acting appropriately. Be prepared to take notes and ask questions.

The telephone can provide you with a link to job leads through employer **job lines,** taped announcements of current openings. Many large facilities maintain job lines that include information about how to apply for the jobs described. Check the help-wanted ads for telephone numbers or call the personnel department at the facility in which you are interested to inquire whether they have this service.

Direct Employer Contacts. Calling or visiting employers to inquire about job openings can be a successful strategy. These actions demonstrate motivation and self-confidence, the very qualities that can help win you a job. When making telephone calls, find out the name or title of the person who does the hiring. Use your best telephone manners, and be considerate of the person's time. He or she may be busy with patients or paperwork and may not have time to answer more than a quick inquiry. Your goal is to find out whether there are job openings, how to apply, and whether you can schedule an interview.

Telephone calls can be especially helpful if you are relocating to a new area. They provide an efficient way to contact a large number of employers. Explain that you will be moving and are unfamiliar with the area. If the facility contacted has no openings, ask whether they can refer you to anyone else in the area.

Dropping in on employers gets the word out that you are looking for a job. Visiting all the offices in a large medical facility can be a productive way to spend a day. It gives you a chance to introduce yourself to at least one staff member and personally distribute your resume. If the person who greets you has time, ask for information about the facility. If this is not possible, ask who does the hiring, leave your resume, and express your appreciation. While you should be dressed as if you were attending an interview, do not ask for one at this time if you don't have an appointment.

Large medical facilities, such as hospitals, often coordinate hiring through their human resources office. All resumes and applications must be submitted to this office. It can be worthwhile to also contact or visit the department where you wish to work. Ask for the supervisor and, if available, let him or her know that you have applied for work through human resources and are very interested in working in that department. Explain why you want to work there and ask that your application be given consideration. If the supervisor is not available, ask to make an appointment. Don't be discouraged, however, if you are unable to make direct contact. Health care professionals today are extremely busy and simply may not have the time.

Using the Internet

The Internet is the newest job search tool. It greatly expands your job search possibilities by being available 24 hours a day. It offers a wide range of how-to information, job postings, and facts about specific occupations and employers. So much information is available, in fact, that it's easy to get lost in cyberspace. You may suddenly realize that you've spent 3 hours moving from one interesting site to another without actually adding much to your job-search efforts!

If you don't have much experience searching the Internet, online tutorials are available to help you develop good research skills. A web site produced by The University of Albany, one of the State Universities of New York, has links to many good teaching sites. (**Note:** This University's web site, as well as all others referred to in this chapter, can be directly accessed through Elsevier's *EVOLVE* web site.)

General Job Search Information. You can find general information about the economy and employment trends on web sites such as Business Week. Another good resource, Health Careers USA, has articles about trends in health care employment, projections of the future needs of employers, and a list of fast-growing health care occupations.

Many web sites contain good advice about topics such as resume writing, interviewing, and negotiating a salary offer. The following web sites are good starting points for the job seeker:

The Riley Guide: hundreds of links to good articles about all aspects of the job search

Career Magazine: many good articles about career-search topics

Job Hunters' Bible: companion web site for Richard Bolles' classic book *What Color Is Your*

Parachute?, the best-selling job search book ever written

Job Star: created originally for the State of California with federal funds, this site has expanded over the years and contains great information for everyone

Health Care Facility Web Sites

Many large health care facilities have web sites that include photos, maps, information about the services they offer patients, job postings, and forms to fill out to apply for jobs online. Use a search engine, such as Google (www.google.com), and enter the name of the company or facility. Web sites for organizations may include photographs of the facility, details about the services they offer, statements of their goals and mission, lists of open positions, and online applications. (Chapter 10 contains information about submitting electronic resumes and completing online applications.)

Job Postings. Job openings are listed on hundreds, perhaps thousands, of web sites. Although some web sites are easier to use than others, most organize jobs by occupational fields, such as health care, and geographic location. Here are five popular general employment web sites:

1. **America's Job Bank**
   This web site is produced by the United States Department of Labor and state employment offices. It draws from almost 2000 databases and contains over one million job listings.
2. **Monster**
   Originally called the Monster Board, this web site is one of the original online job resources. It is very comprehensive and easy to use.
3. **Career Builder**
   This web site has also been in business for a number of years and offers links to thousands of jobs around the world.
4. **Hot Jobs**
   Sponsored by Yahoo!, the health care category is well organized and easy to access.
5. **Nation Job**
   Sponsored by Nation Job Network, this site is very easy to use and contains lists of health care jobs from a variety of employers.

You can view the job listings on these sites without registering. If you wish to post your resume, however, you must register by supplying information such as your name, address, and telephone number. You then select a username and password to access your account each time you visit the web site. A feature available to those who register on these sites is the assistance of a "search scout," an automated search that matches jobs to your resume and e-mails the results to you.

The following web sites are specific to health care:

1. **Absolutely Health Care** (also known as Health Jobs US)
   Over 900 health care companies advertise openings on this web site. You can post your resume and receive e-mail notification of matches.
2. **America's Health Care Source**
   This web site has thousands of job openings posted, but like Absolutely Health Care, the lists are limited to companies who become clients of the service.
3. **Medzilla**
   In addition to job lists, resume posting, and e-mail notification of matches, Medzilla contains articles of interest to the health care job seeker.

Most professional organizations maintain web sites, and some offer placement assistance for members. For example, the American Health Information Management Association (AHIMA) maintains job postings online for members.

Many web sites exist for specific cities and states. Many of these sites include job lists and opportunities to post your resume. The number of jobs posted varies, but these sites are worth checking. Many contain valuable information, such as job fair announcements and facts about local employers. Most newspapers are available online, including the employment ads. These web sites are especially helpful if you are relocating to a new area.

Keep in mind that new web sites are continually being developed and old ones are merging, being deleted, or being moved to a different "address." Some of the addresses given in this book and in others may have changed by the time you try them. And it is certain that new web sites will have been created.

Networking. The Internet provides opportunities for sharing information and ideas with others through mailing lists and newsgroups. **Mailing lists** (also known as Listservs and e-mail discussion groups) operate through e-mail. Each list is devoted to a specific topic: occupations, hobbies, health conditions, and so on. Once you have subscribed, you receive e-mail messages to which you can respond. Your e-mail is then sent to all other subscribers. Mailing lists offer a way to learn what other job seekers are doing and what's happening in your field around the country. A comprehensive directory of the thousands of mailing lists is available from Topica, Inc. Another source of mailing list groups is available from Yahoo! called Yahoo! Groups.

Newsgroups offer another way to network online. A newsgroup is basically an online discussion group for a specific topic. Anyone can join and participate by reading and posting messages. Messages that address the same topic are called a "thread" and each time a different topic is introduced, a new thread is started. Most web browsers have a search capacity called a "newsreader" that organizes the many newsgroups and allows you to post a message.

If you decide to use either mailing lists or newsgroups, it is important to learn the proper "netiquette" for participating. Experts suggest that you read a group's messages for at least 2 weeks before submitting anything. That way, you'll know the type and quality of material that is expected. It is also recommended that you check the "Frequently Asked Questions" or FAQs section to avoid asking something that has already been covered. This is because all subscribers, not just you, receive the answer to your question and may find it annoying to receive information they already know and that is available elsewhere. When you do send messages, keep them short and to the point.

Web forums are another form of online discussion group offered through a variety of web sites. You only need an e-mail address and web browser to participate. Lists of discussion groups are available on the Internet. For example, Microsoft maintains a web site (MSN Groups) with links to thousands of discussion groups organized by category. Over 6000 of the groups are related to medicine, health, and wellness. (**Note:** Links to the web sites of resources mentioned in this section are available on Elsevier's web site *EVOLVE*.)

One important newsgroup rule is never to send advertising or use these groups to ask for a job. You may, however, find someone in the group who you can contact personally via e-mail for possible assistance, just as you would other professional contacts. Good people to write to are those who have posted messages demonstrating that they have knowledge of or work in the occupational area you wish to enter. In your e-mail, identify yourself and the interests you have that seem related to what this person has said in his or her electronic messages to the group. Do not ask the person for a job. The purpose of this contact is to ask for—or better yet, share—information about something you may have in common. Once a relationship is developed online, and this person seems to have useful knowledge and is willing to share it, it is appropriate to ask for information and career advice.

Success Tips for Using the Internet

☐ **Learn More.** If you are not already proficient at using the Internet, take a class or get a copy of one of the many books on how to use it. If your school does not offer instruction, look for adult education classes in your community. Many are offered free of charge.

☐ **Be Patient.** The Internet is a developing technology and still has a few bugs. You may get bumped offline just as you find what you are looking for. A promising-sounding web site may have disappeared. But the wealth of information available is worth the time it takes to search.

☐ **Monitor Where You Are.** It's easy to get lost in a maze of links that takes you far from the original site. When you access a major site, write down its name and address so you can find it again.

☐ **Mark Favorite Sites.** Most Internet-access software allows you to create personalized lists of useful sites so you can find them later. Also, save information in your job search notebook from any online groups you join about how to unsubscribe and the name and e-mail address of the person who manages the list.

☐ **Watch the Time.** Using the Internet can be addictive. You can wander for hours linking and looking and actually accomplishing very little. If you find sites that look interesting but are unrelated to the task at hand, write down or mark their addresses and return to them later.

☐ **Beware of Scams.** Take care when posting your resume or sending private information. If a web site makes claims about jobs that seem too good to be true, it may simply be a means of getting personal information about you. Stick with major employment web sites and the web sites of employers whose existence you can verify in other ways.

☐ **Don't Exceed 25%.** Remember that the Internet is only one tool for your job search. Use it wisely as a supplement to other methods.

Prescription for Success 9–1
Updating Your Self-Assessment

1. List any areas in which you believe you still need improvement:

   _____

   _____

   _____

   _____

   _____

   _____

2. What are some actions you can take to improve in these areas and increase your chances for success in both getting and then keeping a job?

   _____

   _____

   _____

   _____

   _____

   _____

3. Now think of at least two examples from previous employment, school, or your personal life that illustrate how you have applied each competency.

   Competency   **Examples**
   1. Creative thinking   a. _____

   _____

                             b. _____

   _____

   2. Decision making   a. _____

   _____

                             b. _____

   _____

   3. Problem solving   a. _____

   _____

                             b. _____

   _____

Prescription for Success 9–1
Updating Your Self-Assessment—cont'd

Competency   **Examples**

4. Continuous learning a. _____

   _____

   b. _____

   _____

5. Responsibility   a. _____

   _____

   b. _____

   _____

6. Self-worth   a. _____

   _____

   b. _____

   _____

7. Empathy   a. _____

   _____

   b. _____

   _____

8. Self-management   a. _____

   _____

   b. _____

   _____

9. Integrity   a. _____

   _____

   b. _____

   _____

10. Honesty   a. _____

   _____

   b. _____

   _____

Prescription for Success 9–2
My Support System

Think about the people in your life who are qualified to help your job search efforts. Who can you ask to help you with each of the following?

1. Proofreading your resume and other written materials

_____

_____

_____

2. Interview practice

_____

_____

_____

3. Postinterview evaluations

_____

_____

_____

4. Encouragement

_____

_____

_____

Prescription for Success 9–3
What's Going On?

Use your research skills to find answers to the following questions:

1. What is the unemployment rate in your area?

_____

2. Who are the major health care employers?

_____

_____

_____

3. What are the current hiring trends in health care?

_____

_____

_____

4. How might these conditions affect your occupation?

_____

_____

_____

5. How might they influence your job search strategies?

_____

_____

_____

Prescription for Success 9–4
Create a Targeted Response

Find an ad in the employment section of your local newspaper. Identify the employer's requirements and write a response that demonstrates how you meet these requirements.

(Attach ad)

Your Response:

_____

_____

_____

_____

_____

_____

Prescription for Success 9–5
Learning from the Ads

Read the health care employment ads in two recent Sunday newspapers. Health care occupations may be listed under a variety of headings: dental, medical, nursing, rehabilitation, occupational and physical therapy, and so on. Answer as many of the following questions as possible based on what you learn from the ads.

1. In which health care occupations do employment opportunities seem to be growing the fastest in your area?

   _____

   _____

   _____

2. How many openings are posted for each of the following employment settings?

   Home care _____   Private offices _____

   Long-term care _____   Other _____

   Acute care _____

3. How much experience is generally required for the position you have targeted as your long-term career goal? _____

4. How might you acquire this experience? _____

5. How many positions are seeking bilingual applicants? _____

   Which language(s)? _____

6. Do any of the ads contain telephone numbers for job lines? _____ Yes _____ No

7. If you answered "yes" to question 6, call at least one job line. What information is given on the recording?

   _____

   _____

   _____

8. Do any of the ads contain web site addresses? _____ Yes _____ No

9. If you answered "yes" to question 8, and you have access to the Internet, look at the web sites. What information is available? Can you submit an application online?

   _____

   _____

   _____

10. List the announcements, if any, of job fairs, open houses, or informational meetings found in the newspaper, on job lines, or on web sites.

    _____

    _____

    _____

Chapter 10

Writing Your Resumé

PRODUCTION: THE SECOND "P" OF MARKETING

"You have to take life as it happens, but you should try to make it happen the way you want to take it."
—OLD GERMAN SAYING

In Chapter 1, you read about the first step in the marketing process, planning. The second of the "5 Ps of Marketing" is production: using the information gathered from market research to design and put together a product that meets the needs of the customer. Accepting responsibility for creating your own life—with you as the product—can lead to an empowering and satisfying experience.

Human beings have the unique ability to create their own lives. They can generate ideas, form mental images, and plan ways to achieve what they imagine. You have already generated the idea of becoming a health care professional and have completed the first step toward achieving that goal by enrolling in school. Whether you graduate and find satisfactory employment will depend, to a great extent, on your belief in your ability to succeed and your willingness to take the necessary actions to achieve your goals.

Henry Ford, who not only created fame and riches for himself but changed the history of transportation, is quoted as saying, "Whether you think that you can, or you can't, you are right." The tendency for people to get what they expect is known as the self-fulfilling prophecy. Our beliefs about ourselves—what we can achieve—are more important than any other factor. Many prominent Americans, such as Abraham Lincoln and Thomas Edison, experienced many failures before finally achieving great success. Lincoln had business failures and lost elections before becoming one of our most famous presidents. And Edison conducted thousands of experiments before perfecting the electric light bulb, an invention that dramatically changed the world.

You can use the principle of expecting success as you begin your career journey. All achievements begin as ideas, and what you picture mentally can become your reality. Positive images of you succeeding as a student act as powerful motivators. In addition to visual suggestions, your self-talk influences your success—or lack of it. We are continually holding conversations with ourselves that either give us encouragement ("I know I can pass this test.") or put ourselves down ("I'll never be able to get this report finished."). By taking control of the pictures and words in your mind, you can apply their power to help you create the life you want.

A related and very powerful concept you can apply to your life is to act as if you already are what you hope to become. For example, you can increase your chances of becoming a successful health care professional if you start approaching life as if you already were that person. Practice behaviors now that you know will be expected on the job. For example, because accuracy and efficiency are important characteristics for the health care professional, complete all class assignments as if the well-being of others depended on their accuracy. Working effectively with others as part of a team will be required in your work, so start using every opportunity to develop your teamwork skills. Strive to cooperate with your classmates and instructors. Imagining yourself as a health care worker can promote behaviors that lead to achievement of your career goals. Be **proactive** and look for opportunities to increase your personal and professional growth. Turn mistakes into lessons and learn from them. Approach personal difficulties as opportunities to learn and to grow. By the time you graduate, you will have become the health care professional you aspire to be.

PACKAGING

Even an excellent product may not sell if it is poorly packaged. Companies know this and invest a lot of time and money to make their products visually appealing to customers. Appearance can make the difference between whether a product sells or collects dust on the shelf. Most of us package ourselves to impress others or to fit into a specific social group. Americans spend billions of dollars annually on clothing, cosmetics, accessories, and hair care in an effort to create what we believe to be a pleasing appearance.

Appearance is especially important in the health care field because many patients form their opinions about the competence of health care professionals based on their appearance. Your effectiveness in meeting patient needs can be influenced by your appearance because patient satisfaction increases when health care professionals "look like they know what they are doing."

What is expected of the health care professional? How do you look competent? There are several ways. The first is to be fairly conservative in dress and grooming. This means avoiding fashion trends that are outside the mainstream of society, such as brightly colored hair, tattoos, and body piercing. While these may simply represent a current style and a fun way to look, they may be interpreted as signs of rebellion, immaturity, and lack of common sense. Many patients are offended or even frightened by this type of appearance. Even clothing that is not extreme may be inappropriate for work. Dressing for work is different than dressing casually for play or for social functions.

A second consideration is to strive for an appearance that radiates good health. An important responsibility of the health care professional is to promote good health and this is partly achieved by example. If you smoke or are overweight, putting you at risk for serious health problems, this would be a good time to adopt new healthy living habits. Other conditions, such as teeth that need dental work, badly bitten fingernails, and dandruff indicate a lack of self-care, which is inappropriate in a profession that encourages the practice of good personal health habits. The way you present yourself reflects your approach to life and your opinion of yourself. Failure to care for yourself can project a lack of self-confidence and undermine patient faith in your effectiveness.

Third, the issues of cleanliness and **hygiene** are vitally important for professionals whose work requires them to touch others. Patients literally put themselves in the hands of health care professionals and must feel assured that they will benefit from, and not be harmed by, any procedures performed. It is natural to want the professional to look clean and neat and to be free from unpleasant odors. For example, while the hands of the dental assistant may be clean and gloved, a dirty uniform or shoes (or even shoe strings!) give an unfavorable impression to the patient who may wonder whether proper attention was given to sterilizing the equipment and cleaning the work area.

Finally, professionals must consider the safety and comfort of both patients and themselves. Perfumes and scented personal products cannot be tolerated by many patients. Long fingernails, flowing hair, and large dangling earrings may be attractive and appropriate for a social event. But in a health care setting they can scratch patients, contaminate samples, get caught in equipment, or be grabbed by a young patient. Safety on the job cannot be compromised to accommodate fashion trends. Some clothing customs are determined by our cultures, such as head coverings and flowing skirts. These customs may also have to be modified to ensure the safety of both you and the patient.

Take a Moment to Think—Journal Entry

1. Are there any aspects of my appearance that might be inappropriate for the health care setting?

_____

_____

_____

_____

a. Fashion trends

_____

_____

_____

b. Health habits

_____

_____

_____

c. Cleanliness and hygiene

_____

_____

_____

d. Safety issues

_____

_____

_____

2. How am I willing to change the way I dress, at least during working hours?

_____

_____

_____

_____

_____

3. Is there anything I need to start doing now to improve my professional appearance?

_____

_____

_____

_____

_____

_____

Note: *If you are not sure about aspects of your appearance or grooming, speak privately with your instructor or someone else you trust. Dealing with these issues now will give you time to take care of them before you begin your job search.*

PRESENTATION

Your **resumé,** a written outline of your qualifications for work, is an important method for presenting yourself and what you have to offer to prospective employers. The main purpose of a resumé is to convince an employer to give you an interview, and in this chapter you will learn how to write and organize an effective resumé. The focus of the rest of this chapter is on learning about the content of the resumé and how you can use it as a guideline to create your professional self. Starting to plan your resumé now will help you:
1. Recognize what you already have to offer an employer.
2. Build self-confidence.

3. Motivate yourself to learn both the technical and nontechnical skills that contribute to employment success.
4. Identify things you want to improve about yourself.
5. Know ahead of time what kinds of experiences will enhance your employability.
6. Get a head start gathering information and collecting examples to demonstrate your value and skills.

YOUR RESUMÉ AS A GUIDE TO SUCCESS

"Begin with the end in mind."
—STEPHEN COVEY

Thinking about your resumé at the beginning instead of waiting until the end of your educational program turns your resumé into a checklist of "To Dos" for creating a product—your professional self—that you'll be able to offer with confidence to prospective customers: health care employers. The various components of a resumé are explained in this chapter, along with suggestions on how to make them work for you while you are still in school.

Building Block #1 CAREER OBJECTIVE. A brief description, often only one sentence long, of the position or job title you are seeking.

In addition to the job you are seeking, you may include the type of facility and environment you prefer. Here are a couple of examples:
☐ Obtain a position as an administrative and clinical medical assistant in a fast-paced office that offers challenging work and opportunities to acquire additional knowledge and learn new skills.
☐ Work as an occupational therapy assistant in a pediatric facility.

As we discussed earlier, it is wise to have reasonable expectations for your first employment positions. Set positive long-term goals, but be realistic when starting out. Your first job is your chance to work with real people who have real problems. The wider range of jobs you are willing to accept when first entering the field, the better your chances of obtaining employment.

As you go through your training, learn as much as possible about the various jobs for which you might qualify. You may be unaware of jobs that closely match your interests. It is not uncommon to rewrite objectives more than once before beginning the actual job search. Use the Resumé Building Block #1 Career Objective to begin defining the kind of job you want.

Building Block #2 EDUCATION. A list of all your education and training, with emphasis on health care training.

Start your list with the school you attended most recently. Include grade point average and class standing (not all schools rank their students by grades) if they are above average. Use the Resumé Building Block #2 Education form as a motivator to do your best academically.

Building Block #3 PROFESSIONAL SKILLS AND KNOWLEDGE. The skills and knowledge that contribute to successful job performance.

The way you organize this section when you actually write your resumé depends on your educational program and the number and variety of skills acquired. You can list them individually if there are not too many (such as "Take vital signs") or as clusters of related skills (such as "Perform clinical duties").

Listing individual skills or clusters of skills is a good idea if your previous work experience is limited and you want to emphasize the recent acquisition of health care skills as your primary

---

Resumé Building Block #1
CAREER OBJECTIVE

Employers want to know what kind of job you are looking for. You need to know this, too! You may change your objective for your first job several times as you learn new subjects and get ideas from your lab and clinical experiences.

TO DO NOW
Write at least two sentences that describe your objective, as you see it now, for your first job in health care.

1. _____

_____

_____

2. _____

_____

_____

Add new ideas here:

_____

_____

_____

_____

_____

WRITING YOUR RESUMÉ

OBJECTIVE:

_____

_____

_____

_____

_____

Resumé Building Block #2
EDUCATION

Your education is more than a list of schools you've attended. Take the steps to get all you can out of your training program.

TO DO NOW

List five things you can do to get the most from your education.

1. _____
2. _____
3. _____
4. _____
5. _____

Write 3 academic goals.

1. _____
2. _____
3. _____

What study skills would help you achieve your goals?

_____
_____
_____
_____
_____

WRITING YOUR RESUMÉ

List the schools you have attended, starting with the most recent.

_____
_____
_____
_____
_____

qualification. It is also helpful if you have trained for one of the newer positions in health care that is not familiar to all employers. For example, "Patient Care Technician" is a relatively new multi-skilled worker who can be employed in a variety of health care settings. Even if you decide not to include a skills list on your resume, starting a list now will keep you aware of what you know and have to offer an employer. Employers report that many recent graduates don't realize just how much they really know and therefore, fail to sell themselves at job interviews.

Find out whether your school provides lists of program and course objectives and/or the competencies you will master. Some instructors give their students check lists to monitor the completion of assignments and demonstration of competencies. Other sources of information include handouts from your instructor, such as **syllabi** and course outlines; the objectives listed in your textbooks; and lab skill sheets. Develop your own inventory of what you have learned, using the Resumé Building Block #3 Professional Skills and Knowledge form to begin a personal inventory of your skills. An additional benefit of tracking your progress is the sense of accomplishment you gain as you see the results of your hard work. You will be amazed by how much you are learning!

Resumé Building Block #3
PROFESSIONAL SKILLS AND KNOWLEDGE

TO DO NOW

Track the skills you are learning by keeping an inventory for each of your subjects. Fill in this form as you progress through your program. Here are some examples of the kinds of skills to include:

- Set up dental trays for common procedures
- Accurately complete medical insurance claim forms
- Create presentations using PowerPoint
- Teach a patient to use different ambulatory devices

COURSE TITLE   SKILLS ACQUIRED

1. _____   _____
2. _____   _____
3. _____   _____
4. _____   _____
5. _____   _____
6. _____   _____
7. _____   _____
8. _____   _____
9. _____   _____
10. _____   _____

WRITING YOUR RESUMÉ

You can organize your professional skills and knowledge into clusters or write a list of individual skills.
_____
_____
_____
_____

Building Block #4 WORK HISTORY. A list of your previous jobs including the name and location of the employer, your job title and duties, and the dates of employment.

You can benefit from this section of your resumé even if you have no previous experience in health care. There are three ways to do this. The first is to review the duties and responsibilities you had in each job you have held in the past. Which ones can be applied to health care work? Skills that are common to many jobs are called **transferable skills.** Here are a few examples of both general and more technical skills common to many jobs:

☐ Work well with people from a variety of backgrounds.
☐ Create efficient schedules that reduce employee overtime.
☐ Purchase supplies in appropriate quantities and at competitive prices.
☐ Resolve customer complaints satisfactorily.
☐ Perform word processing.
☐ Manage accounts receivable.
☐ Provide customer service.
☐ Provide appropriate care for infants and toddlers.

Identifying transferable skills is especially important when you are entering a new field in which you have little or no experience. There is actually a type of resumé that emphasizes skills and abilities rather than specific job titles held. It is called a "functional resumé," and the format is described later in this chapter. At this time, start compiling a list of possible transferable skills.

The second way to maximize the value of the Work History section of your resumé is to mention what you achieved in each job. In a phrase or two, describe how you contributed to the success of your employer. When possible, state these achievements in measurable terms. If you can't express them with numbers, use active verbs that tell what you did. Here are some examples:

☐ Increased sales by 20%.
☐ Designed a more efficient way to track supplies.
☐ Worked on a committee to write an effective employee procedure manual that is still in use.
☐ Trained five employees to use office equipment correctly.

A third way to add value to this section is to include your clinical experience. While you must clearly indicate that this was a part of your training and not paid employment, it still serves as evidence of your ability to apply what you learned in school to practical situations. For many new graduates, this is their only real-world experience in health care. Students sometimes make the mistake of viewing their clinical experience as simply an add-on to their program, just one more thing to get through. They fail to realize the impact their performance can have on their career. Remember that clinical supervisors represent future employers. (In some cases, they are future employers because some students are hired by their clinical sites.) Their opinion of you can help successfully launch your self-marketing efforts or cause them to fizzle, so commit to doing your best during your clinical experience. The inclusion of a successful clinical experience on your resumé increases your chances of getting the job you want.

Use the Resumé Building Block #4 Work History form to start compiling your work history.

Note: *Do not be concerned if your work experience is limited or you can't think of any achievements. You may have finished high school recently or perhaps you spent several years working as a homemaker. Employers understand that everyone starts with a first job and you are receiving training to qualify you for work. And homemakers, as well as mothers and others who care for family members, gain experiences that are valuable to employers. Examples include caring for others, time management, and handling family finances.*

Resumé Building Block #4
WORK HISTORY

TO DO NOW
List the jobs you've had in the past and start recording transferable skills and accomplishments.

JOB TITLE	TRANSFERABLE SKILLS	ACCOMPLISHMENTS
_____	_____	_____
_____	_____	_____
_____	_____	_____
_____	_____	_____
_____	_____	_____

WRITING YOUR RESUMÉ
Remember that the different types of resumés (chronological, functional, and combination) described in this chapter will influence what information you include in your Work History section.

WORK HISTORY
_____
_____
_____
_____
_____
_____

Building Block #5 LICENSES AND CERTIFICATIONS. Some professions require you to be licensed or have specific types of approval before you are allowed to work. Nursing is one example. Others include physical and occupational therapy and dental hygiene. Some professions have voluntary certifications and registrations, such as those earned by medical assistants. The kind of approvals needed vary by state and profession. Most licenses and certifications require certain types of training and/or passing a standardized exam. It is important that you clearly understand any professional requirements necessary or highly recommended for your profession.

Learn as much as you can now about the requirements for the occupation you have chosen. It is not advisable to wait until the end of your studies to start thinking about preparing for required exams. Ask your instructors about review classes, books, and computerized material. Check with your professional organization. Become familiar with the topics on the exams and plan your studies accordingly. Knowing the format of the questions (multiple-choice, true-false, etc.) is also helpful. Increase your chances for success by preparing over time, the proven way to do well on exams. Use the Resumé Building Block #5 Licenses and Certifications form to start gathering information about certifications for your occupation.

Resumé Building Block #5
LICENSES AND CERTIFICATIONS

TO DO NOW

Describe the licensing and/or certification requirements for your occupation, if any.

_____

_____

_____

Are there voluntary approvals for which you can test or apply?

_____

_____

_____

Are written and/or practical exams required? What range of content is covered? How are the questions formatted (multiple choice, true/false, etc.)?

_____

_____

_____

Are content outlines, review books, software, and/or practice exams available?

_____

_____

_____

WRITING YOUR RESUMÉ

LICENSE/CERTIFICATION/REGISTRATION (CHOOSE APPROPRIATE HEADING):

_____

_____

_____

_____

Building Block #6 HONORS AND AWARDS. This is an **optional** resumé section. Your school may offer recognition for student achievements and special contributions. Community and professional organizations to which you belong may also give awards. Acknowledgments received for volunteer work can also be included in this section.

Investigate what you might be eligible for and use these rewards as incentives for excellent performance. Keep this in perspective, however. Awards should serve as motivators, not indicators of your value. They are nice to have but certainly not essential for getting a good job.

Use the Resumé Building Block #6 Honors and Awards form to find out about the availability and requirements of awards for which you might qualify.

Resumé Building Block #6
HONORS AND AWARDS

TO DO NOW
List school awards for which you might qualify.
_____
_____
_____

Eligibility requirements:
_____
_____
_____

List community awards for which you might qualify.
_____
_____
_____

Eligibility requirements:
_____
_____
_____

List other awards for which you might qualify.
_____
_____
_____

Eligibility requirements:
_____
_____
_____

WRITING YOUR RESUMÉ

HONORS/AWARDS:
_____
_____

Building Block #7 SPECIAL SKILLS. Special skills are those that don't fit into other sections but do add to your value as a prospective employee. Examples include proficiency in desktop publishing and the ability to use American Sign Language.

Research the needs of employers in your geographic area. Do you already have special skills that meet these needs? Would it substantially increase your chances for employment if you acquired skills outside the scope of your program—for example, to become more proficient on the computer? If (and only if!) time permits, you might decide to attend workshops in addition to your regular program courses, do extra reading, or take a course on the Internet. Use the Resumé Building Block #7 Special Skills form to record any skills that might supplement your qualifications.

Building Block #8 VOLUNTEER ACTIVITIES. Volunteer activities can be included on your resumé if they relate to your targeted occupation or demonstrate desired qualities such as being responsible and having concern for others. If you are already involved in these types of activities, think about what you are learning or practicing that can help you on the job. If you aren't, consider becoming involved if you have a sincere interest and

adequate time. Adult students face many responsibilities outside of class, and the additional activities mentioned in this chapter should be taken as suggestions, not must-dos. Mastering your program content should be your first priority. If applicable, use the Resumé Building Block #8 Volunteer Activities form to investigate opportunities and record your service.

Building Block #9 PROFESSIONAL AND CIVIC ORGANIZATIONS. Professional organizations provide excellent opportunities to network, learn more about your field, and practice leadership skills. Participation in **civic organizations,** groups that work for the good of the community, promotes personal growth and demonstrates your willingness to get involved in your community. Consider joining and participating actively in a professional or civic organization while you are in school. See whether your school or community has a local chapter. Use the Resumé Building Block #9 Professional and Civic Organizations form to record your participation.

Building Block #10 LANGUAGES SPOKEN. In our multicultural society, the ability to communicate in a language other than English is commonly

Resumé Building Block #7
SPECIAL SKILLS

TO DO NOW
Start recording special skills you think may be applicable to a job in health care.

SKILL	METHOD OF ACQUISITION	APPLICATION TO HEALTH CARE

WRITING YOUR RESUMÉ

SPECIAL SKILLS:

Resumé Building Block #8
VOLUNTEER ACTIVITIES

TO DO NOW

List any volunteer activities you might use on your resumé. Do you have time while you are in school for new or additional activities?

ACTIVITY	PERSONAL SKILLS ACQUIRED	QUALITIES DEMONSTRATED
_____	_____	_____
_____	_____	_____
_____	_____	_____
_____	_____	_____
_____	_____	_____

WRITING YOUR RESUMÉ

VOLUNTEER WORK/COMMUNITY SERVICE:

_____

_____

_____

_____

_____

_____

Resumé Building Block #9
PROFESSIONAL AND CIVIC ORGANIZATIONS

TO DO NOW

List any professional and/or civic activities you might use on your resumé. Are there organizations you can join to gain experience and enrich your educational program?

ORGANIZATION	ACTIVITIES	SKILLS ACQUIRED
_____	_____	_____
_____	_____	_____
_____	_____	_____
_____	_____	_____
_____	_____	_____

WRITING YOUR RESUMÉ

PROFESSIONAL AND CIVIC ORGANIZATIONS:

_____

_____

_____

_____

_____

_____

Resumé Building Block #10
LANGUAGES SPOKEN

TO DO NOW

Languages you speak other than English:

_____

_____

_____

_____

Languages spoken by patients in your geographic area:

_____

_____

_____

Opportunities to learn another language (even a few phrases useful in the health care setting):

_____

_____

_____

_____

WRITING YOUR RESUMÉ

LANGUAGES SPOKEN:

_____

_____

_____

included on the resumé. Find out whether many patients speak a language other than English in the area where you plan to work. Consider acquiring at least some conversational ability or a few phrases to use to reassure patients. Also consider learning about the customs, especially the ones related to health practices, of ethnic groups in your community. If your program offers these languages as elective courses, they would be good choices. Patients benefit greatly, during the stress of illness or injury, when health care professionals know at least a few phrases of their native language. Even speaking just a few basic phrases can increase your value to employers. Use the Resumé Building Block #10 Languages Spoken form if you have or plan to acquire knowledge of another language.

PORTFOLIOS

Although resumés are the principal method for job seekers to present their qualifications to potential employers, portfolios are increasingly used to supplement the resumé. A **portfolio** is an organized collection of items that document your capabilities and qualifications for work. A portfolio can give you a competitive edge at job interviews.

Starting to plan your portfolio now can cast your class assignments in a new light. More than work you turn in to your instructor, they can serve as demonstrations of your abilities to an employer. Strive to perform consistently at your highest level, producing work that will represent you well.

As you complete each course, save assignments that might be suitable for your portfolio. Store them in a folder or large envelope so they stay in good condition. In addition to written assignments, there are nontraditional ways to showcase your abilities. The items you collect need not be limited to evidence of your technical skills. For example, it is appropriate to include documentation of other activities, such as organizing an event for charity. No standard list of items to put in your portfolio exists, although your school may have prepared a list for students. In any case, only accurate and neat work should be included.

PROMOTION

Think about how companies use promotional campaigns to give new products maximum exposure. They advertise—sometimes endlessly, it seems!—on television, in magazines and newspapers, and on billboards to spread the word to as many consumers as possible about how the product will fulfill their needs. You will conduct a similar campaign when you conduct your job search. As with your resumé and portfolio, you can begin to prepare now. Networking, references, and the job interview are the three main ways to promote yourself during the job search.

Networking

Networking, as we are using the word here, refers to meeting and establishing relationships with people who work in health care. It is an effective way to learn more about your chosen career. At the same time, it gets the word out about you and your employment goals. Examples of networking opportunities include professional meetings, career fairs, class field trips to health care facilities, and guest speakers who come to your school.

There are many ways to begin networking: at a professional meeting, introduce yourself to other members; after hearing a guest speaker in class, ask questions; at a career fair, ask a local employer for advice about what to emphasize in your studies. Be sure to follow-up with a phone call or thank-you note to anyone who sends you information or makes a special effort to help you.

Another benefit of networking is building your self-confidence as you introduce yourself to people. You can improve your speaking ability and increase your ability to express yourself effectively. These are valuable skills you will use when attending job interviews. Start now to create a web of connections to help you develop professionally and assist you in your future job search and career.

References

References are people who will confirm your qualifications, skills, abilities, and personal qualities. In other words, they endorse you as a product. Professional references are not the same as personal or character references. To be effective, professional references must be credible (believable) and have personal knowledge of your value to a prospective employer. Your best references

have knowledge of both you and the health care field. Examples include your instructors, clinical experience supervisors, and other professionals who know the quality of your work. Previous supervisors, even in jobs outside of health care, also make good references.

Recall the discussion in this chapter about becoming a health care professional by conducting yourself as if you already were one. Start now to project a professional image to everyone you meet, including your instructors and other staff members at your school. Become the person who others will be happy to recommend.

Job Interview

Job interviews provide the best opportunities to promote yourself to prospective employers. Interviewers often ask for examples of how you solved a problem or handled a given situation. Start thinking now about your past experiences and begin to collect examples from your work as a student, especially from your clinical experience, that will demonstrate your capabilities. It is not too early to start preparing so you can approach your future interviews as opportunities to shine, at ease and confident that you are presenting yourself positively. Job interviews are discussed in detail in Chapter 11.

PULLING IT ALL TOGETHER

You are now ready to gather the information in your Resumé Building Blocks to construct a finished product. The steps described in this section will help you to create a document that best highlights your qualifications.

You will see as you progress through this chapter that there is no one best way to write a resumé. Everyone has different talents and experiences. Even students who complete the same program at the same time come from a variety of backgrounds that can be presented in different ways. For example, a young person who graduated from high school shortly before beginning a dental assisting program will benefit from emphasizing different areas than a classmate who worked in sales for 20 years before entering the same program.

There are also local customs and employer preferences regarding resumés. Seek the advice of your instructors, school career service personnel, and professional contacts. They keep in touch with employers and can offer sound advice.

At this busy time in the job-search process, you may be tempted to use a standard resumé format. Filling in the blanks on a "one-type-fits-all" resumé may seem to be a fast and easy way to complete this task. However, the time spent customizing your resumé can pay off in several ways. For example, you will:

1. Better recognize and review your own qualifications
2. Respond to employers' specific needs
3. Be prepared to support your claims with examples
4. Demonstrate your organizational skills
5. Show your initiative and creativity

An effective way to increase your efficiency when putting together your resumé is to use word processing software. This gives you several advantages because you can:

☐ Try different layouts and formats
☐ Change and reorganize content quickly and easily
☐ Check for (most) spelling errors
☐ Change your objective or skill clusters to address specific employer needs
☐ Use special features such as bolding and changing the size and style of the letters
☐ Send your resumé (with some revisions) as part of an e-mail and/or post it on the Internet

If you don't know how to word process, now is a good time to learn if you have a little time. Today's software is quite easy to learn and even nontypists can produce great-looking documents by learning a few basic commands. Spacing, bolding, underlining, moving text, and printing can be accomplished with the click or two of a button. If you can spend a few hours to learn the basics of a word processing program now, it will be a good investment of your time. Not only will this skill support your job-search effort, it will provide you with a valuable workplace skill. Even health care professionals who dedicate most of their time to hands-on patient activities can benefit from knowing how to word process.

10 STEPS FOR ASSEMBLING YOUR RESUMÉ

Whether you create your resumé on a computer or not, following a step-by-step process can help you assemble a resumé to fit your needs. Box 10-1 summarizes the steps that are explained in the following sections.

Box 10-1 A 10-Step Checklist for Assembling Your Resumé

1. Prepare the heading.
2. Add the objective.
3. Select the best type of resumé for you.
4. Decide if you want to include a Qualifications section.
5. Choose which Resumé Building Blocks to include.
6. Plan the order of your Building Blocks.
7. Decide whether you want to add a personal statement.
8. But ... leave out personal information.
9. Plan the layout.
10. Create an attractive and professional-looking document.

STEP ONE
Prepare the Heading. It is not necessary to write the word "Resumé." Instead, clearly label the top of the page with your name, address, and telephone number. Centering your name is good for both appearance and practicality. Placing it on the far left side makes it more difficult for the employer to find if it is placed in a stack of other resumés. Capitalizing your name and/or using a slightly larger font (letter) size than the rest of the document helps it to stand out.

Capitalize and boldface your name and consider using a larger font size. Include ZIP code and area code. Be sure all numbers are accurate. Include e-mail address if you have one.

JAIME RAMIREZ
3650 Loma Alta Lane
San Diego, CA 92137
(619) 123-4567
jrnurse@aol.com

If your resumé is long and you are trying to conserve space, center your name above your full address, phone number, and email address.

STEP TWO
Add the Objective. The objective, from Resumé Building Block #1, should be near the beginning of the resumé so prospective employers can quickly see whether there is a potential match between your goals and their needs. This part of the resumé may change slightly, as discussed before, if

you are trying to match your objective with the stated needs of each employer. Your objective will not change if you have specific requirements you are not willing to change or if you have written a very general objective that meets a number of job targets.

STEP THREE

Select the Best Type of Resumé for You. The three basic types are chronological, functional, and combination. They provide different ways to present your work history and professional qualifications. Your particular background determines which type you should choose.

CHRONOLOGICAL RESUMÉ

The chronological resumé emphasizes work history. It shows the progression of jobs you have held to demonstrate how you have gained increasing knowledge and experience and/or responsibility relevant to the job you want now. This type of resumé is recommended if you have:

- ☐ Held previous jobs in health care
- ☐ Had jobs in other areas in which you had increases in responsibility or a strong record of achievements
- ☐ Acquired many skills that apply to health care (transferable skills)

In the chronological resumé, each job you've had in the past is listed, followed by the duties performed and accomplishments achieved. The Work section is well developed and likely to be longer than most other parts of your resumé.

FUNCTIONAL RESUMÉ

The functional resumé emphasizes skills and traits that relate to the targeted job but which weren't necessarily acquired through health care employment. They can be pulled from both work and personal experiences. For example, if you cared for a sick relative for an extended period of time, this is an experience you might decide to include. Review the transferable skills on Resumé Building Block #4 for ideas. Once you have identified and listed qualifications that fit your target jobs, organize them into three or four clusters with descriptive headings.

Functional resumés are advantageous if you:
- ☐ Are entering the job market for the first time
- ☐ Have held jobs unrelated to health care
- ☐ Have personal experiences you can apply to health care work

The Work History section of a functional resumé consists of a simple list of job titles with each employer's name, city and state, and your dates of employment. A functional resumé may take more time to develop than a chronological one, but the extra effort can really pay off because it allows you to highlight the qualifications that are your strongest bid for employment.

COMBINATION RESUMÉ

The combination resumé, as its name implies, uses features of both the chronological and functional types. The details of the job(s) held in or closely related to health care are listed, along with clusters of qualifications or a list of supporting skills. This resumé is appropriate if you:
- ☐ Have held jobs in health care and
- ☐ Have related qualifications you gained through other, non–health care jobs and experiences or
- ☐ Have held a number of jobs in health care for which you performed the same or very similar duties

Let's look at how a recent occupational therapy assistant graduate who worked for 2 years as a nursing assistant and for 3 years as a preschool aide creates a combination resumé. She decides to:
- ☐ Include a list of the duties she performed in the nursing assistant job
- ☐ Create clusters to highlight her teaching and interpersonal skills, both important in occupational therapy
- ☐ List skills from her teaching and other experiences under each cluster heading

CHOOSING THE BEST RESUMÉ FOR YOU

Review your skills and experiences and use the guidelines in this section to choose the best type of resumé for you. If you decide to use a chronological presentation, copy what you prepared for your Work History in Building Block #3.

If a functional resumé would serve you better, use the following guidelines to create the clusters:

1. Consider the current needs of employers. Check your local help-wanted ads and the National Health Care Skill Standards.
2. Think about the skills and traits that contribute to success in your occupation.
3. Look over your work history, clinical experience, personal experiences, volunteer activities, and participation in professional organizations.
4. Refer to your completed Prescription for Success 10-1 for references and recommendations you can use in clusters.

5. Create three or four headings for clusters that support your job target and give you an opportunity to list your most significant qualifications. The following list contains examples of appropriate clusters for health care occupations:

- ☐ Communication Skills
- ☐ Organizational Skills
- ☐ Teamwork Skills
- ☐ Interpersonal Relations
- ☐ Computer Skills
- ☐ Clerical Skills

6. List appropriate specific skills under each heading.

STEP FOUR

Decide Whether You Want to Include a Qualifications Section. This is an optional section. Its purpose is to list skills that support you as a product but that don't fit well in other sections. For example, you may have decided to use a chronological resumé but have additional experiences that don't belong in the Work History section. Or maybe you are designing a functional resumé, but have single experiences worth mentioning that don't fit any of the headings. Here are some examples:

- ☐ Excellent time-management skills
- ☐ Work calmly under pressure
- ☐ Proven problem-solving ability
- ☐ Cost conscious
- ☐ Enthusiastic team player
- ☐ Work well without supervision
- ☐ Enjoy learning new skills

A qualifications section can also serve as a summary of highlights to draw attention to your most significant features. Such a summary might look like this:

- ☐ Eight years' experience working in health care
- ☐ Up-to-date administrative and clinical medical assisting skills
- ☐ Current CPR certification
- ☐ Fluent in spoken Spanish
- ☐ Excellent communication skills

Popular titles for the Qualifications section include "Summary of Qualifications," "Professional Qualifications," and "Professional Profile." Review the same information sources recommended in Step Four for preparing functional clusters. The difference in preparing the Qualifications section is you can combine different kinds of characteristics. They don't have to fall into neat categories, but only have to demonstrate capabilities, traits, and special skills that relate to the job you want.

Note: *If you are have created clusters and are using them in a functional or combination resumé, you may not need a Qualifications section. The important thing is not to repeat information in your resumé. Step Five talks more about deciding what to include.*

STEP FIVE

Choose Which Resumé Building Blocks to Use. You want your resumé to be comprehensive but, at the same time, you don't want to repeat the same information. For example, if you are using a functional format and have listed a special skill in one of your clusters, don't repeat it under another heading. Group as much as fits well into each Resumé Building Block instead of having many headings with just one item listed. Think about which items fit together. The following are the most appropriate to combine:

1. Licenses and certifications can be placed in their own section, in the Education section, or listed as a Professional Qualification.

2. Honors and awards earned in school can be listed under Education. If you have a variety of awards, it might be better to highlight them by listing them in their own section.

3. Memberships can go under Education if they are limited to school groups or your health care professional organization. If you have been active in the organizations or are involved in several organizations, they can go in their own section.

4. Clinical experience can be listed under either Education or Work History. Wherever you place it, include some information about the duties you performed. For career changers and recent graduates, this may be a significant form of work history. Be sure to indicate clearly, however, that the work was unpaid and part of an educational program.

5. Languages you speak other than English can be listed under Qualifications, Special Skills, or Languages Spoken.

Deciding which headings to use and where to place content depends on the amount of content, how directly it relates to the kind of job you want, and your own organizational preferences. Suppose you speak two languages other than English. If they are spoken by many people in your geographic area, they are likely to be valuable job qualifications and can be listed there. If they are not commonly spoken in your area, they might best be listed under Languages—skills you want to show, but that may not be directly related to the job. Think about the relative importance of your content as you decide how best to organize and label it.

STEP SIX
Plan the Order of Your Building Blocks. Place the sections that contain your strongest qualifications first. For example, if you are changing careers and recent education is your primary qualification, list this section before Work History.

STEP SEVEN
Decide Whether You Want to Add a Personal Statement. In their book *Career Planning*, Dave Ellis and coauthors suggest adding a positive personal statement at the bottom of your resumé. This gives you an opportunity to make a final impression and add an original touch. It is a way to say "Here is something personal and interesting about me that might help you, the employer." If you decide to write a personal statement, be sure it is a sincere reflection of you and not simply something that sounds good. And, as with the entire resumé, be sure it relates to your job target. Here are some examples:

> *"I enjoy being a part of a team where I can make a positive contribution by using my ability to remain calm and work efficiently under stressful conditions."*
>
> *"I get great satisfaction working with people from a variety of backgrounds who need assistance in resolving their health care problems."*

If you decide to include a personal statement, review your reasons for choosing a career in health care along with what you believe are your best potential contributions to prospective employers. It is also a good idea to have someone else, such as your instructor, review your statement.

STEP EIGHT
Leave Out Personal Information. Don't include personal information such as your age, marital status, number of children, and health status. And never include false statements about your education or experience. If these are discovered later, they can be grounds for dismissal from your job.

Although it is important to have a Reference Sheet (list of references) available for potential employers who request it, it is not necessary to write a statement such as "References Available Upon Request."

STEP NINE
Plan the Layout. Each section of your resumé, except the heading at the top and personal statement (optional) at the end, should be labeled: Objective, Education, Work History, and so on. Headings can be flush (aligned) with the left margin, with the content set to the right:

OBJECTIVE	XXXXXXXXXXXXXXXXXXXX
	XXXXXXXXXXXXXXXXXXX
EDUCATION	XXXXXXXXXXXXXXXXXXXX
	XXXXXXXXXXXXXXXXXXX

Alternatively, you can center your headings and list the information beneath and flush left.

OBJECTIVE
XXXXXXXXXXXXXXXXXXXXXXXXXXXXX
XXXXXXXXXXXXXXXXXXXXXXXXXX

EDUCATION
XXXXXXXXXXXXXXXXXXXX
XXXXXXXXXXXXXXXXXXXXXXXX
XXXXXXXXXXXXXXX

The information you list under the headings can be arranged in a variety of ways. The design should be based primarily on whether you need to use or save space on the page. The second consideration is personal preference. However you choose to lay out your resumé, strive for a balanced, attractive look. Note the varied use of capitalization and boldface to draw attention to the job title in the following examples:

WORK HISTORY Medical Transcriptionist
1997–Present
Hopeful Medical Center,
Better Health, NJ

or

MEDICAL TRANSCRIPTIONIST
1997–Present
Hopeful Medical Center,
Better Health, NJ

or

Medical Transcriptionist
Hopeful Medical Center,
Better Health, NJ
1997–Present

STEP TEN
Create an Attractive and Professional-Looking Document. Selecting and organizing content is the most time-consuming part of writing your resumé. Don't waste your efforts by failing to attend to the details of appearance. The following tips will help you achieve a professional look:

☐ Leave enough white space so the page doesn't look crowded. Double-space between the sections.

☐ It is recommended that you limit your re-sumé to one page. It is better to use two pages, however, than to crowd too much information on one page. If you do use two pages, write "More" or "Continued" at the bottom of the first page and your name and contact information and "Page 2" or "Page Two" at the top of the second.

☐ Capitalize headings.

☐ Use bullets to set off listed items.

☐ Try using boldface for emphasis.

☐ Make sure your spelling and grammar are perfect.

☐ Leave at least a 1-inch margin on all sides.

☐ Use good quality paper in white, ivory, or very light tan or gray.

☐ Whether printing from the computer or us-ing a copy machine, make sure the print is dark and clear. If you don't have access to a computer printer or a good copy ma-chine, consider paying to have your resumé printed. Although this limits your flexibility in customizing the resumé for various em-ployers, it will provide professional quality copies.

Your basic resumé can serve you throughout your health care career. Think of it as a living document on which you continually record your experiences and new skills.

See Figures 10-1, 10-2, and 10-3 for examples of completed resumés. Yours will look different, of course, but these might give you some ideas.

RUDY MARQUEZ
1909 Franklin Blvd.
Philadelphia, PA 19105
(610) 765-4321   MAmarquez@aol.com

OBJECTIVE   Position as a clinical medical assistant in an urgent care setting

QUALIFICATIONS

- 13 years experience as a certified medical assistant
- Current certifications in CPR and Basic Life Support
- Proven ability to communicate with patients and staff
- Proactive employee who anticipates office and physicians' needs
- Fluent in Spanish and Italian

WORK HISTORY   Medical Assistant   2000-present
Founders Medical Clinic   Philadelphia, PA
- Perform clinical and laboratory duties
- Assist physicians with exams, procedures, and surgeries
- Reorganized patient education program, including selection of updated brochures, videos
- Provide patient education and present healthy living workshops
- Train and supervise new medical assistants

Medical Assistant   1994-2000
North Side Clinic   Pittsburgh, PA
- Performed clinical and laboratory duties
- Developed system for monitoring and ordering clinic supplies that resulted in annual savings of over $25,000
- Received commendation for providing outstanding patient service

Medical Assistant   1992-1994
Dr. Alan Fleming   Erie, PA
- Assisted Dr. Fleming with procedures and minor office surgeries
- Prepared treatment and examining rooms
- Took vital signs and administered injections
- Performed routine laboratory tests
- Handled computerized recordkeeping tasks
- Assisted in researching and purchasing new office computer system

EDUCATION   Associate of Science in Medical Assisting   1992
Emerson College of Health Careers, Erie, PA

Recently Completed Workshops and Continuing Education Courses
- Health Care Beliefs of Minority Populations
- Medical Spanish
- New Requirements for Maintaining Patient Confidentiality

ORGANIZATIONS   American Association of Medical Assistants (AAMA)
Pennsylvania Association of Medical Assistants
Philadelphia Lions Club

Figure 10-1 Example of a chronological resumé.

HEATHER DIETZ
10532 Cactus Road
Yuma, AZ 85360
(520) 321-7654   thedietz@linkup.com

OBJECTIVE
Entry-level position in health information management in which I can apply up-to-date knowledge and skills. I especially enjoy applying my organizational skills and working on challenging tasks that must be complete and accurate.

EDUCATION
Associate of Science in Health Information Technology   2004
Desert Medical College   Yuma, AZ

COMPUTER SKILLS
- Created electronic spreadsheet to track fund raising for Sage Elementary School PTA
- Taught self to efficiently use leading brand software programs in the following areas: word processing, database, spreadsheets, and accounting
- Set up and managed electronic accounting system for family-owned construction business
- Taught computer classes at Girl Scout summer day camp

ORGANIZATIONAL SKILLS
- Created system to monitor all church collections and fund-raising projects
- Initiated and developed computer career awareness program for Girl Scouts
- Secretary for college HIT student organization
- Completed HIT associate degree program with perfect class attendance while working part-time and managing family life

CLERICAL/ADMINISTRATIVE SKILLS
- 7 years bookkeeping experience
- Keyboarding speed of 78 wpm
- Excellent written communication skills

WORK HISTORY
Unpaid Internship at St. John's Medical Center, Yuma, AZ   2004
Medical Records Department

Bookkeeper   1998-2002
Buildwell Construction Company, Yuma, AZ

Bookkeeper   1993-1998
Perfect-Fit Cabinetry, Yuma, AZ

Secretary   1990-1993
Caldwell Insurance Company, Yuma, AZ

ORGANIZATIONS
Desert Medical College Health Information Technology Student Organization, Secretary
Sage Elementary School PTA, Treasurer
Faith Community Church, Member of Social Service Committee

Figure 10-2   Example of a functional resumé.

DISTRIBUTING YOUR RESUMÉ

Make the best use of your printed resumé by distributing it to people who have jobs—employers—and people who might know about jobs. Here are some suggestions to get you started:
- Employers who place help-wanted ads
- Employers who have unadvertised openings you have heard about
- Your networking contacts
- Friends and relatives
- Anyone who indicates that he or she knows someone who might be hiring
- Your school's career services department

Keep enough copies of your resumé on hand to respond to unexpected opportunities. Take copies to interviews (even if you have sent a copy in advance), career fairs, and the human resource departments of health care facilities. Be sure to have plenty on hand if you decide to drop in on employers as described earlier. A well-prepared resumé in many hands is an effective way to get the word out that you are a serious job candidate.

It is usually not recommended, however, that you send resumés to dozens of employers in the hope of locating one that has a job opening. One exception is when there are more job openings than applicants. This can occur when there is a shortage, such as the current nationwide shortage of registered nurses. When there is a shortage, you are more likely to receive responses when sending unsolicited resumés. A second exception is

EMILY COLLINS
8215 Mile High Drive
Denver, CO 80201
(303) 987-6543

OBJECTIVE   Position as an Occupational Therapy Assistant working with clients who have physical disabilities

EDUCATION   Associate of Science   Occupational Therapy Assistant   2005
Salud College   Denver, CO
Graduated with Honors
Passed national certification exam
Fieldwork completed at Central Rehabilitation Hospital

Certificate   Nursing Assistant   2000
San Juan Medical Center   Denver, CO

HEALTH CARE WORK EXPERIENCE
Nursing Assistant   2000-2003
GoodCare Nursing Home, Denver, CO
• Encouraged patients to achieve their maximum level of wellness, activity, and independence
• Demonstrated interest in the lives and well-being of patients
• Helped patients to perform prescribed physical exercises
• Organized and participated in activities with patients
• Assisted patients with basic hygiene and dressing

INTERPERSONAL SKILLS
• Provided daily care for parent with Alzheimer's disease for 18 months
• Answered telephone, directed calls, and took messages for busy sporting goods manufacturer
• Received Connor Memorial Award from Salud College for making positive contributions and assisting classmates

TEACHING SKILLS
• Teach swim classes to all ages at YMCA
• Conduct CPR instruction for the American Heart Association
• Organize holiday programs and outings for nursing home residents (volunteer)
• Planned and supervised craft and play activities for school-age children
• Tutored ESL students at Salud College

WORK HISTORY
Preschool Aide   1999-2000
Bright Light Preschool, Denver, CO

Swim Instructor (part-time)   1999-present
YMCA, Denver, CO

Receptionist   1995-1999
Sportrite Manufacturing Co., Denver, CO

ORGANIZATIONS
American Occupational Therapy Association
American Heart Association, Chair of Local Fundraising Committee

Figure 10-3 Example of a combination resumé.

when you are moving to a new area. Sending a large number of resumés, along with a cover letter explaining that you are relocating, may be more economical and productive than calling many potential employers.

New Developments in Resumés

The capacities of the computer to sort and organize data, along with the speed and convenience of the Internet, have resulted in new forms of resumés and ways for job searchers and employers to connect.

PREPARING A SCANNABLE RESUMÉ

Some employers enter all the resumés they receive into a computerized database. Each resumé is then reviewed electronically and key words are identified. When there is a job opening, the computer searches for resumés that contain key words that match those in the job description. If there is a possibility your resumé will be scanned, make the following revisions to your basic resumé to ensure that it has the best chance of being selected from the database for the jobs you want. You will note that some changes require you to do exactly the opposite of the directions given in the previous sections to create an attractive printed resumé.

☐ Prepare a list of keywords that relate to your job target. Fifteen to 30 words are recommended. Place this list at the top of the resumé in place of the objective. Think about which key words most nearly describe the jobs for which you want to be considered. If possible, secure job descriptions from potential employers. Read ads or job announcements and visit facility web sites. The Occupational Outlook Handbook, a government publication that contains descriptions of thousands of jobs, is a good source. Good key words are nouns that name specific skills, such as insurance billing, laboratory tests, and patient care.

☐ Do not use special features such as boldface, italics, or special styles of type. These do not always scan well.

☐ Use 12-point font.

☐ Use regular printer paper and submit only originals, not photocopies.

☐ Do not fold or staple the pages.

☐ Make sure the print is clear and sharp so the scanner can read it accurately. Make sure there are no extra marks on the page, not even small ones like the holes left by removed staples.

POSTING YOUR RESUMÉ ON THE INTERNET

There are many types of web sites on which you can post your resumé. Some are general employment sites, such as Monster. Others are specific to health care. And still others are employer web sites that allow you to apply electronically for specific job openings. Deciding whether to place your resumé on the Internet and which type of web site to choose depends on your job target and the kind of employer you are seeking. While many web sites allow job searchers to post their resumés for free, they charge employers to place help-wanted ads online and to view the resumés in their databases. Therefore, larger organizations are the ones most likely to pay for this service. A physician's office or small clinic may not be able to justify the expense for its relatively small number of hires. Organizations with many employees, such as Kaiser Permanente or even a single hospital, may have their own web sites and online application capabilities.

Spend some time considering whether to post your resumé on the Internet. Although posting on a large web site, such as Monster, makes your resumé available to millions of viewers, you are also competing with millions of other job seekers. Experts suggest that posting your resumé on a few carefully chosen sites is worth some of your time but not as likely to help you find a job as methods such as networking and applying directly to specific employers. (The web sites referred to here are general employment services, such as Monster and Career Builder, not the web sites of employers who are requesting resumés for specific job openings. It is highly recommended that you do submit a resumé or application for any employer-listed jobs for which you qualify.)

If you decide to post your resumé, you may have to convert your printed version to what is called a "plain text" version. Similar to what must be done to make a resumé scannable, you'll need to remove the bullets, bolding, tabs, and other features (such as italics) that make the printed version attractive. Even the type of quote marks you use (curly versus straight) is important. If you paste the resumé you have created in a program, such as Word, in an e-mail or post it on the Internet, it may become scrambled and full of strange symbols. It is important that you follow the instructions on the web site(s) you choose, read about how to convert documents in books such as the *Guide to Internet Job Searching,* or find information on web sites such as susanireland. com. Some web sites, especially those sponsored by companies who are listing their own job openings, provide an online application you can fill out to create a standardized resumé. Whatever the format, it is extremely important that your resumé or answers to the questions be error-free. Once posted, they are on display for literally millions of people to view. As a courtesy to those who are looking for applicants, remove your resumé from all web sites on which you have it posted once you become employed.

Deciding on which web sites to post your resumé should also receive careful consideration. In general, experts recommend that you don't pay to have your resumé distributed. Many of these "services" simply send out mass e-mails containing the resumés of anyone who pays them. The resumés may or may not match the jobs (if indeed, the targeted employers have job openings) and it is reported that resumés are often sent without contact information, such as your name and telephone numbers, so employers cannot reach you even if they are interested in learning more about you. You must explore web sites for yourself, but starting with the recommendations of well-known job-search experts will help you avoid unreliable web sites. Richard Bolles recommends the following list in the latest edition of his long-running bestseller, *What Color Is Your Parachute?:*

1. Monster
2. Hot Jobs (Yahoo!)
3. Career Builder
4. Salary.com

Note: *The web sites referred to in this chapter can be directly accessed through Elsevier's* EVOLVE *web site.*

The following suggestions can help you choose an appropriate web site:

☐ Do not use web sites that won't allow you to review at least a sample of their job lists before you provide personal information or your resumé.

☐ Read the privacy policy! Some web sites sell or give your information to other businesses. Important: NEVER put your social security number on your resumé.

☐ Check the wording. Do the lists provided include real jobs or are they examples of what the web site claims to be trying to fill?

☐ Check for currency. Are there dates on the jobs listed? Are they recent?

☐ Look for information about who sponsors the site. Do they have credentials and/or experience in the job-search industry?

☐ If you do not get any responses to your resumé within 45 days, remove it and find another web site on which to post it.

INTRODUCING YOUR RESUMÉ: COVER LETTERS

A cover letter should be sent along with your resumé. The purpose of a cover letter is to provide a brief personal introduction. It should be short, informative, persuasive, and polite. The fact that you write a letter can be persuasive in itself. It shows that you took the time and made the effort to consider why and how you meet this particular employer's qualifications. You did more than simply put a resumé in an envelope or send it electronically.

Cover letters can be customized for different circumstances. Before discussing the different types, let's look at a few how-tos common to all cover letters:

1. Use a proper business letter format.
2. Be sure your spelling and grammar are error-free.
3. Direct your letter to a specific person whenever possible. Look for a name in the employment ad, ask your contact for the name of the appropriate person, or call the facility and ask. If you are writing in response to an unadvertised position, having a name on your correspondence is especially important. Letters without names can get misdirected or discarded. Busy facilities don't have time to determine to whom to direct your inquiry.
4. Write an introduction. State who you are, why you are writing, who referred you or what ad you are responding to, and what position you are applying for. Employers may have more than one position open, so don't assume they will know which job you are applying for.
5. Develop the body of the letter. Explain why the employer should interview you. Summarize your qualifications for the job. Do your best to match them with what you believe the employer is seeking. Avoid repeating the same information that is on your resumé.
6. Include a closing paragraph. Ask the employer to call you for an interview or state that you will call for an appointment.
7. If you are sending your cover letter electronically (in the body of an e-mail, for example), keep the format simple: don't use bolding, bullets, or other special features and avoid using tabs to indent text.

Letter for an Advertised Position

Earlier, we discussed responding to employment ads in a way that demonstrates how you meet the employer's needs. Use language in your letter that mirrors the words used in the ad or job announcement.

Letter for an Unadvertised Opening

You may learn about unadvertised job openings through your school or from your networking contacts. Mention your source of information in the introduction of your cover letter. (Be sure to obtain permission from the contact person before using his or her name!) Before writing the letter,

10752 Learning Lane
Silver Stream, NY 10559
July 22, 2005

Ms. Sandra Walters, Manager
Caring Clinic
7992 Oates Road
Greenville, NY 10772

Dear Ms. Walters:

I am writing to inquire about job openings at Caring Clinic. My husband and I are relocating to Greenville in September and I am looking for a position in which I can apply my up-to-date skills as a phlebotomy technician. Caring Clinic has a reputation for excellent service to the health needs of the Greenville community and I would be proud to be a contributing member of your team.

As a recent graduate of Top Skill Institute, I had the opportunity to perform my internship at Goodwell Laboratory Services, an affiliate of Caring Clinic. I understand the importance of combining technical excellence with attention to customer service. While at Goodwell, my technical skills were highly praised by my supervisor, Mr. Jaime Gutierrez. In addition, I consistently received top ratings on patient satisfaction surveys.

My resume is enclosed for your review. I will call you in early September to see if I can set up an appointment to meet with you. Thank you for your consideration.

Respectfully,

Carla Martinez
Carla Martinez

Figure 10-4 A cover letter used to inquire about possible job openings.

learn as much as possible about the job. Sources of information include the person who told you about it, the employer's web site, or an inquiry call to the facility.

Letter of Inquiry

There may be a facility where you would like to work, but you don't know if it has any job openings. Perhaps you have a friend who is happily employed there and has recommended it as a great place to work. Or it may have a reputation for excellent working conditions and educational and promotional opportunities. When you are not

responding to a specific job opening, state your general qualifications that meet the current needs in health care. Explain why you are interested in working at the facility. Learn as much as possible about the facility so you can emphasize specific contributions you can make (Figure 10-4).

APPLICATIONS

Applications are commonly requested of job applicants, even if they have submitted a resumé. Applications provide the employer with complete, standardized sources of information. Once you are hired, the application is placed in your personnel file and can serve as a legal document and record of information about you and your previous employment.

Some applications contain important statements you are required to read and sign. For example, employers of home health care workers may protect themselves from **liability** if employees have an accident when they are driving to and from job assignments. Read all statements carefully before signing. Applications and employment contracts may contain legal language and unfamiliar words. Don't hesitate to ask for an explanation of anything you don't understand.

After the work of constructing a resumé, filling out an application may seem easy. But don't take it for granted. Take time to read the instructions, and fill it out as accurately and neatly as possible. This is especially important when applying for health care positions because neatness and accuracy are job requirements. Use this opportunity to demonstrate that you meet these requirements.

Success Tips for Filling Out Job Applications

☐ Read the entire application before you begin to fill it in.
☐ Fill out all sections completely. Do not leave blanks or write in "See resumé."
☐ Use black or blue pen, never pencil.
☐ Print neatly.
☐ Go to interviews prepared to fill out an application. Take complete information with you, including the following:
  ○ Social Security number
  ○ Education, including dates and locations
  ○ Work history, including names of employers and dates of employment
  ○ Military service
  ○ References
☐ Proofread what you have written before submitting it.
☐ Be honest when answering questions. Giving false information can be grounds for dismissal if you are hired.
☐ For questions that don't apply to you, write "N/A" instead of leaving them blank. This way it is clear that you saw the question and didn't accidentally skip over it.
☐ Many entry-level jobs have a set salary. If the one you are applying for does not, it is best to write "negotiable."
☐ Be sure to sign and date the application.

Electronic Applications

Many employers now have application forms on their web sites. When applying electronically, it is especially important to follow the directions and check your entries carefully before pushing the "send" button. Once the application is sent, it is difficult to change incorrect information. In some cases, the online application takes the place of sending a resumé. As with traditional written materials, what you submit is a reflection of you as a professional.

REFERENCE SHEETS

References are people who will vouch for your qualifications and character. Good references can be a key factor in tipping the hiring scales in your favor. Give careful consideration to whom you ask to serve as references. They must be considered believable. Take care not to ask people who may be competing for the same jobs. Friends and relatives are not generally accepted as good work references, but they are often acceptable if you are asked to provide character references. In addition to being credible, references must:
  ☐ have the time and be willing to speak on your behalf to potential employers
  ☐ be able to speak positively about you
  ☐ have the ability to speak clearly and in an organized way
The following people are good candidates to be work references:
  ☐ Instructors
  ☐ Other school personnel
  ☐ Clinical/externship/internship/fieldwork supervisor(s)
  ☐ Previous employers
  ☐ Supervisors at places where you have performed volunteer work
  ☐ Professionals with whom you have worked on committees or projects
Contact each person you want to serve as a reference. Do this before you begin your job search. Never give out a name and then ask the person for permission afterwards. This can put the person on the spot and makes it difficult if he or she prefers not to be a reference. Inform your references about the types of jobs you are applying for and what qualifications are important. This will enable them to be prepared to answer the potential employer's questions.

Create a written list of at least three references. At a minimum, include their names, titles, telephone numbers, and e-mail addresses. You may also want to include their addresses. Ask them if they can be contacted at work. If not, provide recommended times to call. It is essential that the telephone numbers be current and accurate. If you list a work number and the person is no longer employed there, your credibility can be questioned. Potential employers don't have time to call you back or make numerous calls trying to locate your references. Make it easy for them. This makes it easier for them to hire you.

Organize your reference list in an easy-to-read format and print it on the same kind of paper as your resumé. Write "References for (your name)" at the top of the page. The reference sheet should not be mailed with your resumé unless it is specifically requested. Take copies with you to interviews to give to potential employers who ask for it. If you are visiting a human resource department, take a copy with you, because many employment applications have a section for listing references.

Be sure to let your references know when you are hired. Thank them for their willingness to assist you. Keep them posted of your career progress. In the future, you may be in a position to help them, and that is what true networking is all about—mutual career support.

LETTERS OF RECOMMENDATION

Another type of reference is provided through letters of recommendation. These letters are usually written by supervisors or people in authority, such as instructors, who write statements about your work record, skills, and personal qualities. It is a good idea to request reference letters from employers throughout your career because they can serve as a record of endorsements and achievements over the years. As you leave each job (on good terms, it is hoped!), ask for a letter of recommendation from your supervisor.

Make copies of your letters of recommendation to place in your portfolio and/or to give to potential employers who request them. It is

appropriate at interviews to mention that you have them available.

As with other references, be considerate. Ask only those people who you believe can write a positive letter. Also, try to give people enough time to compose a letter. Avoid giving one day's notice. Finally, let your references know what kind of job you are seeking so they can phrase their letters appropriately. Prescription for Success 10-1 will assist you in starting to develop professional references.

THE PORTFOLIO: SUPPORTING WHAT YOU SAY

Look over the items you have been collecting to put in your portfolio. Choose the ones that represent your best work and support the qualifications needed for your target jobs. Think about others you can include. For example, you might add a list of the courses you have taken if your educational program included classes not commonly offered in your program of study.

Organize your materials in a logical order, grouping related items together in sections. Place them in a binder or presentation folder using plastic protection sheets. It is not necessary to go to a lot of expense, but the folder should be well made and in a plain, conservative color. Prepare a title page labeled "Professional Portfolio" and include your name, address, and telephone number. If you have a large number of items, number the pages and prepare a table of contents.

You need to make only one portfolio if it is rather large; if it consists of only a few pages, make a few copies in case a potential employer asks you to leave it after the interview. Portfolios are not generally sent with your resumé, but are taken to interviews. You may mention to the interviewer that you have a portfolio. Don't simply hand it to the employer and expect him or her to read it (unless you are asked for it, of course). It is to be used during the interview to demonstrate your capabilities. For example, if you are asked about your knowledge of coding, you could show assignments in which you accurately coded a variety of diagnoses and procedures. Chapter 11 contains a section on using your portfolio at interviews.

Prescription for Success 10–1
Planning Ahead

1. Who do you already know who would be a good professional reference?

   _____

   _____

   _____

2. What can you start doing now to ensure that you have access to at least four positive recommendations when you begin your job search?

   _____

   _____

   _____

   _____

   _____

Chapter 11

Interviewing for Jobs

THE INTERVIEW—YOUR SALES OPPORTUNITY

Finally! The words you have been hoping to hear: "When can you come in for an **interview**?" Your job search efforts are paying off. But wait a minute! You begin to worry: "What if I can't think of anything to say?" "What if I don't have the skills they are looking for?" "What if they ask me about … ?"

The purpose of this chapter is to help you put the "what if's" to rest and see the interviewing process as an opportunity to present yourself at your best. In Chapter 2, we discussed the power of attitude and how, with practice, you can choose your reaction to any situation. Many applicants view interviews as opportunities to be rejected. But you have another choice. You can view an interview as an opportunity to determine an employer's needs and show how you can meet them.

Think about it. Employers are busy people who don't have time to conduct interviews with people who are unlikely job candidates. You obviously meet the minimum qualifications. The interviewer wants to see whether you are a likable person who can back up your qualifications, communicate, and fit in with the organization.

By learning what will be expected of you at an interview and practicing your presentation skills, you can attend each interview with confidence. The most common reason for not being hired is lack of preparation for the interview. And this is a factor over which you, not the interviewer, has control.

THE CUSTOMER'S NEEDS

Good sales presentations are based on showing customers—employers—how they can benefit by buying a product—in this case, by hiring you. Identifying the customer's needs is an important step for students who are beginning a program of career preparation. As we pointed out, it doesn't make sense to create a product that no one needs.

In the same way, if you attend an interview without knowing anything about what the employer is looking for, you put yourself at a disadvantage. This is because in order to be at your best during the interview, the following preparations must be completed in advance:

- ☐ Anticipate what types of questions might be asked.
- ☐ Practice answering them.
- ☐ Create examples to demonstrate your mastery of needed skills.
- ☐ Prepare appropriate questions to ask.

All employers have general qualities they look for in applicants. And health care employers have expressed their needs through the National Health Care Skill Standards. In addition, individual employers have requirements based on factors such as patient population, services offered, size of facility, budgets, and so on. It is important for you to learn as much as possible before attending the interview. Here is a checklist of possible sources of information:

- ☐ Direct contact by phone or in person: ask questions, request a job description, observe the facility
- ☐ Brochures produced by the organization
- ☐ People who work there, such as friends, classmates, or networking contacts
- ☐ The local newspaper: large facilities are sometimes the subject of news articles
- ☐ The employer's web site
- ☐ Your school's career services department

☐ The Chamber of Commerce and other organizations that have information about large employers

☐ The local chapter of your professional organization

☐ Information gathered at career fairs and employer orientation meetings

☐ Employment ad if the position was advertised

If the facility is small, such as a one-physician office, you should know, at a minimum, the type of specialty practiced and the patient population served. When you are unable to learn very much before the interview, it is especially important that you listen carefully to the employer and ask good questions. How to do this is discussed later in this chapter.

The Interviewer Is Human, Too

"Research into interviewing shows that the person conducting the interview is often more stressed than the candidate."
—ALLAN-JAMES ASSOCIATES

In addition to knowing the employment needs of the employer, consider the personal situation of the interviewer. Many applicants view the interviewer as a person of great confidence who has all the power in the hiring process. Applicants mistakenly see themselves as the underdogs in a game they have little chance of winning. In reality, interviewers may be experiencing a number of pressures:

☐ Concern about finding the right candidate who can perform the job as needed

☐ An extremely busy schedule

☐ Lack of interviewing skills

☐ A demanding supervisor who will hold them responsible for the performance of the person who is hired

☐ Concern about finding the time and resources to orient and train a new employee

Understanding the interviewer's point of view requires empathy—attempting to see the world through the eyes of others. This may not seem easy in a job interview when you are nervous and concentrating on presenting yourself well. But it is this very shift of focus—from yourself to the interviewer—that leads to a more successful interviewing experience. It is through this attempt to understand and then show how you can help solve the employer's problems that you best present yourself as the candidate for the job.

HEADS UP! KNOWING WHAT TO EXPECT

Some interviews are highly structured, meaning that each candidate is asked the same set of prepared questions. Others are more like a conversation, with topics and questions generated freely. Most interviews fall somewhere between these patterns, with interviewers preparing at least a few questions in advance. Some questions have become the "golden oldies" of the employment world, and knowing them gives you an opportunity to plan possible responses. It is essential, however, to focus your answers on the needs of the health care industry in general and the specific needs of the employer. This means that even if you are asked the same question, the same answer will not necessarily be appropriate at every interview.

General Interview Questions. Table 11-1 contains commonly asked interview questions.

These are only a few examples of commonly asked questions. You can see that a thorough knowledge of your skills and personal characteristics, along with an awareness of employer needs, are the sources of good answers.

Work Preference Questions. You may be asked about your job preferences. In addition, be prepared to answer questions such as:

☐ Whether you want full-time or part-time work

☐ The hours you are willing to work

☐ The length of shift you prefer

☐ The days and time of day you can work

Remember to be realistic when applying for jobs. Don't waste employers' time—or your own—interviewing for jobs with conditions you already know are absolutely impossible for you to meet.

Occupation-Specific Questions. Questions in this category explore your specific knowledge, skill mastery, willingness to learn new procedures, and the general content of your training. The type of question will vary:

☐ Describe how to perform a specific procedure.

☐ Explain how to operate certain equipment.

☐ Describe appropriate action to take in a given situation.

☐ Suggest how to solve a health care problem.

☐ Explain how you plan to keep your skills updated.

TABLE 11-1 Commonly Asked Interview Questions

Question	Response Guidelines
1. Why are you applying for this job?	Explain why you are interested in working in health care and specifically at this facility.
2. What do you consider your greatest strengths?	Choose from among technical or personal traits. Explain how they relate to the job and will benefit the employer.
3. What are your weaknesses?	It is not a good idea to say "none," as this is unrealistic and gives the impression that you don't know yourself very well. Prepare an honest answer that displays a weakness that has a positive side or for which you have an improvement plan in place that you can describe. (Examples: "I tend to take on too many tasks. I have been working on knowing how much I can accomplish well in the time I have available and to better organize my time." "I really enjoy working on my own, but I have concentrated on developing good teamwork skills in my lab classes. I realize how much I can learn from others and how much a group of people who work together can accomplish.")
4. What do you know about this organization/facility/specialty?	Do your research! And be clear about what it is that interests you *and* how you believe you can make a contribution.
5. Why should we hire you?	Explain how you can make a positive contribution to the organization. Mention specific skills, attitudes, interests, personal characteristics, and so on.
6. What do you enjoy most in school?	Describe how your favorite class, subject, or activity relates to the job you are applying for.
7. Where do you want to be in 5 years?	This is a good opportunity to think about your long-term goals (*before* the interview, of course). Examples: seek increasing responsibility in the same profession, move into supervisory work, or pursue additional education to move up the career ladder. You don't want to give the impression, however, that you plan to stay at this job for only a short time.
8. How do you work under pressure? Do you manage your time well? Do you work well with others?	Be prepared to give examples showing *how* you have worked well under pressure, used your time well, and so on. Use examples from work, school, and/or your personal life.

☐ Discuss how you would resolve a conflict with a coworker or supervisor.

☐ What do you know about ... ? (a theory, new procedure, etc.)

☐ Why do you want to work in pediatrics/dermatology/children's dentistry, etc?

Some employers give practical skill tests or ask you to physically demonstrate your knowledge. Examples of these tests include a keyboarding speed test, filing or record-keeping exercise, spelling test, calculating drug dosages, or demonstrating a procedure. An increasingly popular interview question presents you with a scenario or problem and asks you how you would solve it. If you are asked to perform a practical test that is appropriate for your level of training, do so willingly. Don't apologize that you "might not do well" or give signs of annoyance. Use the request to show that you have confidence in your abilities and can handle stress.

Computerized Job Interviews

Yes, believe it or not, some employers are conducting interviews with the help of a computer. The advantage for the employer, in addition to saving time, is to prepare a set of questions, often up to 100, to ask of every applicant. Most interview programs consist of answers to be checked. This enables the comparison of "apples with apples" when deciding whom to interview in person. The advantage for you, the applicant, is you have more time to think about your answers and can, through the type of questions asked, learn a little about the organization before coming face-to-face with a human interviewer.

Answer the questions carefully and honestly. Computers are able to notice inconsistencies in your answers.

Most computer-assisted interviews must be completed in a certain length of time, so be sure you know how much time you have and keep track of it as you move through the questions.

Other uses of the computer in the hiring process include scenarios in which applicants explain what they would do in a given situation, skills tests, integrity tests, and personality tests. Some organizations administer computerized interviews and tests on their own computers at their facility; others make them available on the Internet and provide applicants with a password to gain access to their web sites.

Practice: Your Key to Success

"Successful interviews usually depend on good preparation."
—JOHN D. DRAKE

Of course, you cannot anticipate the exact questions that interviewers are going to ask. What you can do is prepare yourself to answer a variety of questions. Here are some things you can practice to improve your interviewing skills:

- ☐ Listening carefully
- ☐ Asking for clarification when necessary
- ☐ Thinking through your "inventory" of capabilities and characteristics that apply when answering questions
- ☐ Finding examples to back up your answers
- ☐ Projecting self-confidence

Preparation means practice—actually answering questions, aloud, under conditions as close to those of an actual interview as possible. The best way to practice is to role-play with someone who acts as the interviewer. This can be an instructor, mentor, networking contact, friend, or family member. Many schools require mock (pretend) interviews as part of professional development classes. Take advantage of these opportunities, and do your best to conduct yourself as if you were at a real interview. Videotaping or having an observer take notes can be helpful, even if it's a little nerve-wracking. It's better to make a few mistakes now and avoid them at interviews.

If you believe that you might be asked to demonstrate skills or react to a scenario, include them in your practice sessions. The career services personnel at your school may be familiar with the interviewing practices of facilities in your area and can give you additional information about what to expect and how to best prepare.

The goal of "interview rehearsals" is not to memorize answers you can repeat. It is to develop a level of comfort about the interviewing process and have facts fresh in your mind that you can call on as needed to respond to questions intelligently and confidently.

Be Prepared: What to Take Along

Having everything you might need at the interview will help you feel organized and confident. It also demonstrates to employers that you are organized and think ahead, valuable qualities for health care professionals. Although your own list will be different, here are some suggestions for what to take along:

- ☐ Extra copies of your resumé
- ☐ Your portfolio
- ☐ Copies of licenses, certifications, and so on
- ☐ Proof of immunizations and results of health tests
- ☐ Reference sheet
- ☐ Any documentation of skills and experience not included in your portfolio (or if you have chosen not to create a portfolio)
- ☐ Pens
- ☐ Small notepad
- ☐ Your list of questions (discussed later in this chapter)
- ☐ All information needed to fill out an application (see Chapter 10)
- ☐ Appointment calendar/planner/electronic organizer
- ☐ Anything you have been requested to bring
- ☐ For your eyes only: extra pantyhose, breath mints, other "emergency supplies"

A small case or large handbag is a convenient way to carry your papers and supplies. It can be inexpensive, but it should be a conservative color, in good repair, and neatly organized so you can quickly find what you need.

First Impressions: Make Them Count!

"The way in which we think of ourselves has everything to do with how our world sees us."
—ARLENE RAVEN

Just 30 seconds! That's how long you have to make a lasting impression. The average person forms a strong opinion of another in less than 1 minute. This is why so much emphasis is placed on professional appearance both during the job search and later, on the job. While it is possible to eventually reverse a negative first impression, it's a lot easier to make a good one in the first place.

In Chapter 10, we discussed the messages that dress and grooming communicate. When applying for a job in health care, appropriate appearance can let the interviewer know that you:

- ☐ Understand the impact of your appearance on others (patients, other professionals).
- ☐ Know what is appropriate for the job.
- ☐ Apply the principles of good hygiene.
- ☐ Respect both yourself and the interviewer.
- ☐ Take the interview seriously.

There is no universal agreement about the proper clothing to wear when applying for health care jobs. Some schools encourage their students to wear a clean, pressed uniform. Other schools advise them to wear neat, everyday clothing that is not too casual. It is important to pay attention to the professional advice of the staff at your school. The best choices for clothing are generally conservative colors and simple styles.

There are a few don'ts that apply wherever you live. Never wear jeans or clothing that is revealing or intended for sports and outdoor activities. Don't wear a hat or sunglasses during the interview. If you're not sure about what to wear, ask your instructor or someone in your school's career service department for help. If extra money for interview clothes is a problem, ask if your school has a clothes-lending program. Many cities have excellent thrift shops that sell nice clothes at reasonable prices. Some even specialize in helping people dress for job interviews.

You may arrive at an interview and discover that most people at the facility are dressed very casually. Don't worry. It is far better to be overdressed in this situation than underdressed. You can adjust your style later, after you get the job.

Here are some additional guidelines that apply to all health care job applicants:

Be Squeaky Clean. Take a bath or shower, wash your hair, scrub your fingernails, and use a deodorant or antiperspirant.

Save the Fashion Trends for Later. Hair and nails should be natural colors, tattoos covered up, and visible rings and studs from piercings removed. Limit earrings to one set. Women should apply makeup lightly for a natural, not painted, look.

Show That You Know What Is Acceptable for the Health Care Professional. Avoid long fingernails, free-flowing hair, and dangling accessories that can be grabbed by patients or caught in machinery. Wear closed-toe shoes. Strive to be odor-free. For example, don't smoke on the way to the interview. Even the fragrances in perfumes and other personal products, intended to be pleasant, should not be worn because many patients find them disagreeable or have allergic reactions.

- ☐ Men who wear facial hair should groom it neatly.

Your appearance may be perfect, but if you arrive late for an interview, it may not matter. Being late is a sure way to make a poor impression. Time management is an essential health care job skill, and you will have failed your first opportunity to demonstrate that you have mastered it. In addition, arriving late is a sign of rudeness and inconsideration for the interviewer's time. Make a few advance preparations to ensure that this doesn't happen to you:

- ☐ Write down the date and exact time of the appointment.
- ☐ Verify the address and ask for directions, if necessary.
- ☐ If the office is in a large building or complex, get additional instructions about how to find it.
- ☐ Inquire about parking, bus stops, or subway stops.
- ☐ If you are unsure of the location and it is not too far away, go there a couple of days before the interview to be sure you can find it.
- ☐ Allow extra time to arrive, and plan to be there about 10 minutes before the appointed time.

If there is an emergency that can't be avoided (a flat tire or unexpected snow storm), call as soon as possible to offer an explanation and reschedule the interview.

Many job applicants don't realize that the interview actually starts before they sit down with the person asking the questions. That's right. From the first contact you made to inquire about a job opening or set the appointment, you have been making an impression. If you arrive for the interview and are rude to the receptionist, you may have already failed in your bid for the job. You cannot know what information is shared with the hiring authority. (Keep in mind, too, that these may be your future coworkers!)

Learn the name of the person who will be conducting the interview. Be sure you have the correct spelling (for the thank-you note, discussed later in this chapter) and pronunciation. When introduced, the following actions express both courtesy and self-confidence:

1. Make and maintain eye contact.
2. Give a healthy (not limp or hesitant) handshake.
3. Express how glad you are to meet him or her and how much you appreciate the opportunity to be interviewed.
4. Don't sit down until you are offered a chair or the other person is seated.

Courtesy during the Interview

Maintaining eye contact (without staring, of course) while the other person is speaking indicates that you are interested in what he or she is saying. When you are speaking, it is natural to look away occasionally. Most of the time, however, you should look at the listener. This is a sign of openness and sincerity. The following is a summary of behaviors to definitely avoid (even if the interviewer engages in them):

☐ Interrupting
☐ Cursing
☐ Using poor grammar (such as the word "ain't") or slang
☐ Gossiping, such as commenting on the weaknesses of other facilities, professionals, or your previous employer
☐ Telling off-color jokes
☐ Putting yourself down
☐ Chewing gum
☐ Appearing to snoop by looking at papers or other materials on the interviewer's desk, shelves, and so on
☐ Discussing personal problems

You don't want to come across as stiff or stuffy, but you do want to come across as professional. Try to be at ease and act natural while maintaining your best "company manners."

Apply Your Communication Skills

A successful job interview depends on the effective use of communication. An interview is essentially a conversation between two people who are trying to determine whether they fit each other's employment needs. As a job applicant, you must take responsibility for making sure that you understand the employer's needs, questions, and comments. At the same time, you have to express yourself clearly so that the interviewer understands you.

Active Listening. Understanding begins by listening actively. The importance of carefully listening to the interviewer cannot be overemphasized. So many times we become so caught up in thinking about what we're going to say next that we fail to fully hear, let alone actively listen to, the other person. This is especially true in an interview when we are nervous and worried about whether we are saying the right thing. But this is the very situation in which we can most benefit from listening carefully so we can base what we say on what we hear.

Active listening consists of paying attention, focusing on the speaker's words, and thinking about the meaning of what is said. This takes practice. When you participate in the mock interviews suggested earlier, do not look at the questions the person role-playing the interviewer is going to ask. Instead, focus on listening carefully to the questions and then formulating an appropriate response. Pausing to think and compose a good answer will be appreciated by interviewers. You are more likely to be evaluated on the quality of your answer, not on how quickly you gave it.

Mirroring. An effective communication technique for interviews is known as **mirroring.** This means you observe the communication style of the interviewer and then match it as closely as possible. This does not mean mimicking or appearing to make fun of the other person. It does mean adapting a style that will be most comfortable for the interviewer.

Feedback. Whatever the style of the interviewer, use feedback when necessary to ensure that you understand the message. Feedback, as you recall from Chapter 3, is a communication technique used to check your understanding of the speaker's intended message. It is not necessary—or even desirable—to repeat everything the speaker says. It is annoying to speakers to have everything they say repeated and you don't want to sound like a parrot. Using feedback unnecessarily will use up time better spent learning about the job and presenting your qualifications. Used when needed, however, feedback can help you understand the other person so you can respond appropriately and intelligently.

Organization. When speaking, do your best to present your ideas in an organized manner so they are easy for the listener to follow. This can be difficult when you are nervous, so take your time to think before you speak. Sometimes we feel uncomfortable with silence and feel that we have to talk to avoid it. But taking a few moments to consider your content will result in better answers. Saying something meaningful after a pause is more important than simply responding quickly.

Nonverbal Communication: It Can Make You or Break You

"If you want a quality, act as if you already had it."
—WILLIAM JAMES

You can speak smoothly and answer questions correctly and yet fail in your communication efforts. What has gone wrong? Your actions have betrayed you. That's right: what you do communicates as much as—or even more than—what you say. As we discussed in Chapter 3, our movements, posture, gestures, and facial expressions usually reveal our true feelings. You can enthusiastically claim that you would love the challenge of working in a fast-paced, think-on-your-feet clinical environment. But if your face and body language reflect fear, anxiety, or subtle expressions of "yuck!," your verbal message will not ring true. Remember that more than half of the content of our messages is communicated nonverbally. This is why videotaping yourself is very helpful when practicing interviewing skills. You can observe your nonverbal language, and catch inappropriate facial expressions and other behaviors that you will want to work on.

The point is not to suggest that you should try to mask your true feelings and put on an act to impress interviewers. Rather, the purpose of this discussion is to encourage you to be aware of how important your actions are and what they say about you. If there are aspects of a job you know you can't or don't want to perform, this is the time to find out. Keep in mind that one of your goals in an interview is to learn about the job and the organization so you can decide whether this is the place for you.

Developing a positive attitude about the interviewing process and having confidence in your own abilities will help ensure that your body language communicates appropriate positive messages. At the same time, developing the body language of a positive, confident person will help you become that person.

Using Your Portfolio Wisely

Portfolios are gaining popularity among job seekers, including those in the health care field. They can be a very effective way to support your claims of competence by providing evidence of your accomplishments and qualifications.

Not all employers are familiar with portfolios. Announcing at the beginning of interviews that you have brought one and asking interviewers if they would like to see it may not be the most effective way of using it to your advantage. Remember that one of your main goals at the interview is to show how you meet the employer's needs. You won't know enough about these needs until you spend a little time listening. Then you may be able to use your portfolio constructively. The following interviewer questions and statements might be answered with material in your portfolio:

1. Asks a question about your skills and abilities
   "Can you … ?"
   "Have you had experience … ?"
2. States what skills are needed or provides a job description
   "This job requires …"
   "We need someone who can use medical terminology correctly and chart accurately."
3. Shares a problem or concern
   "One of our problems has been with ensuring accurate documentation …"
   "We have difficulties with …"
4. Isn't familiar with the contents of your training program
   "Did your program include … ?"
   "What skills did you learn … ?"
5. Asks for verification of licenses, certifications, and so on
   "Have you passed the _____ exam?"
   "Are you a certified medical assistant?"
   "Are you licensed in this state?"

It isn't necessary—or even a good idea—to try to back up everything you say with your portfolio. In fact, if overused, a portfolio loses its effectiveness. And many questions are better answered with an oral explanation and/or example.

Become very familiar with your portfolio's contents so you can find items quickly. If necessary, create an easy-to-read table of contents. Frantically flipping through pages to find something will make you look (and feel) unprepared and disorganized. You will also waste valuable time, a very limited resource in most interviews.

Use your portfolio to give a brief summary presentation if you are given an opportunity at the end of the interview. For example, the interviewer might say, "Tell me why I should hire you," or ask, "What else should I know about you?" Use this presentation to quickly review your qualifications or to point out those that haven't been mentioned.

You may attend interviews where you don't use your portfolio at all. This is okay. It is always better—both during the job search and on the job—to be overprepared. This prevents you from missing opportunities when they do present themselves.

Handling Sticky Interview Situations

In spite of your best efforts, some interviews can be a little rocky. Remember, not every employer is skilled at interviewing. Consider this: you may have prepared and practiced more than the person conducting the interview! Table 11-2 contains difficult situations and suggestions for handling them gracefully. Keep in mind that the questions reveal something about the interviewer and possibly about the organization, so consider them when deciding if this is a place you want to work.

TABLE 11-2 Handling Difficult Interview Situations

If the Interviewer	What You Can Do
Keeps you waiting a long time.	If you are interested in the job, *do not* show annoyance or anger. It is best not to schedule interviews when you have a very limited amount of time. Remember, this person may be overworked, and that's exactly why there is a potential position for you! Keep in mind that health care work does not always proceed at our convenience. A patient with an emergency, for example, will certainly have priority over an interviewee.
Allows constant interruptions with phone calls and/or people coming in.	Again, do not show that you are irritated. This person may be very busy, disorganized, or simply having a difficult day. (This could be another good sign that this employer really needs your help.)
Does most of the talking and doesn't give you an opportunity to say much about yourself.	Listen carefully and try to determine how your qualifications relate to what you are hearing. Being a good listener in itself may be the most important quality you can demonstrate.
Seems to simply make conversation. Doesn't discuss the job or ask you questions.	Try to move the discussion to the job by asking questions: "Can you tell me about what you are looking for in a candidate?" "What are the principal duties that this person would perform?" It is possible that this is a test to see your reaction, so take care to be courteous.
Tries to engage you in gossip about school, etc.	Say you don't really know about the person or other professionals, facilities, or situation and cannot comment. Ask a question about the job to redirect the conversation.
Allows long periods of silence.	This may be a test to see how you react under pressure. Don't feel that you have to speak, and do your best to remain comfortable. (Say to yourself: "This is just a test, and I'm doing fine.") If it goes on too long, you can ask: "Is there something you'd like me to tell you more about? Discuss further?"
Doesn't seem to understand your training or qualifications.	Explain as clearly as possible. Use your portfolio, as appropriate, to illustrate your skills.
Makes inappropriate comments about your appearance, gender, ethnicity, etc.	Depending on the nature of the comment and your interpretation of the situation, it may be best to excuse yourself from the interview. For example, comments of a sexual nature or racial slurs should not be tolerated. You should discuss this situation with your instructor or career services for advice on how to proceed.
Is very friendly, chatty, and complimentary about you.	Why in the world, you ask, is this a problem? It may not be. But be careful not to get so comfortable that you share personal problems and other information that may disqualify you for the job.

Dealing with Illegal Questions. It is illegal for employers to **discriminate** against an applicant on the basis of any of the following factors:

- ☐ Age (as long as the applicant is old enough to work legally)
- ☐ Arrests (without a conviction, being proven guilty)
- ☐ Ethnic background
- ☐ Financial status
- ☐ Marital status and children
- ☐ Physical condition (as long as the applicant can perform the job tasks)
- ☐ Race
- ☐ Religion
- ☐ Sexual preference

Questions that require the applicant to reveal information about these factors are illegal. They are sometimes asked anyway. Some employers are ignorant of the laws. Or the interview becomes friendly and conversational, and personal information is shared. ("Oh, I went to Grady High School, too. What year did you graduate?") Employers may take the chance that applicants won't know the questions are illegal. And a few will ask because they know that most applicants will not take the time to report them for discrimination. It may not be obvious from the questions that answering them will, in fact, reveal information that cannot be considered when hiring. Some examples are listed in Box 11-1. Also, take a look at the following examples:

Question	What It Can Reveal
What part of town do you live in?	Financial status
Do you own your home?	Financial status
Where are your parents from?	Ethnic background
Which holidays do you celebrate?	Religion
When did you graduate from high school	Age

Illegal questions put you in a difficult situation, and there are no easy formulas for handling them. In deciding what to do, you need to ask yourself several questions:

- ☐ Is the subject of the question of concern to me?
- ☐ Do I find the question offensive?
- ☐ Does the interviewer appear to be unaware that the question is illegal?
- ☐ What is my overall impression of the interviewer and the facility?
- ☐ Would I want to work here?
- ☐ How badly do I want this particular job?
- ☐ If this person is to be my immediate supervisor, is the question an indication that this is a person I don't really want to work with?
- ☐ What do I think the interviewer's real concern is? Is it valid?

Based on your answers, there are several ways you can respond to the interviewer:

1. Answer honestly.
2. Ask the interviewer to explain how the question relates to the job requirements.
3. Respond to the interviewer's apparent concern rather than to the question.
4. Ignore the question and talk about something else.
5. Refuse to answer.
6. Inform the interviewer that the question is illegal.
7. Excuse yourself from the interview and leave.
8. State that you plan to report the incident to the Civil Rights Commission or Equal Employment Opportunity Commission.

Employers do have the right—as well as the responsibility—to make sure that applicants can

Box 11-1	**Examples of Illegal Questions**	
Question	**Possible Concern**	**Suggested Responses**
Do you have young children?	Your attendance and dependability	Explain your childcare arrangements, good attendance in school and on other jobs, and your dedication to employers.
Where do you live?	Reliable transportation or punctuality	Describe your transportation and good attendance record in school.
Which religious holidays are you unable to work?	Scheduling problems	Explain that you are a team player and committed to ensuring that all workdays are covered. You are willing to work and cover when coworkers have a holiday that you do not observe.

both physically and legally perform the job requirements. Sometimes there is only a small difference in wording between a legal and an illegal question, as in the following examples:

Illegal	Legal
How old are you?	Are you over 18?
Where were you born?	Do you have the legal right to work in the United States?
What is your maiden name?	Would your work records be listed under another name?
Have you ever been arrested?	Have you ever been convicted of a crime?

Are you beginning to understand how employers can get confused and ask illegal questions? It is possible to be an excellent dentist or physical therapist but not an expert in the details of employment law. However you choose to respond to questions you believe are illegal, it is best to remain calm and courteous. You may decide you don't want to work there, but conduct yourself professionally at all times.

Many employment experts recommend that you respond to the employer's concerns rather than the questions. This requires that you determine what the concerns are. Here are some examples:

One recommended strategy for handling common employer concerns is to bring them up before the interviewer does. This gives you the opportunity to present them in a positive light. Employers may be uncomfortable addressing certain issues and will simply drop you from the "possible hire" list. By taking the initiative, you gain the opportunity to defend your position and stay on the list. Table 11-3 contains suggestions for showing the employer the positive aspects of various employment "problems."

Stay Focused on the Positive

"Employers are hiring based on attitude: "Give me a 'C' student with an 'A' attitude."
—MELVA DURAN, MARIC COLLEGE, SAN DIEGO

Interviews are a time to do your best to stay positive. They are not the place to bring up problems, or what you believe you can't do or don't want to do. Be positive and future-oriented and prepared to emphasize:

☐ What you can do
☐ How you can help
☐ Ways you can apply what you've learned

As mentioned before, you should never criticize a previous employer, instructor, or anyone else. Potential employers realize they may someday be your previous employer and don't want to be the subject of your comments to others in the profession. It is also possible that the interviewer is a friend of the person you are criticizing!

Keep in mind that every interview is a sales presentation. A sales presentation is not the time to point out the product's faults. You want to emphasize the positive aspects of your skills and character, not your weaknesses. However, if you sincerely feel that you are not qualified for a job (and this is an important consideration in health care), you should never pretend that you are. Lacking needed skills is not a negative reflection on you as a person. It simply means that this job is not appropriate for you. Other jobs will be. In fact, there may be many reasons why jobs and applicants do not match. After all, that's the whole purpose of job interviews—for you and the employer to make that determination.

Personal problems should always be avoided. You are there to help solve the employer's problems, not find solutions to your own. Employers

TABLE 11-3   Point Out the Positives

The Problem	The Bright Side
You're very young, with little work experience.	You are energetic, eager to learn, "trainable," and looking for long-term employment ("One of the advantages of being young is ...").
You have a criminal record.*	You have learned from your mistakes and are eager to have an opportunity to serve others.
You're over age 40.	You are experienced, have good work habits, and are patient.
You've had many jobs, none for very long.	You have a variety of experiences, are flexible, can adjust to the working environment, and have now found a career to which you want to dedicate your efforts.

*Note: Some states do not allow individuals who have been convicted of specific crimes to work in certain health care occupations. In some cases, these individuals are not even allowed to take certification exams.

are looking for independent problem solvers. Bringing your own problems to the interview will not give them a good impression of your capabilities in this area. (There are exceptions. For example, if you are responsible for a disabled family member and need some consideration regarding your work schedule, it would appropriate to mention this at the interview.)

Focusing on your own needs is negatively received by employers. Giving the impression that you are more concerned with what you can get from the job than what you can give is a sure way to get nothing at all. The following questions send the message "What's in it for me?" and should be avoided until you know you are actually being considered for the job:

☐ How much does the job pay?
☐ What are the other benefits?
☐ How many paid holidays will I get?
☐ Is Friday casual day?
☐ Can I leave early if I finish my work?
☐ When will I get a raise?

It is acceptable to inquire about the work schedule, duties, and other expectations. The time to negotiate specific conditions, including your salary, is after you have been offered the job. (This is discussed later in this chapter.)

It's Your Interview, Too

Interviews are not only for the benefit of employers. You have the right, and the responsibility, to evaluate the opportunities presented by the jobs you are applying for. This may seem to contradict what we discussed in the previous section, but it doesn't. In fact, well-stated questions about the job communicate motivation and interest.

When you are in class, it is generally true that "there are no stupid questions." However, at a job interview, the quality of your questions does count. There is a difference between the ones that should be avoided and ones that demonstrate that you:

☐ Have a sincere interest in the job
☐ Want to understand the employer's needs
☐ Understand the nature of health care work
☐ Have thought about your career goal
☐ Want information that will enable you to do your best

What you ask will depend on the job, the interviewer, and how much you already know about the job and the organization. It is a good idea to prepare, in advance, a list of general questions, along with a few that are specific to the job and the facility. This will help you remember what you want to ask. As we pointed out earlier, it is easy to forget when we feel under pressure, as may happen in the interview situation. Not everyone is skilled at "thinking in the seat," especially when it feels like the hot seat!

Here are some suggested questions to get you started:

1. How could I best contribute to the success of this facility?
2. What are the most important qualities needed to succeed in this position?
3. What is the mission of this organization/facility?
4. What are the major problems faced by this organization/facility?
5. How is the organization structured? Who would I be reporting to?
6. What values are most important?
7. I want to continue learning and updating my skills. What opportunities would I have to do this?
8. How will I be evaluated and learn what I need to improve?
9. Are there opportunities for advancement for employees who work hard and perform well?

It is perfectly acceptable to ask questions throughout the interview where they fit in. This will be more natural and lead to a smoother interview than asking a long list at the end. You don't have to wait until you are invited to ask them.

In addition to asking questions, observe the facility and the people who work there. Does this "feel" like a place you would want to work? Is it clean? Organized? Does it appear that safety precautions are followed? What is the pace? Are the people who work there courteous and helpful? How do they interact with patients? If your interview is with the person who would be your supervisor, do you think you would get along? Do you believe you would fit in?

It may not be possible for you to see anything other than the interviewer's office. In fact, at a large facility, your first interview may take place in the personnel office. You won't see the area where you would work. If this is the case, you will want to ask for a tour if you are offered a job. (More about this later in this chapter.)

Leaving Graciously

The end of the interview provides you an opportunity to make a final impression, so make it a good one. It is important to be sensitive to any signals the interviewer gives that it is time to wrap up. Failure to do so shows a lack of consideration for his or her time, and this is definitely not the parting message you want to leave. Some interviewers will make it obvious the interview is almost over by:

☐ Telling you directly

☐ Asking whether you have any "final" questions

☐ Telling you that everything has been covered

Less obvious signs include looking at their watch, clock, appointment book, or papers on their desk; pushing their chair back; or saying that they have "taken enough of your time." Show respect for their time by moving along with the final steps of the interview:

1. Ask any final questions (limit these to a couple of the most important ones that haven't been answered).
2. Make a brief wrap-up statement.
3. Thank them for their time.
4. Inquire about what comes next.

If you are interested in the job, say so in the wrap-up statement. Tell the interviewer why: you believe you can make a contribution; what impressed you about the organization; why you believe your qualifications fit the position; and so on. Express your enthusiasm about working there and state that you hope you are chosen for the position.

Whether you want the job or not, always thank the interviewer for his or her time. This applies even if the interview did not go well. Health care professionals and personnel staff are extremely busy. Let them know how much you appreciate being given the opportunity to present your qualifications.

Finally, if you aren't told about the next step in the application process, don't hesitate to ask. Inquire about when the hiring decision will be made. Find out if there is anything you need to send. If asked, give the interviewer your reference sheet. Be sure to get the interviewer's last name and correct title. An easy way to do this is to ask for his or her business card. And be sure that he or she has your telephone number and any other information needed to contact you. Then smile, give a firm handshake, and leave as confidently as you entered, regardless of how you believe the interview went.

Completing an Important Step

"You wouldn't be nervous if you didn't care."
—ROBERT LOCK

You may be feeling a little—maybe very—overwhelmed at this point. "How can I remember all this and act natural and maintain eye contact and give good examples and …" It is a lot, and that's why it is so important to spend time learning about the interviewing process, preparing, and practicing. Take every opportunity to role-play. Make your practice sessions as realistic as possible. Figure 11-1 contains a summary list of positive interview behaviors.

When you inventoried your skills, were you surprised at how much you can do now that you would never have attempted before you started your educational program? You learned these skills by studying and practicing them—over and over. If you have been working on developing these skills, this is your chance to use them for job success. You are almost certainly more qualified for the job search than you realize. And using your skills to get a job will reinforce your ability to use them once you are on the job.

A final note: It's okay to be nervous. It can even be a good thing, because it means you are not taking this experience for granted. Interviewers know you are nervous, and it tells them that this job is important to you and that you care about the outcome. This is a positive message to communicate.

Reward Yourself

"Celebrate all successes on the job search journey."

Attending an interview is a success, whether or not you are hired for this particular job. You have qualifications that were worthy of the interviewer's time, you prepared well, and you met the challenge of presenting yourself one-on-one to a potential employer. Take a moment to reward yourself for completing this important step.

Maximize the Interview Experience

"Nothing is a waste of time if you use the experience wisely."
—AUGUSTE RODIN

Making the most of every interview means that you view each one as an experience that provides

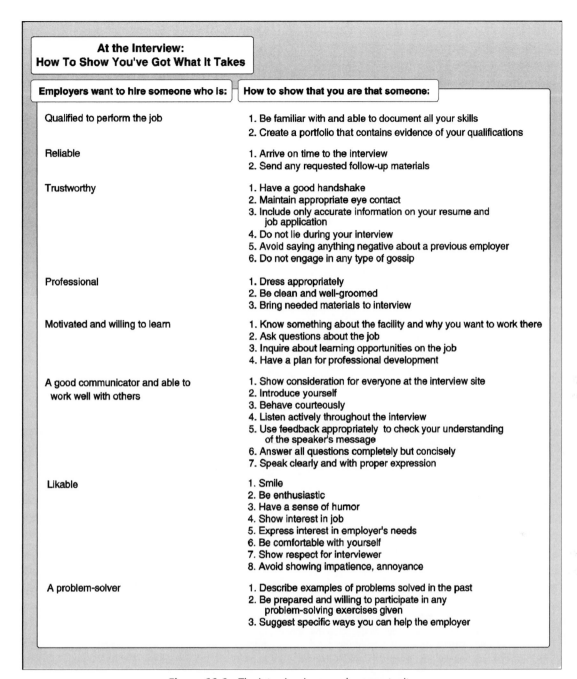

At the Interview:
How To Show You've Got What It Takes

Employers want to hire someone who is:	How to show that you are that someone:
Qualified to perform the job	1. Be familiar with and able to document all your skills 2. Create a portfolio that contains evidence of your qualifications
Reliable	1. Arrive on time to the interview 2. Send any requested follow-up materials
Trustworthy	1. Have a good handshake 2. Maintain appropriate eye contact 3. Include only accurate information on your resume and job application 4. Do not lie during your interview 5. Avoid saying anything negative about a previous employer 6. Do not engage in any type of gossip
Professional	1. Dress appropriately 2. Be clean and well-groomed 3. Bring needed materials to interview
Motivated and willing to learn	1. Know something about the facility and why you want to work there 2. Ask questions about the job 3. Inquire about learning opportunities on the job 4. Have a plan for professional development
A good communicator and able to work well with others	1. Show consideration for everyone at the interview site 2. Introduce yourself 3. Behave courteously 4. Listen actively throughout the interview 5. Use feedback appropriately to check your understanding of the speaker's message 6. Answer all questions completely but concisely 7. Speak clearly and with proper expression
Likable	1. Smile 2. Be enthusiastic 3. Have a sense of humor 4. Show interest in job 5. Express interest in employer's needs 6. Be comfortable with yourself 7. Show respect for interviewer 8. Avoid showing impatience, annoyance
A problem-solver	1. Describe examples of problems solved in the past 2. Be prepared and willing to participate in any problem-solving exercises given 3. Suggest specific ways you can help the employer

Figure 11-1   The interview is your sales opportunity.

opportunities to improve your presentation skills and to learn more about the health care world. This knowledge can help you in future interviews and work-related situations such as performance evaluations. When you leave the interviewer's office, your reaction may be "Whew! That's over!" and the last thing you want to do is spend more time thinking about it. This is especially true if you feel the interview didn't go well. But this is precisely when you need to spend some time thinking about and evaluating the experience and your performance. Using an interview evaluation sheet will help you focus on the important factors that determine the success of an interview and create a plan for improvement.

You might want to discuss your self-evaluation with someone you trust. Sometimes we are too hard on ourselves and need a second point of view to help us see the real situation. Review the interview with your instructor, career services personnel, or mentor. You may have friends and family members who can provide insight and support. Create an improvement plan and practice so you'll feel more confident at the next interview.

When seeking help or discussing interviews with others, it is best not to make negative remarks about the interviewer or the facility. This serves no purpose, unless you are seeking advice about whether to accept a job you have doubts about. A friend may have a friend who works there and your words, said "in confidence," may be passed along to the wrong party.

You may believe you will receive a job offer. You very well might. But don't cancel or turn down other interviews until you are formally hired. You may have done a superb job and the facility plans to hire you. Then the next day, your soon-to-be supervisor is informed of a facility-wide hiring freeze. You don't want to be left out in the cold with no other options. You may even find something better before they make the offer. Stay actively involved in the search until you have a job.

Thank You

Whether the interview went like a dream or a nightmare, send a thank-you note. This courtesy is something many job seekers don't do. Yet it is a simple action that can set you apart from the others. Suppose the employer interviewed nine people in two days, in addition to carrying on a normal workload. Tired? Very likely. Able to remember each candidate clearly and recall who said what? Maybe. But why take the chance of being lost in the crowd?

If you know for sure that you don't want the job, send a thank-you note anyway. Keep it simple, say something positive about the interview, and express your appreciation for the time taken to meet with you. Do not say that you are not interested in the job. Figure 11-2 is an example of this kind of note.

1642 Windhill Way
San Antonio, TX 78220
October 18, 2005

Nancy Henderson, Office Manager
Craigmore Pediatric Clinic
4979 Coffee Road
San Antonio, TX 78229

Dear Ms. Henderson:

Thank you so much for the time you spent with me yesterday. You have a busy schedule, and I appreciate the time you took to describe the opening for a medical assistant at Craigmore Pediatric. The Clinic enjoys a good reputation in San Antonio for the services it provides children in the community, and it was a pleasure to learn more about it.

Sincerely,

Karen Gonzalez
Karen Gonzalez

Figure 11-2   Simple thank-you letter.

Why, you might ask, would you write if you don't want to work there? There are at least three good reasons:

1. The employer may know someone else who is hiring. Impressed by your follow-up, he or she recommends you.
2. An opening for a job that you do want becomes available at this facility. You are remembered for your thoughtfulness.
3. At this time, when courtesy and consideration for others are disappearing, it is the right thing to do.

Thank You–Plus. If you want the job (see the next section for how-tos on making that decision), then take the time to write a thank-you–plus letter. The "plus" refers to a paragraph or two in which you do at least one of the following:

☐ Briefly summarize your qualifications in relation to the job as it was discussed in the interview.
☐ Point out specifically how you can make a positive contribution—again, based on details you learned.

Let the employer know you want the job and hope to be the candidate selected. Include your full name and telephone number.

Thank-you notes should be sent no later than the day following the interview. Consider keeping a box of cards in the car and writing the note immediately after you leave the interview. Interviewers will be impressed when they receive your note the very next day.

For some jobs, such as administrative positions, e-mailing a thank you may be acceptable because it demonstrates computer proficiency. Take the same care you would with a written letter: include a salutation, write complete sentences, use correct grammar, spell all words correctly, and use a proper closing.

Alert Your References

If you left a reference sheet with the interviewer, call your references as soon as possible to tell them they may receive a call. Of course, they already know that you have given their names out as references. (You did ask them, right?) Give them the job title, nature of the work, and type of facility. Add anything you learned about the type of candidate the employer is seeking. This gives your references an opportunity to stress those features that best support your bid for the job. Help them to help you by keeping them informed.

When to Call Back

Following up after an interview is a kind of balancing act: you don't want to be considered a pest by calling too soon and too frequently. On the other hand, you took the time to attend the interview and have a right to be informed when the hiring decision is made.

The best strategy is to wait until the day after you were told a decision would be made. Call and identify yourself and inquire about the decision. If none has been made, ask when you might expect to hear. Use your best telephone manners. This is still part of the interview, and courtesy counts. Never express impatience about a delay. You want to show interest but not pressure the employer for a decision he or she is not ready to make. Sometimes the interviewer is deciding between two candidates and the decision may be influenced by your follow-up.

Is This the Job for You?

Jobs are usually not offered on the spot during the first interview. If this does happen to you, it is a good idea to ask when a decision is needed and say that you are very interested (if you are) but need a little time to make a decision. There are exceptions, of course. You may have performed your clinical work at this site and know for sure that this is the place for you. In this case, the interview may be a formality and it makes sense to accept the position immediately.

Interviewers will usually give you a time range during which a hiring decision will be made. You, too, need to make a decision: if this position is offered, will you accept it? Many factors will influence your decision. We discussed how the job market is affected by various economic and governmental conditions. When the unemployment rate is high, you probably can't be as choosy about the job you take. In fact, you may have very few choices, because there will be more candidates competing for a limited number of positions. You can be more selective when the unemployment rate is low. Of course, your location and specific occupation will influence the number of opportunities available to you. Some parts of the country are highly desirable places to live, and competition is intense. And some occupations will be in either high or low demand, depending on current health care trends.

While you should consider these questions carefully, remember that the job that is "exactly what you want" probably doesn't exist. Finding the right job for you is a matter of finding a close match on the most important elements. You are starting a new career, and there are certain factors that will help your long-term success. Working with someone who is interested in teaching you, for example, may be a better choice than choosing a slightly higher-paying position that offers no opportunities for acquiring new skills. Many health care facilities make it a practice to promote from within. If there is a facility where you want to work, consider taking a job that gets you in the door.

Discussing Salary: When and How

Most career experts recommend that you not discuss salary with a potential employer until you have been offered the job. In many cases, this won't be an issue because salaries are predetermined and not negotiable. Some occupations, such as nursing, have labor unions, and the employer cannot change agreed-upon salaries for specific positions.

Doing your research before you attend an interview may provide you with this information. If a range of salary is given for a position, the amount offered to you will most likely depend on the experience you bring to the job. Recent graduates tend to start at the low end of a range, earning more as they gain experience.

Considering an Offer

A job offer may be extended in a telephone call, at a second or even third interview, or in a letter. Even if you feel quite sure that this is the right job, you still need to be sure that you have all the information needed to make a final decision. It is essential that you understand:

☐ The exact duties you will be required to perform. If you haven't seen a written job description, ask for it now. If there is no written description, ask for a detailed oral explanation if this wasn't done in the interview.

☐ **Start date.** Be sure you are clear about the exact date and time you are to report for work.

☐ The days and hours you will work. Ask about the likelihood of required overtime and any change of hours or days that might take place in the future.

☐ Your salary. Earnings are expressed in various ways: hourly, weekly, biweekly, monthly, or

annual rates. If you are quoted a rate that you aren't familiar with, you might want to convert it to one you know. For example, if you are accustomed to thinking in terms of amount per hour but are given a monthly salary, you may want to calculate the hourly equivalent.

☐ **Orientation and/or training given.** This is especially important for recent graduates. Learning the customs and practices of the facility can make a big difference in your success. Letting the employer know that you are interested in learning as much as possible about the facility and the job communicates the message that you are motivated and interested in being prepared to do your best.

You may have received all this information in the interview(s). Don't hesitate, however, to ask about anything you don't fully understand. It is far better to take the time now rather than to discover later that the job or working conditions were not what you expected. If you didn't have an opportunity to see any more than the interviewer's office, be sure to ask for a complete tour of the facility before deciding whether or not to accept the job.

Understanding Benefits

Benefits can represent a significant portion of your **compensation.** Health insurance, for example, can cost hundreds of dollars per month for a family of four. If full family coverage is offered by the employer, this may be worth thousands of dollars each year. Find out if you must pay part of the cost of the premiums and what type of coverage is provided. Health insurance for individuals (or families) is often more expensive than the group rates available through an employer. And many individuals find it difficult to qualify on their own. Health insurance is becoming an increasingly important benefit to consider when choosing where to work. There are other types of insurance, too, that can add value to the benefits package, including dental, vision, life, and disability.

If you are planning to continue your education, tuition benefits might be important to you. Some employers cover all or part of educational expenses if the studies are related to your work and you receive a grade of C or better. Time off to take classes and workshops is an additional advantage. This benefit is especially helpful for health care professionals who are required to earn continuing education units on a regular basis. Related professional expenses that some employers cover are the dues for professional organizations and required uniforms.

Other benefits to consider when calculating your overall compensation include the number of paid vacation, holiday, and personal days offered and whether there is a retirement plan such as a **401(k) plan.** With this plan, you choose an amount to be deducted from your earnings each pay period. You pay no taxes on this money until you withdraw it anytime after you reach age 59½. The money is invested, often in mutual funds. Some employers match a certain percentage of the money you save, which is like giving you an additional, tax-free salary.

When considering the compensation offered by an employer, think in terms of the total package. One job may offer a higher hourly rate but require you to pay part of your health insurance premium. You may end up financially ahead by accepting the lower salary. On the other hand, if you are included on your spouse's group plan, this might not be significant. Salary alone should not be the determining factor when deciding whether a job "pays enough."

Let's look at an example: suppose you are offered Job A, which pays $24,000 and includes medical insurance, for which the employer pays $2700. The total value of this package, then, is $26,700. Another employer offers you Job B at $27,000 in salary with no insurance benefits. You need insurance and plan to pay for it yourself with the extra salary you will earn. Assuming that everything else about the two jobs is equal, with which one would you come out ahead financially? Almost certainly Job A. Let's see why.

1. You will pay taxes on wages of $24,000 rather than $27,000. (Health insurance benefits are not taxed.)
2. The $2700 for medical insurance is the cost for a member of a group plan. If you buy insurance as an individual, it may cost you even more. (And you may have to qualify medically, which makes it more difficult to get.)

Job A

$24,000 − $7200 (standard tax deduction and single exemption)	=	$16,800 (taxable income)
$16,800 × 15% tax rate	=	$2520 (taxes)
$24,000 − $2520	=	$21,480 (amount of money you keep)

Job B

$27,000 − $7200	=	$19,800 (taxable income)
$19,800 × 15%	=	$2970 (taxes)
$27,000 − $2970	=	$24,030
$24,030 − $2700 (amount spent on health insurance)	=	$21,330 (amount of money you keep)

The lesson here is to collect information and consider all aspects of the compensation plan. While this was just an example, it shows how important it is to do the math. If you are unsure about how to do these calculations, ask for help. Your long-term financial health depends on it.

Accepting an Offer

When you accept a job, express your appreciation and enthusiasm. In addition to responding orally, write a letter of acceptance. The letter should include a summary of what you understand to be the terms of employment.

When speaking with the employer, inquire about any necessary follow-up activities. It is also a good idea to disclose any future commitments or other factors that will affect your work. For example, if your son is scheduled for surgery next month and you know you will need to take several days off to take care of him, let the employer know this during the hiring process. It is a sign of integrity to make important disclosures before the hiring is completed. There may be little risk of losing the job by revealing reasonable, unavoidable future commitments. If the employer does refuse to accommodate you, it is better to learn now that this job lacks flexibility regarding family needs. You may want to reconsider your acceptance. (Be aware, however, that employers cannot grant repeated requests for days off due to family responsibilities. Their first responsibility must be to the patients they serve.)

You may want this job but need to negotiate some conditions. For example, suppose the work hours are 8:00 a.m. to 5:00 p.m. You have a 3-year-old child who cannot be left at day care before 7:45 a.m., and it takes at least 25 minutes to drive to work. It is better to ask if you can work from 8:30 a.m. to 5:30 p.m. than to take the position and arrive late every day. Many problems on the job can be avoided by discussing them openly in advance. (Again, you must also consider the employer's needs. Accommodations like this are not always possible if they disrupt the facility's schedule and patient flow.) And sometimes, having a "Plan B" will save the day—in this case, having someone reliable who can take your child to day care.

What to Expect

Once you are hired, employers can ask questions that were unacceptable during the hiring process. Information that cannot be used to make hiring decisions is often necessary to complete personnel requirements. Examples include the following:

1. Provide proof of your age (to ensure you are of legal age to work).
2. Identify your race (for affirmative action statistics, if applicable in your state).
3. Supply a photograph (for identification).
4. State your marital status and number and ages of your children (for insurance).
5. Give the name and address of a relative (for notification in case of emergency).
6. Provide your Social Security number (for tax purposes).

There may be mandatory health tests and immunizations. In addition, some employers require drug tests and background checks for all employees.

If you are asked to sign an employment contract, read it carefully. As with all other employment issues, ask about anything you don't understand. Also, be sure to ask for a copy of anything you sign.

Turning Down a Job Offer

After careful consideration, you may decide not to accept a job offer. It is not necessary to explain your reasons to the employer. Do express your appreciation and thanks for the opportunity, and do send a thank-you note. In addition to being an expression of courtesy, this leaves a positive impression on all employers. You may want to work at this facility in the future.

If You Don't Get the Job

"Failure is a delay, but not a defeat. It is a temporary detour, not a dead-end street."
—WILLIAM ARTHUR WARD

It can be difficult when you are not selected for a job you really want. There are many reasons why

applicants don't get hired. Some you can't change and must simply accept, such as the following:

☐ There was another applicant with more experience or skills that more closely met the employer's current needs.
☐ An employee in the organization decided to apply for the job.
☐ The employer believed that someone else was a better "match" for the organization in terms of work style, preferences, and so on.
☐ Budget cuts or other unexpected events prevented anyone from being hired at this time.

On the other hand, you may have lost this opportunity for reasons you can change. How do you know? First, do an honest review of your postinterview evaluation, school record, and resumé. Are you presenting yourself in the best possible way? Second, look over the list in Box 11-2. Health care employers and career services personnel name these as major reasons why job applicants fail to get hired. Do you recognize anything that might apply to you?

You must be honest with yourself and commit to improving your attitude and/or job search skills. If necessary, seek advice from your instructor, career services personnel, or mentor. Work on creating a winning attitude that will help you develop the interviewing skills it takes to get hired. Seek support from friends and family members if you are feeling down. They can help you keep your perspective and boost your self-confidence if it's a little low.

Although you may not feel enthusiastic about writing a note to an employer who chooses another

---

Box 11-2 Why Job Applicants Fail to Get Hired

1. Failure to sell themselves by clearly presenting their skills and qualifications
2. Too much interest in what's in it for them rather than what they can give
3. Unprofessional behavior or lack of courtesy
4. Lack of enthusiasm and interest in the job
5. Poor appearance
6. Poor communication skills
7. Unrealistic job expectations
8. Negative or critical attitude
9. Arrived late, brought children or the person who provided transportation, or other demonstrations of poor organizational skills

applicant, consider this: you may have come in a close second. The next opening may be yours! So take a few moments and demonstrate your high level of professionalism by thanking the employer and letting him or her know that you are still interested in working for the organization.

If you fail to get hired after attending an interview that you think went well, ask for assistance from an instructor or career services personnel.

You may be able to get good feedback. Or perhaps this person could call the employers on your behalf to find out how you might improve your presentation or to see if you appeared to lack needed skills. Employers are sometimes more willing to share reasons with school personnel so they can better assist their students. Be willing to listen to any constructive criticism offered and to make any needed changes.

Chapter 12

Code of Ethics and Standards of Practice

Code of Ethics and Standards of Practice

Ethical Principles
- Respect for the dignity of people—Massage professionals will maintain respect for the interests, dignity, rights, and needs of all clients, staff, and colleagues.
- Responsible caring—Competent, quality client care will be provided at the highest standard possible.
- Integrity in relationships—At all times the professional will behave with integrity, honesty, and diligence in practice and duties.
- Responsibility to society—Massage professionals are responsible and accountable to society and shall conduct themselves in a manner that maintains high ethical standards.

Standards of Practice Based on Ethical Principles
In compliance with the principles of the code of ethics, massage professionals will perform the following:
1. Respect all clients, colleagues, and health professionals through nondiscrimination regardless of age, gender, race, national origin, sexual orientation, religion, socioeconomic status, body type, political affiliation, state of health, personal habits, and life-coping skills.
2. Perform only those services for which they are qualified and honestly represent their education, certification, professional affiliations, and other qualifications. The massage professional will apply treatment only when a reasonable expectation exists that it will be advantageous to the client's condition. The massage professional, in consultation with the client, will continually evaluate the effectiveness of treatment.
3. Respect the scope of practice of other health care and service professionals, including physicians, chiropractors, physical therapists, podiatrists, orthopedists, psychotherapists, counselors, acupuncturists, nurses, exercise physiologists,

athletic trainers, nutritionists, spiritual advisors, and cosmetologists.
4. Respect all ethical health care practitioners and work with them to promote health and healing.
5. Acknowledge the limitations of their personal skills and, when necessary, refer clients to an appropriately qualified professional. The massage professional will require consultation with other knowledgeable professionals when:
   - A client requires diagnosis and opinion beyond a therapist's capabilities of assessment
   - A client's condition is beyond the scope of practice
   - A combined health care team is required
   If referral to another health care provider is necessary, it will be done with the informed consent of the client.
6. Refrain from working with any individual who has a specific disease process without supervision by a licensed medical professional.
7. Be adequately educated and understand the physiologic effects of the specific massage techniques used to determine if any application is contraindicated and to ensure that the most beneficial techniques are applied to a given individual.
8. Avoid false claims about the potential benefits of the techniques rendered, and educate the public about the actual benefits of massage.
9. Acknowledge the importance and individuality of each person, including colleagues, peers, and clients.
10. Work only with the informed consent of a client and professionally disclose to the client any situation that may interfere with the massage professional's ability to provide the best care to serve the client's best interest.

Code of Ethics and Standards of Practice—cont'd

11. Display respect for the client by honoring a client's process and following all recommendations by being present, listening, asking only pertinent questions, keeping agreements, being on time, draping properly, and customizing the massage to address the client's needs.

Note: Draping is covered later in this chapter. The Ontario guidelines give these requirements for draping:

- It is the responsibility of the massage professional to ensure the privacy and dignity of the client and to determine if the client feels comfortable, safe, and secure with the draping provided.
- The client may choose to be fully draped or clothed throughout the treatment.
- The female client's breasts are not undraped unless specified by referral from a qualified health care professional and the massage professional is working under the supervision of such a health care professional.
- The genitals, perineum, and anus are never undraped.

The consent of the client is required for work on any part of the body, regardless of whether the client is fully clothed, fully draped, or partly draped.

12. Provide a safe, comfortable, and clean environment.
13. Maintain clear and honest communication with clients and keep client communications confidential. Confidentiality is of the utmost importance. The massage professional must inform the client that the referring physician may be eligible to review the client's records and that records may be subpoenaed by the courts.
14. Conduct business in a professional and ethical manner in relation to clientele, business associates, acquaintances, governmental bodies, and the public.
15. Follow city, county, state, national, and international requirements.
16. Charge a fair price for the session. A gift, gratuity, or benefit that is intended to influence a referral, decision, or treatment may not be accepted and must be returned to the giver immediately.

17. Keep accurate records and review the records with the client.
18. Never engage in any sexual conduct, sexual conversation, or any other sexual activities involving clients.
19. Avoid affiliation with any business that uses any form of sexual suggestiveness or explicit sexuality in advertising or promoting services or in the actual practice of service.
20. Practice honesty in advertising, promoting services ethically and in good taste and advertising only techniques for which the professional is certified or adequately trained.
21. Strive for professional excellence through regular assessment of personal strengths, limitations, and effectiveness and through continuing education and training.
22. Accept the responsibility to oneself, one's clients, and the profession to maintain physical, mental, and emotional well-being and to inform clients when the professional is not functioning at best capacity.
23. Refrain from using any mind-altering drugs, alcohol, or intoxicants before or during professional massage sessions.
24. Maintain a professional appearance and demeanor by practicing good hygiene and dressing in a professional, modest, and nonsexual manner.
25. Undergo periodic peer review.
26. Respect all pertinent reporting requirements outlined by legislation regarding abuse.
27. Report to the proper authorities any accurate knowledge and its supportive documentation regarding violations by massage professionals and other health or service professionals.
28. Avoid interests, activities, or influences that might conflict with the obligation to act in the best interest of clients and the massage therapy profession and safeguard professional integrity by recognizing potential conflicts of interest and avoiding them.

Governmental Credentials and Regulations

Licensing
- Requires a state or provincial board of examiners
- Requires all constituents who practice the profession to be licensed
- Legally defines and limits the scope of practice for a profession
- Requires specific educational courses or an examination
- Protects title usage (e.g., only those licensed can use the title massage therapist)

Governmental Certification
- Administered by an independent board
- Voluntary but required for anyone using the protected title (e.g., massage therapist); others can provide the service but cannot call themselves massage therapists
- Requires specific educational courses and an examination

Governmental Registration
(Not to be confused with private registration processes)
- Administered by the state Department of Registry or other appropriate state agency

Voluntary
- Does not necessarily require a specific education, such as a school diploma; often other forms of verification of professional standards, such as years in practice, are acceptable
- Does not provide title protection

Exemptions
- Means that a practitioner is not required to comply with an existing local or state regulation
- Excuses practitioners who meet specified educational requirements from meeting current regulatory requirements
- Does not provide title protection

Steps for Complying with Licensing Requirements

1. Find out whether your state or province requires licensing. Contact the Department of Licensing and Regulation, Occupational Licensing Division, for this information. If state licensing is required, find out what educational requirements must be met to take the examination.
2. If your state does not have licensing, contact the local government where you intend to work to inquire about local ordinances. Obtain a copy of the ordinances and read them carefully. Look especially for the educational, zoning, and facility requirements. Whether you live in a city, township, or similar government unit, the clerk's office is the department that usually has this information. **Note:** Even if there is no state or local regulation, it is a good idea to attend only a licensed school or an approved training program. Other states or local governments may require this type of education, and without it you cannot practice in their areas.
3. Shop carefully for your school of massage training. Contact the state Department of Education and confirm that the school is licensed and in compliance with state regulations.
4. Before renting, buying, or setting up the actual massage practice, contact the local government concerning zoning requirements and building codes. If you are considering a home office, check the zoning ordinances to make sure you will be in compliance. Again, your city or township officials (usually the clerk) are your best sources of information.
   - Zoning permits require a public hearing. Your neighbors are notified by mail, and the hearing is advertised in the newspaper. Contact the zoning department to find out what action is required. Whether you are establishing your business in a home office or a business zone, contact the neighbors to explain your business and find out their response. Without their approval, or at least lack of opposition, you are unlikely to obtain a permit. Attend the hearing at all costs. Remember: **no permit = no business.** Zoning permits may require 6 to 8 weeks to complete. If you start your business without proper permits, you could be shut down at any time by government authorities.
5. Before you actually rent space or begin your business, contact the local government and apply for any necessary permits or business licenses. Make sure you meet all regulations. Fees can run anywhere from $25 to $500.

The National Certification Board for Therapeutic Massage and Bodywork Code of Ethics

The Code of Ethics of the National Certification Board for Therapeutic Massage and Bodywork (NCBTMB) specifies professional standards that allow for the proper discharge of the massage therapist's and/or bodyworker's responsibilities to those served, that protect the integrity of the profession, and that safeguard the interest of individual clients.

Those practitioners nationally certified in therapeutic massage and bodywork in the exercise of professional accountability will conduct themselves as follows:

1. Have a sincere commitment to provide the highest quality of care to those who seek their professional services.
2. Represent their qualifications honestly, including education and professional affiliations, and provide only those services that they are qualified to perform.
3. Accurately inform clients, other health care practitioners, and the public of the scope and limitations of their discipline.
4. Acknowledge the limitations of and contraindications for massage therapy and bodywork, and refer clients to appropriate health professionals.
5. Provide treatment only when there is reasonable expectation that it will be advantageous to the client.
6. Consistently maintain and improve professional knowledge and competence, striving for professional excellence through regular assessment of personal and professional strengths and weaknesses and through continued educational training.
7. Conduct their business and professional activities with honesty and integrity, and respect the inherent worth of all people.
8. Refuse to unjustly discriminate against clients or other ethical health professionals.
9. Safeguard the confidentiality of all client information, unless disclosure is required by law, court order, or absolutely necessary for the protection of the public.
10. Respect the client's right to treatment with informed and voluntary consent. The NCBTMB practitioner will obtain and record the informed consent of the client, or client's advocate, before providing treatment. This consent may be written or verbal.
11. Respect the client's right to refuse, modify, or terminate treatment regardless of prior consent given.
12. Provide draping and treatment in a way that ensures the safety, comfort, and privacy of the client.
13. Exercise the right to refuse to treat any person or part of the body for just and reasonable cause.
14. Refrain, under all circumstances, from initiating or engaging in any sexual conduct, sexual activities, or sexualizing behavior involving a client, even if the client attempts to sexualize the relationship.
15. Avoid any interest, activity, or influence that might be in conflict with the practitioner's obligation to act in the best interests of the client or the profession.
16. Respect the client's boundaries with regard to privacy, disclosure, exposure, emotional expression, beliefs, and the client's reasonable expectations of professional behavior. Practitioners will respect the client's autonomy.
17. Refuse any gifts or benefits that are intended to influence a referral, decision, or treatment and that are purely for personal gain and not for the good of the client.
18. Follow all policies, procedures, guidelines, regulations, codes, and requirements promulgated by the National Certification Board for Therapeutic Massage and Bodywork.

Modified from National Certification Board for Therapeutic Massage and Bodywork: *Code of ethics (adopted 2/17/95) and standards of practice (adopted 2/9/00),* McLean, Va, Author.

The National Certification Board for Therapeutic Massage and Bodywork Standards of Practice

Standard I: Professionalism

The certificant must provide optimal levels of professional massage and bodywork services and demonstrate excellence in practice by promoting healing and well-being through responsible, compassionate, and respectful touch. In his or her professional role the certificant shall commit to the following:

1. Adhere to the NCBTMB Code of Ethics, Standards of Practice, policies, and procedures.
2. Comply with the peer review process conducted by the NCBTMB Ethics and Standards Committee regarding any alleged violations against the NCBTMB Code of Ethics and Standards of Practice.
3. Conduct themselves in a manner in all settings meriting the respect of the public and other professionals.
4. Treat each client with respect, dignity, and worth.
5. Use professional verbal, nonverbal, and written communications.
6. Provide an environment that is safe and comfortable for the client and which, at a minimum, meets all legal requirements for health and safety.
7. Use standard precautions to ensure professional hygienic practices and maintain a level of personal hygiene appropriate for practitioners in the therapeutic setting.
8. Wear clothing that is clean, modest, and professional.
9. Obtain voluntary and informed consent from the client before initiating the session.
10. If applicable, conduct an accurate needs assessment, develop a plan of care with the client, and update the plan as needed.
11. Use appropriate draping to protect the client's physical and emotional privacy.
12. Be knowledgeable of their scope of practice and practice only within these limitations.
13. Refer to other professionals when in the best interest of the client and/or practitioner.
14. Seek other professional advice when needed.
15. Respect the traditions and practices of other professionals and foster collegial relationships.
16. Not falsely impugn the reputation of any colleague.
17. Use the initials NCBTMB to designate his or her professional ability and competency to practice therapeutic massage and bodywork only.
18. Remain in good standing with and maintain NCBTMB certification.
19. Understand that the NCBTMB certificate may be displayed prominently in the certificant's principal place of practice.
20. When using the NCBTMB logo and certification number on business cards, brochures, advertisements, and stationery, do so only in a manner that is within established NCBTMB guidelines.
21. Not duplicate the NCBTMB certificate for purposes other than verification of the practitioner's credentials.
22. Immediately return the certificate to NCBTMB if it is revoked or suspended.

Standard II: Legal and Ethical Requirements

The certificant must comply with all the legal requirements in applicable jurisdictions regulating the profession of massage therapy and bodywork. In his or her professional role the certificant shall commit to the following:

1. Obey all applicable local, state, and federal laws.
2. Refrain from any behavior that results in illegal, discriminatory, or unethical actions.
3. Accept responsibility for own actions.
4. Report to the proper authorities any alleged violations of the law by other certificants.
5. Maintain accurate and truthful records.
6. Report to the NCBTMB any criminal convictions regarding himself or herself and other certificants.
7. Report to NCBTMB any pending litigation and resulting resolution related to his or her professional practice and the professional practice of other certificants.
8. Respect existing publishing rights and copyright laws.

Standard III: Confidentiality

The certificant shall respect the confidentiality of client information and safeguard all records. In his or her professional role the certificant shall commit to the following:

1. Protect the client's identity in social conversations, all advertisements, and any and all other manners unless requested by the client in writing, medically necessary, or required by law.
2. Protect the interests of clients who are minors or who are unable to give voluntary consent by securing permission from an appropriate third party or guardian.
3. Solicit only information that is relevant to the professional client/therapist relationship.
4. Share pertinent information about the client with third parties when required by law.
5. Maintain the client files for a minimum period of four years.
6. Store and dispose of client files in a secure manner.

Standard IV: Business Practices

The certificant shall practice with honesty, integrity, and lawfulness in the business of massage and bodywork. In his or her professional role the certificant shall commit to the following:

The National Certification Board for Therapeutic Massage and Bodywork Standards of Practice—cont'd

1. Provide a physical setting that is safe and meets all applicable legal requirements for health and safety.
2. Maintain adequate and customary liability insurance.
3. Maintain adequate progress notes for each client session, if applicable.
4. Accurately and truthfully inform the public of services provided.
5. Honestly represent all professional qualifications and affiliations.
6. Promote his or her business with integrity and avoid potential and actual conflicts of interest.
7. Advertise in a manner that is honest, dignified, and representative of services that can be delivered and remains consistent with the NCBTMB Code of Ethics.
8. Advertise in a manner that is not misleading to the public by, among other things, the use of sensational, sexual, or provocative language and/or pictures to promote business.
9. Comply with all laws regarding sexual harassment.
10. Not exploit the trust and dependency of others, including clients and employees or co-workers.
11. Display or discuss schedule of fees in advance of the session that are clearly understood by the client or potential client.
12. Make financial arrangements in advance that are clearly understood by and safeguard the best interests of the client or consumer.
13. Follow acceptable accounting practices.
14. File all applicable municipal, state and federal taxes.
15. Maintain accurate financial records, contracts and legal obligations, appointment records, tax reports and receipts for at least 4 years.

Standard V: Roles and Boundaries
The certificant must comply with all the legal requirements in applicable jurisdictions regulating the profession of massage therapy and bodywork. In his or her professional role the certificant shall commit to the following:
1. Recognize his or her personal limitations and practice only within these limitations.
2. Recognize his or her influential position with the client and shall not exploit the relationship for personal or other gain.
3. Recognize and limit the impact of transference and countertransference between the client and the certificant.
4. Avoid dual or multidimensional relationships that could impair professional judgment or result in exploitation of the client or employees and/or co-workers.

5. Not engage in any sexual activity with a client.
6. Acknowledge and respect the client's freedom of choice in the therapeutic session.
7. Respect the client's right to refuse the therapeutic session.
8. Refrain from practicing under the influence of alcohol, drugs, or any illegal substances (with the exception of prescribed dosage of prescription medication, which does not significantly impair the certificant).
9. Have the right to refuse and/or terminate the service to a client who is abusive or under the influence of alcohol, drugs, or any illegal substance.

Standard VI: Prevention of Sexual Misconduct
The certificant shall refrain from any behavior that sexualizes, or appears to sexualize, the client/therapist relationship. The certificant recognizes that the intimacy of the therapeutic relationship may activate practitioner and/or client needs and/or desires that weaken objectivity and may lead to sexualizing the therapeutic relationship. In his or her professional role the certificant shall commit to the following:
1. Refrain from participating in a sexual relationship or sexual conduct with the client, whether consensual or otherwise, from the beginning of the client/therapist relationship and for a minimum of 6 months after the termination of the client/therapist relationship.
2. In the event that the client initiates sexual behavior, clarify the purpose of the therapeutic session, and if such conduct does not cease, terminate or refuse the session.
3. Recognize that sexual activity with clients, students, employees, supervisors, or trainees is prohibited even if consensual.
4. Not touch the genitalia.
5. Only perform therapeutic treatments beyond the normal narrowing of the ear canal and normal narrowing of the nasal passages as indicated in the plan of care and only after receiving informed voluntary written consent.
6. Only perform therapeutic treatments in the oropharynx as indicated in the plan of care and only after receiving informed voluntary consent.
7. Only perform therapeutic treatments into the anal canal as indicated in the plan of care and only after receiving informed voluntary written consent.
8. Only provide therapeutic breast massage as indicated in the plan of care and only after receiving informed voluntary consent from the client.

Modified from National Certification Board for Therapeutic Massage and Bodywork: *Code of ethics (adopted 2/17/95) and standards of practice (adopted 2/9/00)*, McLean, Va, Author.

Chapter 13

Medical Terminology

TABLE 13-1   Common Root Words

Root (Combining Vowel)	Meaning	Root (Combining Vowel)	Meaning
Abdomin (o)	Abdomen	Neur (o)	Nerve
Aden (o)	Gland	Ocul (o)	Eye
Adren (o)	Adrenal Gland	Orth (o)	Straight, normal, correct
Angi (o)	Vessel	Oste (o)	Bone
Arteri (o)	Artery	Ot (o)	Ear
Arthr (o)	Joint	Ped (o)	Child, foot
Bronch (o)	Bronchus, bronchi	Pharyng (o)	Pharynx
Card, cardi (o)	Heart	Phleb (o)	Vein
Cephal (o)	Head	Pnea	Breathing, respiration
Chondr (o)	Cartilage	Pneum (o)	Lung, air, gas
Col (o)	Colon	Proct (o)	Rectum
Cost (o)	Rib	Psych (o)	Mind
Crani (o)	Skull	Pulm (o)	Lung
Cyan (o)	Blue	Py (o)	Pus
Cyst (o)	Bladder, cyst	Rect (o)	Rectum
Derma	Skin	Sten (o)	Narrow, constriction
Duoden (o)	Duodenum	Stern (o)	Sternum
Encephal (o)	Brain	Stomat (o)	Mouth
Enter (o)	Intestines	Therm (o)	Heat
Fibr (o)	Fiber, fibrous	Thorac (o)	Chest
Gastr (o)	Stomach	Thromb (o)	Clot, thrombus
Gyn, gyne, gyneco	Woman	Thyr (o)	Thyroid
Hem, hema, hemo, hemat (o)	Blood	Toxic (o)	Poison, poisonous
Hepat (o)	Liver	Trache (o)	Trachea
Hydr (o)	Water	Ur (o)	Urine, urinary tract, urination
Hyster (o)	Uterus	Urethr (o)	Urethra
Ile (o), ili (o)	Ileum	Urin (o)	Urine
Laryng (o)	Larynx	Uter (o)	Uterus
Mamm (o)	Breast, mammary gland	Vas (o)	Blood vessel, vas deferens
My (o)	Muscle	Ven (o)	Vein
Myel (o)	Spinal cord, bone marrow	Vertebr (o)	Spine, vertebrae
Nephr (o)	kidney		

TABLE 13-2   Common Prefixes

Prefix	Meaning	Prefix	Meaning
a-, an-	Without or not	intro-	Into, within
ab-	Away from	leuk-	White
ad-	Toward	macro-	Large
ante-	Before, forward	mal-	Bad, illness, disease
anti-	Against	mega-	Large
auto-	Self	micro-	Small
bi-	Double, two	mono-	One, single
circum-	Around	neo-	New
contra-	Against, opposite	non-	Not
de-	Down, from, away from, not	para-	Abnormal
dia-	Across, through, apart	per-	By, through
dis-	Separation, away from	peri-	Around
dys-	Bad, difficult, abnormal	poly-	Many, much
ecto-	Outer, outside	post-	After, behind
en-	In, into, within	pre-	Before, in front of, prior to
endo-	Inner, inside	pro-	Before, in front of
epi-	Over, on	re-	Again
eryth-	Red	retro-	Backward
ex-	Out, out of, from, away from	semi-	Half
hemi-	Half	sub-	Under
hyper-	Excessive, too much, high	super-	Above, over, excess
hypo-	Under, decreased, less than normal	supra-	Above, over
in-	In, into, within, not	trans-	Across
inter-	Between	uni-	One
intra-	Within		

TABLE 13-3 Common Suffixes

-algia	Pain
-asis	Condition, usually abnormal
-cele	Hernia, herniation, pouching
-cyte	Cell
-ectasis	Dilation, stretching
-ectomy	Excision, removal of
-emia	Blood condition
-genesis	Development, production, creation
-genic	Producing, causing
-gram	Record
-graph	Diagram, recording instrument
-graphy	Making a recording
-iasis	Condition of
-ism	Condition
-itis	Inflammation
-logy	Study of
-lysis	Destruction of, decomposition
-megaly	Enlargement
-oma	Tumor
-osis	Condition
-pathy	disease
-penia	Lack, deficiency
-phasia	Speaking
-phobia	Exaggerated fear
-plasty	Surgical repair or reshaping
-plegia	Paralysis
-rrhage, -rrhagia	Excessive flow
-rrhea	Profuse flow, discharge
-scope	Examination instrument
-scopy	Examination using a scope
-stasis	Maintenance, maintaining a constant level
-stomy, -ostomy	Creation of an opening
-tomy, -otomy	Incision, cutting into
-uria	Condition of the urine

TABLE 13-4 Common Abbreviations

Abbreviation	Meaning	Abbreviation	Meaning
ABD	Abdomen	IBW	Ideal Body Weight
ADL	Activities of daily living	ICT	Inflammation of connective tissue
ad lib	As desired	Id.	The same
alt. dieb	Every other day	L	Left, length, lumbar, liter
alt. hor	Alternate hours	lig	ligament
alt. noct	Alternate nights	M	Muscle, meter, myopia
AM (AM, am)	Morning	ML	Midline
a.m.a.	Against medical advice	meds	Medications
ANS	Autonomic nervous system	n	Normal
approx	Approximately	NA	Nonapplicable
as tol	As tolerated	OB	Obstetrics
BM	Bowel movement	OTC	Over-the-counter
BP	Blood pressure	P	Pulse
Ca	Cancer	PA	Postural analysis
CC	Chief complaint	PM (PM, pm)	Afternoon
c/o	Complains of	PT	Physical therapy
CPR	Cardiopulmonary resuscitation	Px	Prognosis
CSF	Cerebrospinal fluid	R	Respiration, right
CVA	Cerebrovascular accident, stroke	R/O	Rule out
DM	Diabetes mellitus	ROM	Range of motion
DJD	Degenerative joint disease	Rx	Prescription
Dx	Diagnosis	SOB	Shortness of breath
ext	Extract	SP, spir	Spirit
ft	Foot or feet	Sym.	Symmetric
fx	Fracture	T	Temperature
GI	Gastrointestinal	TLC	Tender loving care
GU	Genitourinary	Tx	Treatment
h (hr)	Hour	URI	Upper respiratory infection
H_2O	Water	WD	Well-developed
Hx	History	WN	Well-nourished

Chapter 14

Sanitation Practices

Sanitation Practices for Massage Professionals

The following sanitation requirements for practicing massage professionals have been developed from the Oregon model:

- The massage professional must clean and wash the hands and forearms thoroughly with an antibacterial/antiviral agent before touching each client. Any professional known to be infected with any communicable disease or to be a carrier of such disease or who has an infected wound or open lesion on any exposed portions of the body is excluded from practicing massage until the communicable condition is alleviated.
- The professional must wear clean clothing. If at all possible, lockers or closets for personnel should be maintained apart from the massage room for the storage of personal clothing and effects.
- All doors and windows opening to the outside must be tight fitting and must ensure the exclusion of flies, insects, rodents, or other vermin. All floors, walks, and furniture must be kept clean, well maintained, and in good repair.
- All rooms in which massage is practiced must meet the following requirements: (1) heating must be adequate to maintain a room air temperature of 75°F; (2) ventilation must be sufficient to remove objectionable odors; and (3) lighting fixtures must be capable of producing a minimum of 5 foot-candles of light at floor level; this level of lighting should be used during cleaning.
- All sewage and liquid waste must be disposed of in a municipal sewage system or approved septic system. All interior water distribution piping should be installed and maintained in conformity with the state plumbing code. The water supply must be adequate, deemed safe by the health department, and sanitary. Drinking fountains of an approved type or individual paper drinking cups should be provided for the convenience of employees and patrons.

- Every massage business must have a sanitary toilet facility with an adequate supply of hot and cold water under pressure, and it must be conveniently located for use by employees and patrons. Bathroom doors must be tight fitting, and the rooms must be kept clean, in good repair, and free of flies, insects, and vermin. A supply of soap in a covered dispenser and single-use sanitary towels in a dispenser must be provided at each lavatory installation, as well as a covered waste receptacle for proper disposal; a supply of toilet paper on a dispenser must be available for each toilet.
- Lavatory and toilet rooms must be equipped with fly-tight containers for garbage and refuse. These containers should be easily cleanable, well maintained, and in good repair. Any refuse must be disposed of in a sanitary manner.
- Massage lubricants, including but not limited to oil, alcohol, powders, and lotions, should be dispensed from suitable containers, to be used and stored in such a manner as to prevent contamination. The bulk lubricant must not come in contact with the massage professional. It should be poured, squeezed, or shaken into a separate container or the massage professional's hand. Any unused lubricant that comes into contact with the client or massage professional must be discarded.
- The use of unclean linen is prohibited. Only freshly laundered sheets and linens should be used for massage. All single-service materials and clean linens should be stored at least 4 inches off the floor in shelves, compartments, or cabinets used for that purpose only. All soiled linens must be placed in a covered receptacle immediately and kept there until washed in detergent and an antiviral cleaning agent (e.g., a 10% bleach solution, or one part bleach to nine parts water) in a washing machine that provides a hot water temperature of at least 140° F.

Sanitation Practices for Massage Professionals—cont'd

- Massage tables must be covered with impervious material that is cleanable and must be kept clean and in good repair. Equipment that comes into contact with the client must be cleaned thoroughly with soap or other suitable detergent and water, followed by adequate sanitation procedures before use with each individual client (a 10% bleach solution, made up daily, is recommended). All equipment must be clean, well maintained, and in good repair.
- When cleaning the massage area, observe the following rules:
  - Do not shake linen, and dust with a damp cloth to minimize the movement of dust.
- Clean from the cleanest area to the dirtiest. This prevents soiling of a clean area.
- Clean away from your body and uniform. If you dust, brush, or wipe toward yourself, microorganisms will be transmitted to your skin, hair, and uniform.
- Used linens must be stored in a closed bag or container while in the massage room or during transport.
- Floors are dirty; any object that falls on the floor should not be used on or for a client.

Standard Precautions

Standard precautions synthesize the major features of universal (blood and body fluid) precautions (designed to reduce the risk of transmission of blood-borne pathogens) and body substance isolation (designed to reduce the risk of transmission of pathogens from moist body substances). Standard precautions apply to (1) blood; (2) all body fluids, secretions, and excretions, except sweat, regardless of whether they contain visible blood; (3) nonintact skin; and (4) mucous membranes. Standard precautions are designed to reduce the risk of transmission of microorganisms from both recognized and unrecognized sources of infection in hospitals.

Hand Washing and Gloving
Hand washing frequently is called the single most important measure to reduce the risks of transmitting organisms from one person to another or from one site to another on the same patient. The scientific rationale, indications, methods, and products for hand washing have been delineated in other areas.

Washing hands as promptly and thoroughly as possible between clients is very important. In addition to hand washing, gloves play an important role in reducing the risks of transmission of microorganisms.

Gloves are worn for two important reasons. First, gloves are worn to provide a protective barrier. Second, gloves are worn to reduce the likelihood that microorganisms are present on the hands of the massage practitioner and will be transmitted to clients. Wearing gloves does not replace the need for hand washing, because gloves may have small, unapparent defects or may be torn during use, and hands can become contaminated during removal of gloves.

Gloves are to be changed and disposed of after each use.

A mask provides protection against the spread of infectious large-particle droplets that are transmitted by close contact and that generally travel only short distances (up to 3 feet) from infected patients who are coughing or sneezing. Massage professionals occasionally use masks.

Gowns and Protective Apparel
Various types of gowns and protective apparel are worn to provide barrier protection and to reduce the opportunity for transmission of microorganisms in medical settings.

Immunocompromised Clients
Use standard precautions, or the equivalent, for the care of all clients.

Hand washing
1. Wash hands after touching blood, body fluids, secretions, excretions, and contaminated items, regardless of whether gloves are worn. Wash hands immediately after removing gloves, between client contacts, and when otherwise indicated to avoid transfer of microorganisms to other clients or environments. It may be necessary to wash hands between tasks and procedures on the same client to prevent cross-contamination of different body sites.
2. Use a plain (nonantimicrobial) soap for routine hand washing.
3. Use an antimicrobial agent or a waterless antiseptic agent if hand washing is not available.

Gloves
Wear gloves (clean, nonsterile gloves are adequate) when touching blood, body fluids, secretions, excre-

Continued

Standard Precaution—cont'd

tions, and contaminated items. Put on clean gloves just before touching mucous membranes and non-intact skin. Change gloves between tasks and procedures on the same client after contact with material that may contain a high concentration of microorganisms. Remove gloves promptly after use, before touching uncontaminated items and environmental surfaces, and before going to another client, and wash hands immediately to avoid transfer of microorganisms to other clients or environments.

Mask, Eye Protection, Face Shield

Wear a mask and eye protection or a face shield to protect the mucous membranes of the eyes, nose, and mouth during procedures and client care activities that are likely to generate splashes or sprays of blood, body fluids, secretions, and excretions.

Gown

Wear a gown (a clean, nonsterile gown is adequate) to protect skin and to prevent soiling of clothing during procedures and client care activities that are likely to generate splashes or sprays of blood, body fluids, secretions, or excretions. Select a gown that is appropriate for the activity and amount of fluid likely to be encountered. Remove a soiled gown as promptly as possible, and wash hands to avoid transfer of microorganisms to other clients or environments.

Modified from the Division of Healthcare Quality Promotion, National Center for Infectious Diseases, Centers for Disease Control and Prevention.

Chapter 15

Preventing the Transmission of HIV, Hepatitis, and Tuberculosis

Using the information presented in this section, the student will be able to perform the following:
- ☐ Define AIDS in detail
- ☐ Identify behavior that could result in transmission of HIV or HBV

ACQUIRED IMMUNODEFICIENCY SYNDROME

A *syndrome* is a group of clinical symptoms that constitute a disease or abnormal condition. (*Clinical* means reported or observed symptoms not discovered by laboratory tests.) With syndromes, an individual need not have all the symptoms. Syndromes may be caused by many different things, but with **acquired immunodeficiency syndrome (AIDS),** the cause is a dysfunction in the body's immune system, one of the body's primary defenses against disease.

The diseases of AIDS are caused by germs we encounter every day. In fact, some of these germs live permanently in small numbers inside the human body. When the immune system weakens, these germs have the opportunity to multiply freely; therefore the diseases they cause are called *opportunistic diseases.*

The **human immunodeficiency virus (HIV),** which seems to be responsible for AIDS, is a retrovirus. As a group, retroviruses can live in the host for a long time without causing any sign of illness. In most animals, retrovirus infections last for life. These viruses die when exposed to heat, they can be killed by many common disinfectants, and they usually do not survive well if the tissue or blood they are in dries up. However, retroviruses have a high mutation rate and consequently tend to evolve very quickly into new strains. HIV shares this and other traits with other known retroviruses.

HIV replicates (lives) in the group of white blood cells called *lymphocytes,* or *T cells.* Among the T cells, HIV's favorite target is the T4 cell. The T4 cell, also called the *helper/inducer T cell,* performs a vital job in the immune system. HIV infection of the T4 cells creates a defect in the body's immune system, which may eventually result in AIDS. Long-term infection with HIV without the development of AIDS is becoming more common. Improved treatment, a better understanding of the disease on the part of health care professionals, increased public education, and less stress from public stigma support this process.

The Mechanics of Transmission

For transmission, HIV must travel from inside one person to the inside of another person. Because viruses are unable to enter the body through intact skin, they must enter through an open wound or one of a number of possible body openings (most of which contain mucous membranes). *Mucous membranes* are thin tissues that protect most openings and passages in the human body. These membranes secrete mucus, which contains antigerm chemicals and keeps the surrounding tissues moist. Mucous membranes can be found in the mouth, inside the eyelids, in the nose and air passages leading to the lungs, in the stomach, along the digestive tract, in the vagina, in the anus, and inside the eye and the opening of the penis. From the surface of a mucous membrane, many viruses can travel through the membrane and enter the tiny blood vessels inside. The mucous membranes of the eyes and mouth often are doorways for highly infectious viruses such as the flu virus. The danger with HIV is very different. The major infection sites for this virus are the bloodstream and the central nervous system. HIV can be found in any body fluid or substance that contains lymphocytes.

The presence of HIV in a substance does not necessarily indicate that the substance is capable of transmitting the infection. In theory, all body fluids are capable of transmitting disease; in reality, however, the most dangerous substances seem to be blood, semen, and preejaculate fluid; cervical and vaginal secretions; and perhaps feces. Despite much research, a clear-cut case of saliva causing transmission has not been found, although kissing theoretically could transmit the virus. The concentration of HIV (i.e., the number of viral particles per unit of volume) is very important in infectivity. If a substance has a high concentration of HIV, it is more likely to transmit the virus. A pregnant woman can transmit the virus to her unborn child. The concentration of HIV in mother's milk and in saliva, urine, and tears is low, but theoretically these are infectious substances that could transmit HIV infection. However, no cases have been reported to be caused by contact with these secretions. Sweat cannot transmit HIV.

HIV Survival Outside the Host. If HIV is present in a substance that leaves the body, the viral particles are capable of remaining infectious until the substance dries up. Depending on the circumstances, this could be a matter of minutes or hours. If the substance stays moist, the viral particles can survive much longer. For example, in water and blood solutions (10% blood, 90% saline), HIV can survive at room temperature for 2 weeks. In refrigerated blood, such as that used for transfusions, HIV can survive indefinitely.

The public has a widespread fear that AIDS can be contracted through casual contact, such as shaking hands, being in the same room with an individual infected with HIV, touching doorknobs, or sharing bathroom facilities. The fear is far, far greater than the risk. Diseases spread by casual contact invariably are spread via saliva or sputum, and they exist in the saliva or sputum in very high concentrations. The concentration of HIV in saliva and sputum is very low, if it exists in these substances at all. After 10 years of documentation of the AIDS epidemic, there are no known cases of AIDS or HIV infection being transmitted by casual social contact, not even among people living in the same household. In some cases household members have even shared toothbrushes with infected housemates without contracting the virus.

To date no medical or health care workers have contracted HIV from casual contact. The contact between the massage professional and the client falls under this classification. We touch only the skin, which is not a transmission route.

HEPATITIS

Hepatitis is an inflammatory process, an infection of the liver caused by a virus. It is classified as type A, B, C, D, E, or G. Hepatitis A, caused by the hepatitis A virus (HAV), is a less serious form and is usually transmitted by fecal contamination of food and water. Hepatitis B is a potentially fatal disease caused by the hepatitis B virus (HBV), which is transmitted through routes similar to those for HIV. HBV is 100 times more contagious than HIV, and it is estimated that more than 1 million people in the United States are carriers of HBV. Two types of vaccine are available for preventing transmission of HBV. Hepatitis C accounts for 86% of new cases of hepatitis each year. The hepatitis D virus (HDV) infects only those who have hepatitis B, and its symptoms are more severe than other forms of hepatitis. Vaccines do not appear to be effective for HDV. Hepatitis E is transmitted through food and water contaminated by fecal material. Hepatitis G is a sexually transmitted virus.

Standard precautions prevent the spread of hepatitis. It is important to be cautious of all behaviors in which body fluids are contacted or unsanitary conditions may be present that may allow transmission of HIV and the hepatitis viruses.

TUBERCULOSIS

Tuberculosis (TB) is an infection caused by a bacterium that usually affects the lungs but may invade other body systems. It is estimated that approximately 1.86 billion people—32% of the world's population—are infected with TB. Transmission is by airborne droplets produced when an infected person coughs, sneezes, or talks. TB can also be spread through contaminated food.

In many infected individuals, tuberculosis is asymptomatic. In others, symptoms develop so gradually that they are not noticed until the disease is advanced. However, symptoms can appear in immune-suppressed individuals within weeks of exposure to the bacillus. Symptoms include fatigue, weight loss, lethargy, anorexia (loss of appetite), and a low-grade fever that usually occurs in the afternoon. A cough that produces purulent sputum develops slowly and becomes more frequent over several weeks or months. Night sweats and general anxiety are often present. Because these are common signs and symptoms of all chronic infections, referral is necessary for diagnosis. Dyspnea, chest pain, and hemoptysis may also occur as the disease progresses.

Tuberculosis is diagnosed by a positive tuberculin skin test (PPD), sputum culture, and chest x-ray. A positive tuberculin skin test indicates that an individual has been infected and has produced antibodies against the bacillus. By itself the positive skin test does not indicate the presence of an active disease. Treatment consists of antibiotic therapy to control active or dormant tuberculosis and to prevent transmission. Massage professionals should be tested yearly because of their contact with the public.

Chapter 16

Effects of Massage

EFFECTS OF MASSAGE

Both mechanical and reflexive responses are linked to massage techniques that deliver moderate to deep pressure, which stimulate pressure receptors. This type of massage is often referred to as *Swedish massage* or *therapeutic massage*. Some of the benefits outlined in this chapter are related to touch, but most are linked to Swedish massage, which is noted. One study implemented deep Swedish massage or deep tissue massage. In this study, massage using light pressure generally produced adverse results. In fact, it was criticized because it stated that massage did not have any effect on circulation but, after closer examination, it was discovered that only light pressure was used for the experimental (massaged) group.

In a study conducted by Cherkin et al, speculation was offered to explain why massage was effective in the treatment of low back pain. As you would expect, effects on soft tissues were noted. Other factors attributed to massage effectiveness were the client spending 1 hour in a relaxed environment, receiving ongoing attention from the therapist, being touched in a therapeutic context, and increased body awareness during and after the massage. Education about exercise and other positive lifestyle changes was another benefit clients received as part of their massage.

Do the effects of massage last? Most benefits cease shortly after the massage treatments are terminated, but this is also true of other health-related treatments such as diet, exercise, and meditation. The key to long-term effects is the education clients receive concerning lifestyle habits and changes. These changes can be a more healthy diet, frequent walks, and increased fluid intake. Clients are also taught other methods of self-care such as how to breathe for relaxation, a basic self-massage routine, or the stretching of muscle groups. Massage does have long-lasting effects on some specific injuries or pathologies. These effects include reducing scar tissue formation, decreasing edema, loosening lung phlegm, and relieving constipation. Chronic conditions often require ongoing massage treatments.

Massage therapy and the response it creates within the body can affect the cardiovascular system, lymphatic/immune systems, skin and related structures, nervous and endocrine systems, muscles, the connective tissues, respiratory system, digestive system, and urinary system. Also noted are miscellaneous effects and indications for specific conditions and individuals. Although most claims made about the benefits of massage therapy are the result of scientific experiments, a few are from empirical clinical observations and speculation based on physiological principles. By examining the effects of massage on each body system, we can understand the scientific application of massage therapy and how it benefits clients.

EFFECTS OF MASSAGE ON THE CARDIOVASCULAR SYSTEM

☐ **Dilates blood vessels.** The body responds to massage by reflexively dilating the blood vessels. This, in turn, aids in improving blood circulation and lowering blood pressure (see the following).

☐ **Improves blood circulation.** Deep stroking improves blood circulation by mechanically assisting venous blood flow back to the heart. The increase of blood flow is comparable to that of exercise. It has been documented that during a massage local circulation increases up to 3 times more than circulation at rest.

☐ **Creates hyperemia.** Increased blood flow creates a hyperemic effect, which is often visible on the surface of the skin.

☐ **Stimulates release of acetylcholine and histamine for sustained vasodilation.** These two substances are released due to vasomotor activity, helping prolong vasodilation.

☐ **Replenishes nutritive materials.** Another benefit of increased circulation, products such as nutrients and oxygen are transported to the cells and tissues more efficiently.

☐ **Promotes rapid removal of waste products.** Not only are nutrients brought to cells and to tissues, but metabolic waste products are removed more rapidly through massage. It is often said that massage "dilutes the poisons."

☐ **Reduces ischemia.** Massage reduces ischemia and ischemic-related pain. Ischemia is also related to trigger point formation and associated pain referral patterns.

☐ **Decreases blood pressure.** Blood pressure is decreased by dilation of blood vessels. Both diastolic and systolic readings decline, a change lasting approximately 40 minutes after the massage session.

☐ **Reduces heart rate.** Massage decreases heart rate through activation of the relaxation response.

☐ **Lowers pulse rate.** As one would expect, a reduced heart rate lowers the pulse rate.

☐ **Increases stroke volume.** Stroke volume is the amount of blood ejected from the left ventricle during each contraction. As the heart rate decreases, more time is available for the cardiac ventricles to fill with blood. The result is a larger volume of blood pushed through the heart with each ventricular contraction, thereby increasing stroke volume.

☐ **Increases red blood cell (RBC) count.** The number of functioning RBCs and their oxygen-carrying capacity are increased. It is speculated that this effect is achieved by (1) promoting the spleen's discharge of RBCs; (2) recruiting excess blood from engorged internal organs into general circulation; (3) stimulating stagnant capillary beds and returning this blood into general circulation. All three events increase RBC count.

☐ **Increases oxygen saturation in blood.** When RBC count rises, a greater oxygen saturation occurs in the blood.

☐ **Increases white blood cell (WBC) count.** The presence of WBCs increases after massage. The body may perceive massage as a mild stressor (an event to which the body must adapt) and recruits additional WBCs. The increase in WBC count enables the body to more effectively protect itself against disease.

☐ **Enhances the adhesion of migrating WBCs.** The surfaces of WBCs become more "sticky" following a massage, increasing their adhesive quality and therefore their effectiveness.

☐ **Increases platelet count.** Gentle but firm massage strokes increase the number of platelets in the blood.

Mini-Lab 16-1
BLOOD PRESSURE AND BLOOD VESSEL DIAMETER

You have two uninflated balloons, a small one and another twice the size of your first. Place a cup of water in each balloon. Which balloon has the lesser amount of pressure, the smaller or the larger? The larger one has the lesser pressure. This illustrates how massage can lower blood pressure through reflex action and increasing the parasympathetic response. By increasing the diameter of the vessel, the pressure inside the vessel decreases.

EFFECTS OF MASSAGE ON THE LYMPHATIC/IMMUNE SYSTEMS

☐ **Promotes lymph circulation.** Lymph is a fluid that moves slowly within its own system of vessels. Lymphatic circulation depends entirely on pressure; from muscle contraction, pressure changes in the thorax and abdomen during breathing, or applied pressure from a massage.

☐ **Reduces lymphedema.** Massage reduces lymphedema (swelling) by promoting lymph circulation, which helps remove waste from the system more effectively than either passive range of motion or electrical muscle stimulation.

☐ **Decreases the circumference of an area affected with lymphedema.** When an area swells, the diameter increases. When the swelling subsides, circumference decreases.

☐ **Decreases weight in patients with lymphedema.** Fluid retention adds weight to a patient. When lymphedema is addressed with massage, weight is consequently reduced.

☐ **Increases lymphocyte count.** Lymphocytes are types of WBCs. This indicates that massage supports immune functions.

☐ **Increases the number and function (or cytotoxicity) of natural killer cells.** Natural killer cells are also types of WBCs. This further suggests that massage strengthens immune functions and might help individuals with immune disorders.

EFFECTS OF MASSAGE ON THE SKIN AND RELATED STRUCTURES

☐ **Increases skin temperature.** Warming of the skin indicates a reduction of stress and other benefits outlined below.

☐ **Improves skin condition.** As superficial blood vessels dilate and circulation increases, the skin appears hyperemic. This brings added nutrients to the skin, improving the skin's condition, texture, and tone. Clinical observations have determined that massage also improves the appearance (i.e., color and texture) of the skin.

☐ **Stimulates sebaceous glands.** Stimulation of the sebaceous (oil) glands causes an increase in sebum production. This added sebum improves the skin's condition and reduces skin dryness.

☐ **Stimulates sudoriferous glands.** Sudoriferous (sweat) gland stimulation increases insensible perspiration. Insensible perspiration is the constant evaporative cooling that occurs as microscopic beads of perspiration evaporate from the skin's surface.

☐ **Improves skin pathologies.** Unless a condition contraindicates massage, skin pathologies may improve by decreasing redness, reducing thickening/hardening of the skin, increasing healing of skin abrasions, and reducing itching.

☐ **Reduces superficial keloid formation.** Massage applied to scar tissue helps reduce the formation of superficial keloids in the skin and excessive scar formation in the soft tissues beneath the site of massage application.

EFFECTS OF MASSAGE ON THE NERVOUS AND ENDOCRINE SYSTEMS

☐ **Reduces stress.** Stress is reduced by activation of the parasympathetic nervous system.

☐ **Reduces anxiety.** Interestingly, a reduction in anxiety is noted in both the person who received the massage and the person who gave the massage.

☐ **Promotes relaxation.** General relaxation is promoted through activation of the relaxation response. Relaxation also has a diminishing effect on pain.

☐ **Decreases beta wave activity.** Associated with relaxation, a decrease in beta brainwave activity occurred during and after the massage (confirmed by electroencephalogram [EEG]).

☐ **Increases delta wave activity.** Increases in delta brainwave activity are linked to sleep and to relaxation; both are promoted with massage (confirmed by EEG).

☐ **Increase in alpha waves.** An increase in alpha brainwave during massage indicates relaxation (confirmed by EEG).

☐ **Increases dopamine levels.** Increased levels of dopamine are linked to decreased stress levels and reduced depression.

☐ **Increases serotonin levels.** Increased levels of serotonin suggest a reduction of both stress and depression. It is believed that serotonin inhibits transmission of noxious signals to the brain, indicating that increased levels of serotonin may also reduce pain.

☐ **Reduces cortisol levels.** Massage reduces cortisol levels by activating the relaxation response. Elevated levels of cortisol not only represent heightened stress but also inhibit immune functions.

☐ **Reduces norepinephrine levels.** Massage has been proved to reduce norepinephrine, a stress hormone; reduced norepinephrine levels are linked to the relaxation response.

☐ **Reduces epinephrine levels.** Epinephrine, another stress hormone, is reduced with massage.

☐ **Reduces feelings of depression.** Both chemical and electrophysiological changes from a negative to a positive mood were noted and may underline the decrease in depression after massage therapy.

☐ **Decreases pain.** Massage relieves local and referred pain caused by hypersensitive trigger points, presumably by increasing circulation, thereby reducing ischemia. Massage also stimulates the release of endorphins (endogenous morphine), enkephalins, and other pain-reducing neurochemicals. General relaxation brought on by massage therapy also has a diminishing effect on pain. The pressure of a massage interferes with pain information entering the spinal cord by stimulating pressure receptors, further reducing pain (see Gate Theory). Massage interrupts the pain cycle by relieving muscular spasms, increasing circulation, and promoting rapid disposal of waste products. Massage also improves sleep patterns. During deep sleep, a substance called somatostatin is normally released. Without this substance, pain is experienced.

☐ **Reduces analgesic use.** Because pain is reduced with massage, so is the need for excessive use of pain medication.

☐ **Activates sensory receptors.** Depending on factors such as stroke choice, direction, speed, and pressure, massage can stimulate different sensory receptors, affecting the massage outcome. For example, cross-fiber tapotement stimulates muscle spindles, which activates muscular contraction while a slow passive stretch activates Golgi tendon organs, which inhibits muscular contraction. Activation of sensory pressure receptors reduces pain (see Gate Theory).

☐ **Faster and more elaborate development of the hippocampal region of the brain.** Development of the hippocampal region, which is part of the limbic system, is related to superior memory performance.

☐ **Increases vagal activity.** Increased activity of the vagal nerve lowers physiological arousal and stress hormones. A decrease in stress hormones leads to enhanced immune functions. One of the branches of the vagus nerve is known as the "smart branch." Stimulation of this nerve branch increases facial expression and vocalization, which reduces feelings of depression.

☐ **Right frontal EEG activation shifted to left frontal EEG activation.** Right frontal EEG activation is associated with a sad affect and left frontal EEG activation is associated

The Gate Theory

In 1965, Wall and Melzack postulated the gate theory of pain relief, which explains why massage, ice, and heat are effective in the treatment of pain. The *gate theory* refers to the exclusion of certain nerve impulses when multiple impulses are competing for the same synaptic "gate" or entry into the central nervous system. To understand this, we will examine the two types of nerve fibers.

The sensory transmitters for pressure, temperature, and sharp acute pain lie close together in large concentrations near the body's surface. Acute refers to those conditions that last for a short time, usually a few days to a few weeks. Acute pain typically has a sudden onset and a severe course. These sensory nerve pathways are composed of long, fast type A nerve fibers, which are important for protecting the body from external harm. Strong stimuli to these surface transmitters generate a quick sensory input to the cord segment, where a reflex-motor impulse is generated to move the affected body part out of harm's way. Touching a needle or a hot pan elicits this type of immediate reflex response.

The sensory transmitters for deep aching pain such as myofascial pain originate in the deeper tissues. These nerve pathways are composed of short, slow type C nerve fibers, which tend to transmit pain that has been present for some time and requires no immediate protective action (i.e., headache or muscular pain). These nerves transmit stimuli that are of lesser importance and lesser consequence to the body. The purpose of type C nerve pathways is to make the conscious mind aware that a problem exists, which can be used to prevent overuse or dependence on an injured body part.

Suppose that an Olympic gymnast is having her performance compromised by pain in her right Achilles tendon. This pain originates from the deeper, slower type C nerve network. When a pressure stimulus such as massage is applied to the calf, the new sensory input travels along the faster, longer type A nerve network and bridges the synaptic gap ahead of the type C sensory input. The synaptic gate is closed, thus excluding the pain information from entry to the spinal cord. The body experiences the pressure of the massage stroke as interruption of pain.

Massage therapists can use the gate mechanism a number of ways including in the application of cold, heat, pressure, vibration, percussion, and superficial rubbing or light stimulation of cutaneous tissue. Any of these applications has the potential to interfere with or interrupt pain signals.

with a happy affect. This implies that the client experienced an improvement of mood during the massage.

☐ **Decreases H-amplitude levels during massage.** A decrease of 60% to 80% was noted. This reduction is crucial for the comfort of patients with spinal cord injuries because it signifies a decrease of muscle cramps and spasm activity.

EFFECTS OF MASSAGE ON THE MUSCULAR SYSTEM

☐ **Relieves muscular tension.** Massage relieves muscular restrictions, tightness, stiffness, and spasms. These effects are achieved by direct pressure and by increasing circulation, resulting in more flexible, supple, and resilient muscle tissues.

☐ **Relaxes muscles.** Muscles relax as massage reduces excitability in the sympathetic nervous system.

☐ **Reduces muscle soreness and fatigue.** Massage enhances blood circulation, thus increasing the amount of oxygen and nutrients available to the muscles. Increased oxygen and nutrients reduce muscle fatigue and postexercise soreness. Massage promotes rapid disposal of waste products, further reducing muscle fatigue and soreness. A fatigued muscle recuperates 20% after 5 minutes of rest and 100% after 5 minutes of massage. A reduction in postexercise recovery time was indicated by a decline in pulse rate and an increased muscle "work" capacity.

☐ **Reduces trigger point formation.** Trigger point formation is greatly reduced by the pressure applied to tissues during a massage, affecting trigger points in both muscle and fascia.

☐ **Manually separates muscle fibers.** Compressive strokes and cross-fiber friction strokes separate muscle fibers, reducing muscle spasms.

☐ **Increases range of motion.** When muscular tension is reduced, range of motion is improved. The freedom of the joints is dictated by the freedom of the muscles.

☐ **Improves performance (balance and posture).** Many postural distortions are removed when trigger points are released and when muscle tension is reduced. Range of motion increases, gait becomes more efficient, the posture is more aligned and balanced, and improved performance is the net result.

☐ **Improves motor skills.** Not surprisingly, if a massage was found to improve performance, balance, and posture, motor skills are also enhanced.

☐ **Lengthens muscles.** Massage mechanically stretches and broadens tissue, especially when combined with Swedish gymnastics (joint mobilization and stretches). These changes are detected by Golgi tendon organs, which inhibit a contraction signal, further lengthening muscles. Massage retrains the tissue from a contracted state to an elongated state, increasing resting length. This is one of the principles behind neuromuscular re-education.

☐ **Increases flexibility.** By lengthening muscles and promoting muscular relaxation, massage has also been shown to increase muscle flexibility.

☐ **Tones weak muscles.** Muscle spindle activity is increased during massage strokes (e.g., tapotement, vibration). An increase in muscle spindle activity creates muscle contractions, helping tone weak muscles. This effect is particularly beneficial in cases of prolonged bed rest, flaccidity, and atrophy.

☐ **Reduces creatine kinase activity in the blood.** Creatine kinase is an enzyme that helps ensure enough adenosine triphosphate (ATP) is available for muscle contraction. By

---

Mini-Lab 16-2
SELF-ADMINISTERED MASSAGE

Sit in a chair with your feet flat on the floor. Moving only your head and neck, look over your left shoulder, and notice how far you can comfortably move. Do the same, looking to the right. Take your right hand and grab the top of your right shoulder. As you apply pressure, slowly move the shoulder up and down ten times. Maintain the pressure, and roll your shoulder back ten times, then forward ten times. Do this same movement with the left shoulder. Squeeze the back of your neck. Without releasing the pressure, turn your head (as if saying no), nod your head (as if saying yes), and circle your nose clockwise and counterclockwise 10 times each. After the "squeeze and move" activity, look over your right and left shoulders again. Notice how much farther you can go. This increase is the result of self-administered massage.

reducing the activity of creatine kinase in the blood, massage indirectly helps decrease muscle contraction and therefore increase muscle relaxation.

- **Improves muscular nutrition.** As a result of an increase in blood-transported nutrients, massage improves muscular nutrition. This hastens muscle recovery and enables muscles to function at maximum capacity after recovery.
- **Decreases electromyography (EMG).** This signifies a decrease in neuromuscular activity and a reduction of neuromuscular complaints.

EFFECTS OF MASSAGE ON CONNECTIVE TISSUES

- **Reduces keloid formation.** Massage applied to scar tissue helps reduce keloid formation in scar tissue.
- **Reduces excessive scar formation.** Deep massage reduces excessive scar formation, helping create an appropriate scar that is strong yet does not interfere with the muscle's ability to broaden as it contracts.
- **Decreases adhesion formation.** The displacement of scar tissue during massage helps reduce formation of adhesions. This, in turn, facilitates normal, pain-free motion of the affected muscles and joints.
- **Releases fascial restrictions.** Pressure and the heat it produces converts fascia from a gel-state to a sol-state (thixotropy), reducing

---

FYI 16–1
For Your Information

The pain-cycle is initiated when painful stimuli result in reflex muscle contraction and localized muscle splinting or guarding. The localized muscle guarding restricts movement and decreases local circulation, which restricts the amount of oxygen available to the tissues and the removal of metabolic wastes. The subsequent swelling creates more pain. From this point, muscle splinting is intensified and the cycle repeats itself. A more generalized secondary pain results that outlasts or exceeds the original discomfort. Massage interrupts the pain cycle on all levels.

---

hyperplasia. Fascia loosens and melts, becoming more flexible and elastic. Softening of the fascia surrounding muscles allows them to be stretched to their fullest resting length, increasing joint range of motion, and freeing the body of restricted movements.

- **Increases mineral retention in bone.** Massage increases the retention of nutrients such as nitrogen, sulfur, and phosphorus in bones.
- **Promotes fracture healing.** When a bone is fractured, the body forms a network of new blood vessels at the break site. Massage increases circulation around the fracture, promoting fracture healing. Increased circulation around a fracture leads to increased deposition of callus to the bone. Callus is formed between and around the broken ends of a fractured bone during healing, and is ultimately replaced by compact bone.
- **Improves connective tissue healing.** Occurring only with deep pressure massage, proliferation and activation of fibroblasts was noted. Fibroblasts generate connective tissue matrix, which promotes tissue healing by increasing collagen production and increasing the tensile strength of healed tissue.
- **Reduces surface dimpling of cellulite.** Massage flattens out adipose globules located under the skin and makes the skin seem smoother. Cellulite, a type of adipose tissue, appears as groups of small dimples or depressions under the skin, caused by an uneven separation of fat globules below the skin's surface, which are displaced by manual manipulation. Massage does not reduce the amount of cellulite below the skin; instead, it temporarily alters the shape and appearance of cellulite.

EFFECTS OF MASSAGE ON THE RESPIRATORY SYSTEM

- **Reduces respiration rate.** Massage slows down the rate of respiration because of activation of the relaxation response.
- **Strengthens respiratory muscles.** The muscles of respiration have a greater capacity to contract, helping improve pulmonary functions.
- **Decreases the sensation of dyspnea.** Dyspnea is shortness of breath or difficult breathing, and is lessened as a result of massage.

☐ **Decreases asthma attacks.** Through increased relaxation and improved pulmonary functions, the client experiences fewer asthma attacks.

☐ **Reduces laryngeal tension.** Laryngeal tension may occur from excessive public speaking or singing. Massage reduces the stress on the larynx and tension on the muscles of the throat.

☐ **Increases fluid discharge from the lungs.** The mechanical loosening and discharge of phlegm in the respiratory tract increases with rhythmic alternating pressures. Tapotement (cupping) and vibration on the rib cage are often used to enhance this effect. Phlegm loosening and discharge is further enhanced when combined with postural drainage (promoting fluid drainage of the respiratory tract through certain body positions) and when the client is encouraged to cough.

☐ **Improves pulmonary functions.** Relaxation plays a big role in how massage improves pulmonary function, but massage also loosens tight respiratory muscles and fascia. The affected pulmonary functions are as follows:

☐ **Increased vital capacity.** This is the amount of air that can be expelled at the normal rate of exhalation after a maximum inhalation, representing the greatest possible breathing capacity.

☐ **Increased forced vital capacity.** This is the amount of air that can be forcibly expelled after a forced inhalation.

☐ **Increased forced expiratory volume.** This is the volume of air that can be forcibly expelled after a full exhalation.

☐ **Increased forced expiratory flow.** This is the volume of air that can be forcibly expelled after a full inhalation.

☐ **Improved peak expiratory flow.** This is the greatest rate of airflow that can be achieved during forced expiration beginning with the lungs fully inflated.

EFFECTS OF MASSAGE ON THE DIGESTIVE SYSTEM

☐ **Promotes evacuation of the colon.** By increasing peristaltic activity in the colon through massage, bowel contents move toward the anus for elimination.

☐ **Relieves constipation.** Because evacuation of the colon is promoted, constipation is relieved.

☐ **Relieves colic and intestinal gas.** Increased peristaltic activity also helps relieve colic and the expulsion of intestinal gas.

☐ **Stimulates digestion.** Massage also promotes activation of the parasympathetic nervous system, which stimulates digestion.

EFFECTS OF MASSAGE ON THE URINARY SYSTEM

☐ **Increases urine output.** Massage activates dormant capillary beds and recovers lymphatic fluids for filtration by the kidney. This in turn increases the frequency of urination and amount of urine produced. Massage is also relaxing. This promotes general homeostasis and increases urine output.

☐ **Promotes the excretion of nitrogen, inorganic phosphorus, and sodium chloride in urine.** Levels of these metabolic wastes are elevated in urine after massage.

MISCELLANEOUS EFFECTS OF MASSAGE

In various research studies, the following effects were noted:

☐ **Reduces fatigue and increases vigor.** Many clients experienced a sense of renewed energy after massage by taking a break from the stresses of the day.

☐ **Improves sleep patterns.** When clients went to sleep, they reported a deeper sleep and felt more rested upon waking.

☐ **Reduces job related and post-traumatic stress.** Massage reduces many types of stress. In particular, job related stress and post-traumatic stress decreased after massage.

☐ **Improves mood.** The mental health status and mood improved in the subjects of the experimental (massaged) group.

☐ **Decreases feelings of anger.** Clients reported a decrease in aggression and feelings of anger with massage.

☐ **Improves body image.** Massage improved body image in clients who stated having a poor body image prior to the massage session.

☐ **Improves self-esteem.** Individuals who received and who gave massages reported enhanced self-esteem.

☐ **Promotes communication and expression.** Individuals who received and gave massages reported an increase in the quantity and quality of their social interactions. They talked more freely and openly and enjoyed themselves more during these social interactions. Massage can also assist the ease of emotional expression through relaxation.

☐ **Improves lifestyle habits.** Following massage, clients reported improved lifestyle habits such as increased activities of daily living (ADLs), fewer cups of coffee, fewer somatic symptoms, fewer doctor visits, and increased levels of exercising (walking).

☐ **Increases physical well-being.** Massage enhances well-being through stress reduction and subsequent relaxation.

☐ **Reduces touch aversion and touch sensitivity.** Massage given to victims of rape and spousal abuse reported a reduction in touch aversion. Hypersensitivity to touch was reduced in other individuals.

☐ **Increases academic performance.** A decrease in math computation time and an increase in math accuracy were noted in massage studies.

☐ **Increases mental alertness.** Massage increases mental alertness by relaxing the body/mind and by removing unwanted stress.

☐ **Satisfies emotional needs.** Clients reported using the therapeutic relationship to satisfy their emotional needs for attention, acceptance, caring, and nurturing touch, which were not being met through their other relationships.

"You can be born with a talent. But you have to acquire a craft to know how to use that talent."
—SID CAESAR

INDICATIONS OF MASSAGE FOR SPECIFIC CONDITIONS AND SPECIFIC INDIVIDUALS

Massage is a relatively low-risk form of therapy. Massage is contraindicated for several conditions, and these are listed later in the chapter. In general, massage is beneficial for just about every other condition that does not fall into the contraindication category. It would be almost impossible to list all the conditions for which massage is indicated. This section focuses on a few conditions that have been scientifically documented to benefit from massage.

☐ **Alzheimer's disease.** Massage decreased physical expressions of agitation (e.g., pacing, wandering) and improved sleep patterns.

☐ **Anemia.** An increase in RBCs and an increase in oxygen saturation in the blood suggest that massage is beneficial for individuals with anemia.

☐ **Asthma.** It was found that massage improved pulmonary functions, and reduced the occurrence of asthma attacks.

☐ **Attention deficit hyperactivity disorder (ADHD).** Individuals diagnosed with ADHD who received massage were observed to be less fidgety and hyperactive, and spent more time completing assigned tasks.

☐ **Autism.** Massaged autistic children spent less time in solitary play and had an increase in attention to sounds and their social relatedness to their teachers. Autistic behavior such as touch aversion was reduced.

☐ **Burn victims.** Burn victims who were massaged experienced a decrease in pain and itching and reduced anxiety before débridement. Massage also lowered feelings of depression and anger.

☐ **Cancer.** Lymphedema, pain, anxiety, and feelings of anger and depression were reduced when cancer patients had routine massages. Massage also increased lymphocyte and natural killer cell counts.

☐ **Cerebral palsy (CP).** Massage promotes circulation of blood and lymph and relieves muscular tension in individuals with CP. Increases in flexibility were also reported.

☐ **Chronic fatigue syndrome (CFS).** Clients with CFS experience reduced feelings of depression and anxiety and fewer somatic symptoms such as fatigue. CFS affects muscle strength; improved grip strength was also documented for clients receiving massages.

☐ **Constipation.** Elimination problems were relieved through massage.

☐ **Diabetes.** Blood glucose levels, anxiety, and depression were reduced with massage. An increase in dietary compliance was also reported.

☐ **Eating disorders.** Anorexia nervosa and bulimia nervosa patients stated a reduction of depression and anxiety. These individuals stated that they experienced an improvement in eating habits and an increase in positive body image with regular massage treatments.

- **Fibromyalgia.** Not only were stress, anxiety, and feelings of depression reduced with massage, but decreases in pain, stiffness, fatigue, and insomnia were documented in individuals with fibromyalgia. Massage was rated more effective than standard physical therapy or prescriptive drugs.

- **Headaches.** Most headaches (muscular, cluster, eye strain, mental fatigue, and sinus) were relieved with massage. Subjects also reported more headache-free days and less analgesic use as a result of pain reduction.

- **High blood pressure.** Massage decreased blood pressure (both systolic and diastolic readings) and helped promote healthy lifestyle habits in patients with hypertension.

- **Individuals infected with the human immunodeficiency virus (HIV).** The number of natural killer cells and their ability to fight pathogens increased after massage. Massage also helped individuals infected with HIV to relax.

- **Hospitalized and hospice patients.** Postoperative pain was reduced and patients had a decline in heart rate and blood pressure, indicating decreased stress and anxiety. Hospice patients experienced the same effects.

- **Infants.** Preterm, cocaine-exposed, HIV-exposed, and full-term infants experienced less colic, less repetitive crying, improved feeding habits, and gained more weight than non-massaged infants in the same categories. Massage was found more effective than rocking for inducing infant sleep.

- **Injuries.** Massage speeds the healing of overuse injuries, sprains, and strains.

- **Insomnia.** Insomnia is alleviated by inducing relaxation.

- **Low back pain.** Low back pain is decreased by addressing trigger points. Medical costs were reduced by about 40% along with reduced analgesic use. Massage increased range of motion and promoted relaxation. Patients reported that massage made them feel cared for, happy, physically relaxed, less anxious, calm, restful, and gave them a feeling of closeness with the individuals who gave massages. Massage was rated more effective than standard physical therapy or prescriptive drugs.

- **Lung disease.** For clients with chronic obstructive pulmonary disease (COPD), massage strengthened respiratory muscles, reduced heart rate, increased oxygen saturation in blood, decreased shortness of breath, and improved pulmonary functions. Respiratory drainage is encouraged through cupping tapotement and vibration. Clients with cystic fibrosis further reported decreased anxiety and improved mood with massage treatments.

- **Lymphedema.** Swelling resulting from lymphedema was reduced with massage if it was not a result of inflammation or disease. Edema resulting from traumatic inflammation may be aided with techniques such as centripetally applied effleurage.

- **Multiple sclerosis (MS).** Individuals with MS who received massages experienced reduced anxiety and depression, improved self-esteem and positive body image, and implemented changes to their lifestyle that promoted health such as exercising and stretching.

- **Nerve entrapment.** Conditions of nerve entrapment that occur when soft tissues constrict the nerve, such as carpal tunnel syndrome, thoracic outlet syndrome, and sciatica, were relieved by release of the myofascial component.

- **Poor circulation.** Massage improved blood circulation.

- **Pregnancy and postpartum.** Massaged pregnant women reported fewer obstetric and postpartum complications, reduced prematurity rates, shorter and less painful labors, and fewer days in hospital after labor and delivery. When nurses, midwives, or spouses massaged the pregnant or laboring women's perineal area, injury such as tearing during fetal delivery was reduced. Feelings of postpartum depression declined with massage. Depressed adolescent mothers reported less stress, anxiety, and depression. These were supported by a reduction in stress hormones in the blood.

- **Premenstrual syndrome.** Massage reduced swelling, reduced pain and anxiety, and improved the mood of women experiencing premenstrual syndrome.

- **Psychiatric patients.** Child, adolescent, and adult psychiatric patients were observed to be better adapted to a group and the medical staff reported better clinical progress with massage treatments. A decrease in depression and anxiety was noted with reduced cortisol levels and norepinephrine blood levels and increased dopamine levels. In many individuals, a decrease in self-destructive behavior was reported and the mental health status in the subjects of the massaged group improved. A decrease in the episodes of dysfunctional behavior was found in patients with dementia.

☐ **Rheumatoid arthritis (RA).** Massage reduced trigger point formation, pain, anxiety, and morning stiffness in individuals with adult and juvenile RA.

☐ **Skin conditions.** Skin problems such as mild dryness and itching were alleviated by massage because of the increase of sebum production and blood circulation.

☐ **Stress and anxiety.** Stress and anxiety are reduced by activation of the parasympathetic nervous system and promotion of the relaxation response.

☐ **Temporomandibular joint (TMJ) dysfunction.** The muscular component of TMJ dysfunction was addressed with massage and reduced pain and dysfunction was the result.

Once the benefits and indications of massage are known, an understanding of contraindications and endangerment sites becomes clear. For instance, by increasing lymph circulation, massage affects the tissue and fluids of the body; because massage increases the circulation of blood, thrombosis must be a contraindication.

CONTRAINDICATIONS FOR MASSAGE THERAPY

This section considers pathologies and symptoms that may contraindicate massage. The professional therapist exercises caution under certain conditions. During the intake process before treatment begins, the therapist conducts a consultation with the client to establish goals, note precautions, and determine any preexisting conditions that might affect treatment. It is the duty and obligation of the therapist to rule out the presence of any conditions in which massage may have harmful effects. However, if the client refuses to disclose his or her medical history, the therapist has the right to refuse treatment.

It is highly recommended that the massage therapist postpone treatment with anyone under the influence of prescription or over-the-counter (OTC) drugs that reduce pain, alcoholic beverages, or any other substance that would inhibit or distort the client's response or ability to give feedback regarding discomfort or pain during treatment.

The two categories of contraindications are *absolute* and *local*. Conditions in which massage is inappropriate, is not advised, and may be harmful to the client are known as absolute contraindications. It is rare that a physician would order massage under these conditions, but some exceptions occur. Note that absolute contraindications are typically contagious viral or bacterial pathologies or chronic ailments in which massage would better serve the client if the ailment were in remission. A physician's clearance is advised. Some of these conditions are so severe that the patient may be hospitalized.

A few contraindications for massage that have been followed by massage therapists for decades are controversial, such as varicose veins and cancer. Physician research refutes the need to consider these two pathologies contradictions to massage. No research currently links massage to increasing varicosities. In fact, massage helps empty veins, aiding circulation. No reported cases exist in which massage has worsened the status of cancer patients. Research proves that massage decreases lymphedema, increases natural killer cell count, and promotes relaxation, which is important because stress impairs immune responses. More research is needed with regard to contraindications. A pathology book may need to be consulted because many conditions have both a common name, such as *boil*, and a medical name, such as *furuncle*.

Many pathologies are local contraindications in which massage can be administered while avoiding the infected area or area in question. These conditions or situations merit caution and adaptive measures to ensure that the massage is safely administered. Each situation must be assessed before a decision is made to either avoid the area or postpone the massage. If a mutual decision has been made to continue with the massage, the therapist should be fastidious about using a closed dispenser of lubricant to prevent cross contamination. Many pathologies can be spread if they are accidentally touched during the massage.

For many conditions massage is fine, but a physician must be consulted. Obtain the physician's "okay" and ask if there are any modifications that can be applied to the client's treatment. Much will depend on the client's vitality. Box 16-1 contains a list of pathologies grouped into three categories: conditions that require a physician's clearance before treatment, local contraindications, and absolute contraindications. Consult a massage and pathology text for further reading.

Some conditions just require adaptive measures to position the client comfortably, reduce pressure, shorten the length of treatment, or increase the frequency of treatments. Examples of adaptive massage are working with pregnant clients or with clients who are chronically ill.

Exercise good judgment and use common sense when identifying these situations. After determining contraindications, you may decide to refer your client to a personal physician for further evaluation and treatment recommendations. As a rule, the therapist should be conservative. If any doubt about a specific condition or injury is evident, ask the client to obtain written medical clearance from a personal physician.

During the massage, monitor the client's response continuously. If the client reports that pain has increased either during or after the massage session, modify or discontinue the massage treatments until further evaluation. If the client becomes ill or nauseated, discontinue treatment immediately.

Box 16-1 Pathologies and Massage Contraindications

Conditions That Require Physician Clearance
- Acromegaly
- Aneurysm
- Atherosclerosis
- Burns
- Cancer
- Cerebrovascular accident
- Chronic obstructive pulmonary disease
- Congestive heart failure
- Coronary artery disease
- Hemophilia
- Hodgkin's disease
- Kidney stones
- Leukemia
- Myasthenia gravis
- Nephrosis
- Peritonitis
- Polycystic kidney disease
- Shingles*
- Uremia

Conditions With Local Contraindications
- Abdominal diastasis (avoid abdomen)
- Abnormal lumps (avoid area)
- Acne vulgaris (avoid infected area)
- Athlete's foot (avoid infected area)
- Blister (avoid area)
- Bruise (avoid bruised area if less than 72 hours old)
- Carpal tunnel syndrome (avoid inflamed area)
- Colitis (avoid abdomen)
- Cretinism (avoid throat area)
- Crohn's disease (avoid abdomen)
- Cystitis (avoid abdomen)

- Decubitus ulcers (avoid ulcerated area)
- Diverticular diseases (avoid abdomen)
- Folliculitis (avoid infected area)
- Foreign objects embedded in the skin such as glass, pencil lead, and metal (avoid area)
- Furuncle/carbuncle (avoid infected area)
- Goiter (avoid throat area)
- Gouty arthritis (avoid infected area)
- Graves' disease (avoid throat region and any enlarged lymph nodes)
- Hernia such as hiatal, femoral, inguinal, and umbilical (avoid herniated area)
- Herpes simplex (avoid infected area)
- Hyperthyroidism (avoid throat area)
- Hypothyroidism (avoid throat area)
- Impetigo (avoid infected area)
- Irritable bowel syndrome (avoid abdomen)
- Local inflammation (avoid inflamed area)
- Onychomycosis (avoid infected area)
- Open wounds (avoid wounded area)
- Paronychia (avoid infected area)
- Phlebitis (lightly over affected area)
- Polyps (avoid abdomen)
- Poison ivy, poison oak, poison sumac (unless affected area is widespread, in which case this is an absolute contraindication)
- (Seborrheic keratosis (avoid infected area)
- Shingles (avoid infected area)*
- Spina bifida (avoid lumbosacral area)
- Swollen lymph glands (avoid swollen area)
- Thrombophlebitis (lightly over affected area; avoid inner thigh region)

*If you, the therapist, have not had the chicken pox, do not massage; it is a contraindication for you.

"It is the heart that understands and the hand that soothes."
—MARTHA ROGERS

ENDANGERMENT SITES

Endangerment sites are areas of the body that contain superficial delicate anatomical structures that are relatively unprotected and are therefore prone to injury. These sites merit caution during treatment. Often, the therapist simply adjusts pressure or avoids sustained pressure. Endangerment sites include such structures as nerves, blood vessels, organs, small or prominent bony projections, and any abnormalities such as cysts. These areas may be treated during a massage session, and often are, but caution must be exercised, working slowly, lightly, and carefully when in or around these sites. Exceptions to this rule would be energy work and techniques with which little or no pressure is used, such as therapeutic touch.

This section examines types of endangerment sites and why caution is warranted. In the next section, areas of the body where most endangerment sites exist will be identified.

☐ **Nerves.** When nerves are compressed during massage, the client may experience numbness, tingling, burning, or shooting pain. It is doubtful that this will damage the nerve, but it may alarm your client or make him or her feel uncomfortable. If the pressure is

---

Box 16-1   Pathologies and Massage Contraindications—cont'd

- Ulcers (avoid abdomen)
- Unhealed burns and abrasions (avoid injured area)
- Urinary incontinence (avoid abdomen)
- Urinary tract infection (avoid abdomen)
- Varicose veins (lightly over affected area)
- Wart (avoid infected area)

Conditions With Absolute Contraindications
- Appendicitis
- Autoimmune diseases or acute inflammatory processes during exacerbation period (or flare-up)
- Cardiac arrest
- Chickenpox
- Cholecystitis (during flare-up)
- Cirrhosis of the liver (if due to viral agent)
- Contact dermatitis (if widespread area is involved)
- Diarrhea (if due to infection)
- Embolism
- Encephalitis
- Fever
- Gallstones (if during a gallbladder attack)
- German measles
- Gout (during acute phase)
- Hemorrhage
- Hepatitis (during acute phase)
- Hives (during acute phase)
- Hypertension (if not controlled by diet, exercise, and/or medication)
- Infectious diseases (many are contained in this list)
- Inflammation
- Influenza
- Intestinal obstruction
- Jaundice
- Laryngitis (if caused by infectious agent)

- Lice
- Lupus (during a flare-up)
- Measles
- Meningitis
- Migraine headache (during the migraine headache episode)
- Mononucleosis
- Multiple sclerosis (during flare-up)
- Mumps
- Pancreatitis (if acute pancreatitis)
- Pericarditis
- Pharyngitis (if due to infection)
- Pleurisy (if caused by infectious agent)
- Pneumonia (during acute phase)
- Preeclampsia
- Psychiatric diagnoses of manic depressive psychosis, schizophrenic psychosis, and paranoid conditions
- Pulmonary embolism
- Pyelonephritis
- Rabies
- Recent injury (wait 72 hours or until medical clearance is given)
- Recent surgery (until medical clearance is given)
- Respiratory distress syndrome
- Rheumatoid arthritis (during flare-up)
- Ringworm
- Scabies
- Scarlet fever
- Scleroderma (during flare-up)
- Severe, acute pain
- Sickle cell disease (during flare-up)
- Tonsillitis
- Tuberculosis

John F. Barnes, PT

"The master therapist is real, calm, nonjudgmental, intelligent, sensitive, strong yet flexible, supportive, compassionate, empathic, and joyful."

One of the major differences between myofascial release and many other forms of bodywork is that, at its best, it allows the therapist to bring more to the table. It is systematic, physiologically grounded, and intuitive without apology. Its founder, John Barnes, is a physical therapist and teacher who values a wide range of modalities like the work of Ida Rolf, Milton Trager, John Upledger, and Paul St. John.

Barnes's father died when he was 3, and he was raised by his mother. He remembers enjoying being alone in the forest and learning to be so quiet that the wildlife would venture out. He studied karate and, as a result, learned about the role of Qi. As a junior in high school, he knew he wanted to be a physical therapist.

With warm eyes, a burly build, and a full beard, he looks like the type to live in a log cabin and love nature and he does. He's been called an old soul and doesn't scoff at the label. He doesn't believe in assembly-line quick fixes. How could he? He knows how insidious pain can be.

As a teen, Barnes was weightlifting and couldn't get out of a dead squat, so he turned a backflip and landed on his tailbone with an extra 300 pounds to boot. It wasn't long afterward that his back locked up

Born February 3, 1939

just as he was about to kiss a girl he was crazy about. Nevertheless, he didn't pay much attention to his condition. He had youth on his side and charged on, until a skiing accident left him in worse condition. Surgery made a big difference, but the pain left an indelible scar.

Robert Calvert of *Massage Magazine* quotes Barnes as saying, "I don't really mean this should happen, but in a way, every physician or therapist should be severely injured, and not just hurt for a week or two or a month, but a couple years. It's a whole different story when you are a prisoner in your own body. I felt broken, and I was broken. It was a horrible, horrible experience."

Yet another injury led him to explore the advantage of alternative therapies that hadn't been offered in his traditional physical therapist training. He began to blend experience with principles from different disciplines and discovered how fascia and energy flow are connected. Basically, myofascial release is based on understanding the role of fascia, a web of inter-

prolonged, the client may experience a temporary loss of motor control.

☐ **Blood vessels.** Pressure applied to superficial blood vessels may cause a temporary reduction in blood flow and may possibly affect blood pressure. When massaging an area where a known or suspected superficial artery is present, apply light pressure and feel for a pulse. If a pulse is felt, avoid prolonged pressure on the specific pulse location. Veins are generally superficially located. Apply gliding movements such as effleurage centripetally (toward the center) to promote venous blood flow.

☐ Caution areas for arteries also include the neighboring veins of the same name with the exception of the aorta, the carotid artery, the great saphenous vein, and the jugular vein. Arteries and veins lie in proximity to

each other, and caution of one generally reflects caution of the other. Note that many of these endangerment sites are common pulse point locations.

☐ **Bony structures.** Compression of certain small, fragile, or prominent bony areas may cause pain, bruising of surface tissues and, in some cases, fracture of the bony projection.

☐ **Organs/glands.** Pressure or striking movements such as tapotement to the kidney or eye area may cause bruising, sharp pain, nausea, or temporary dysfunction. Swollen lymph nodes are also endangerment sites.

☐ **Abnormal findings.** Any abnormal findings such as suspicious lumps, masses, or moles are endangerment sites.

The following specific locations of each type of endangerment site can be located on the endangerment site map (Figure 16-1, A and B). All

John F. Barnes, PT—cont'd

connected tissue that travels the body without interruption. It surrounds individual cells, organs, systems, and then wraps it all up in one huge package, head to toe. This network also serves as the communication medium from cell to cell and organ to organ. Trauma, posture, or inflammation can change the consistency of the web, solidifying and shortening fibers and blocking the flow of messages that are necessary for homeostasis. This web, if pulled too tightly in one place, can leave other areas restricted, creating pressure on nerves, muscles, organs, and bones.

As a physical therapist, Barnes's style had always been focused, slow, and rhythmic. Sometimes his touch was light. Sometimes the tissue beneath his hands granted him deeper access. He didn't know he was practicing *myofascial release,* per se, until he attended a physicians' course on connective tissue. Afterward, he began to see and treat the interrelationship of the whole body (including the mind or spirit) rather than the isolated sore neck, bum knee, or other body part. This shift in thinking enhanced the results of his work, but stirred up emotions that demanded his attention. As his work evolved, so did Barnes. (The goal of myofascial release is not necessarily to incite emotional response, but considering the pervasive nature of the myofascial system and the complex nature of humans, many forms of bodywork are considered and may eventually be proved to be therapeutic for emotional and physical trauma.)

Barnes started teaching others his form of bodywork in the mid-1970s. His task begins by reawakening the therapist's ability to "feel" what is happening with the body. Then he teaches the techniques to evaluate and release restricted areas in a systematic way. In his opinion, a comprehensive program should also include exercise and flexibility programs, movement awareness facilitation techniques, instruction in body mechanics, mobilization and muscle energy techniques, nutritional advice, biofeedback, and psychological counseling.

Even with such a systematic and comprehensive approach, Barnes is realistic about results. Therapists do not "fix" clients. We can offer tools for change not only in the form of bodywork but also in "mindwork." When it gets right down to the nitty gritty, we can't help our clients unless they are ready to help themselves. That's a humbling thought, yet being proficient and humble is a good starting point.

Barnes's advice for beginning massage therapists is to continue learning advanced methods after graduating from the typical 500-hour program. Just reading about a bodywork concept or simply being introduced to a modality isn't sufficient to practice it successfully and in some cases may lead to learning bad habits or faulty techniques. Barnes suggests learning as many forms of bodywork as possible in order to adapt to the wide range of client needs.

---

endangerment sites are bilaterally symmetrical with the exception of those located on the midline of the body. Remember, you can and should work these areas, but be mindful of the following anatomical structures:

- □ **Abdomen.** The structures to be aware of regarding pressure in the abdomen include the abdominal and descending aorta, liver, linea alba (connective tissue band running down the abdominal wall; it can herniate), lumbar plexus, vagus nerve, and xiphoid process.
- □ **Axilla.** The axillary region contains several nerves and blood vessels that can become compressed during massage, such as the axillary and brachial arteries; axillary, median, musculocutaneous, radial, and ulnar nerves; and brachial plexus.
- □ **Elbow.** The areas of endangerment of the elbow are the brachial, radial, and ulnar

(antecubital) arteries; median (antecubital), radial (lateral epicondyles of the humerus), and ulnar (medial epicondyles of the humerus-ulnar notch) nerves, and cubital veins (antecubital).

- □ **Face.** Avoid direct pressure on the eyeball, facial arteries (alongside the upper and lower jaw), and transverse facial arteries (anterior to the ear).
- □ **Femoral triangle/medial thigh.** The borders of the femoral triangle are the gracilis, sartorius, and inguinal ligament. This area contains the femoral arteries and nerves, great saphenous veins, and obturator nerves.
- □ **Low back.** Do not get carried away with the striking tapotement or the electrical massager on the low back. Two structures to watch out for here are the floating ribs and kidneys (located retroperitoneally).

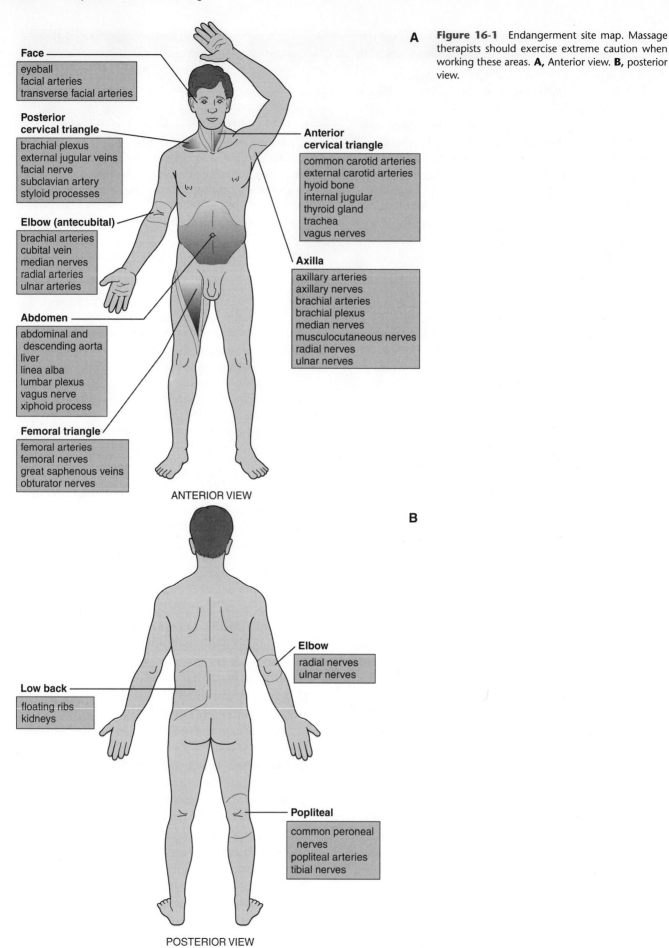

A **Figure 16-1** Endangerment site map. Massage therapists should exercise extreme caution when working these areas. **A,** Anterior view. **B,** posterior view.

Face
eyeball
facial arteries
transverse facial arteries

Posterior cervical triangle
brachial plexus
external jugular veins
facial nerve
subclavian artery
styloid processes

Elbow (antecubital)
brachial arteries
cubital vein
median nerves
radial arteries
ulnar arteries

Abdomen
abdominal and
 descending aorta
liver
linea alba
lumbar plexus
vagus nerve
xiphoid process

Femoral triangle
femoral arteries
femoral nerves
great saphenous veins
obturator nerves

Anterior cervical triangle
common carotid arteries
external carotid arteries
hyoid bone
internal jugular
thyroid gland
trachea
vagus nerves

Axilla
axillary arteries
axillary nerves
brachial arteries
brachial plexus
median nerves
musculocutaneous nerves
radial nerves
ulnar nerves

ANTERIOR VIEW

B

Elbow
radial nerves
ulnar nerves

Low back
floating ribs
kidneys

Popliteal
common peroneal
 nerves
popliteal arteries
tibial nerves

POSTERIOR VIEW

☐ **Popliteal.** Located behind the knee are the common peroneal and tibial nerves and the popliteal arteries.

☐ **Throat.** The throat region contains two triangular regions, the anterior and posterior cervical triangles. The **anterior cervical triangle,** whose defining borders are the trachea, base of the mandible, and sternocleidomastoid, contains seven endangerment sites, which are (1) the common carotid arteries, (2) external carotid arteries, (3) hyoid bone, (4) internal jugular veins, (5) thyroid gland, (6) trachea; and (7) vagus nerves. The **posterior cervical triangle,** which uses the clavicle, sternocleidomastoid, and trapezius as its defining borders, possesses the following endangerment sites: brachial plexus, external jugular veins, facial nerve (just posterior to the mandibular ramus), subclavian artery, and styloid processes of the temporal bone (located anterior to insertion of the sternocleidomastoid and posterior to the mandibular angle).

FYI 16–2 **For Your Information**
When in doubt, don't.

Chapter 17

Anatomy and Physiology

PLANES OF THE BODY

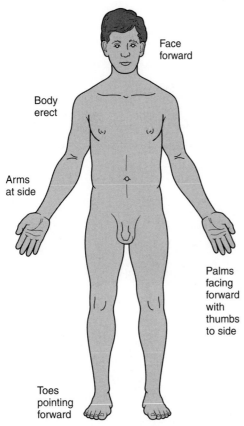

Face forward

Body erect

Arms at side

Palms facing forward with thumbs to side

Toes pointing forward

Figure 17-1 Anatomical position.

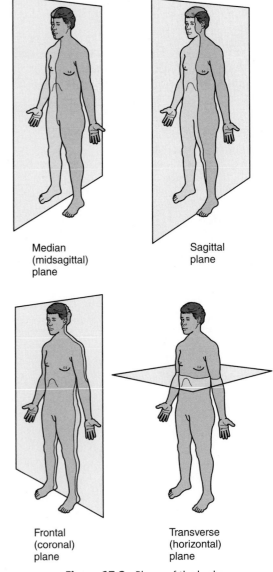

Median (midsagittal) plane

Sagittal plane

Frontal (coronal) plane

Transverse (horizontal) plane

Figure 17-2 Planes of the body.

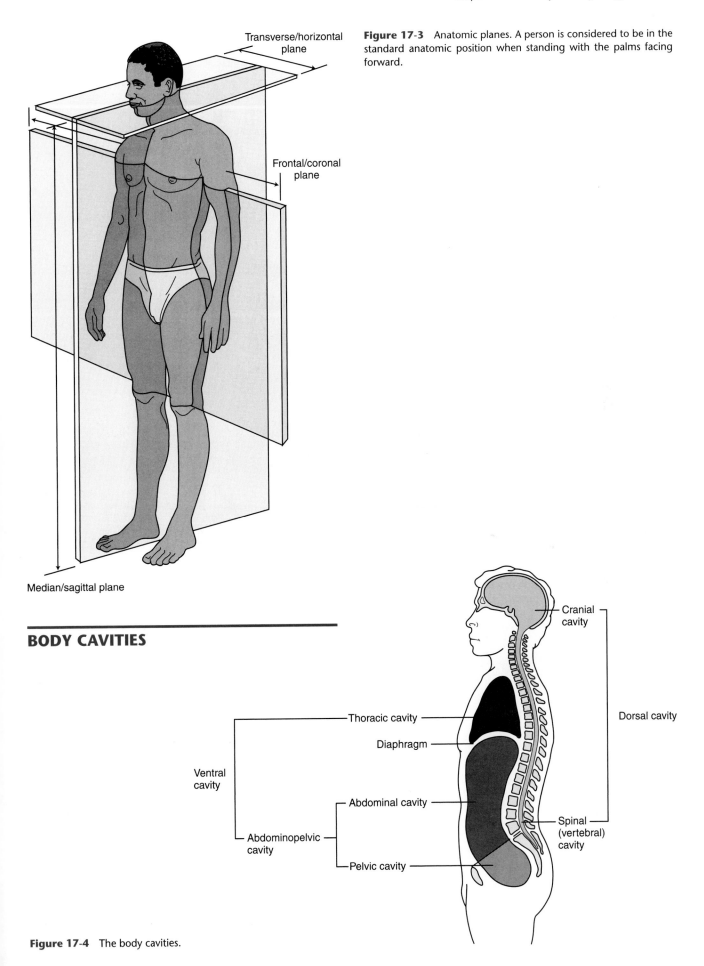

Transverse/horizontal plane

Figure 17-3 Anatomic planes. A person is considered to be in the standard anatomic position when standing with the palms facing forward.

Frontal/coronal plane

Median/sagittal plane

BODY CAVITIES

Thoracic cavity

Diaphragm

Ventral cavity

Abdominal cavity

Abdominopelvic cavity

Pelvic cavity

Cranial cavity

Dorsal cavity

Spinal (vertebral) cavity

Figure 17-4 The body cavities.

DIRECTIONAL TERMINOLOGY

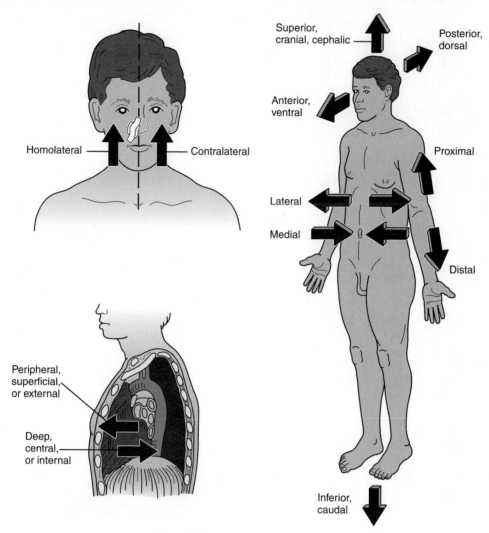

Figure 17-5   Directional terminology.

SKELETON

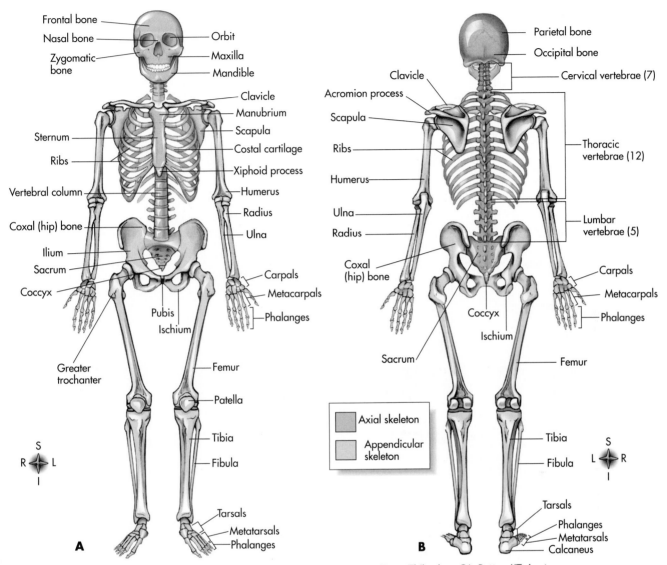

Figure 17-6   Skeleton. **A,** Anterior view. **B,** Posterior view. (From Thibodeau GA, Patton KT: Anatomy and physiology, ed 5, St Louis, 2003, Mosby.)

BONES AND BONY LANDMARKS

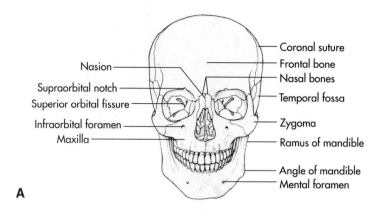

A

Coronal suture
Frontal bone
Nasal bones
Temporal fossa
Zygoma
Ramus of mandible
Angle of mandible
Mental foramen

Nasion
Supraorbital notch
Superior orbital fissure
Infraorbital foramen
Maxilla

Figure 17-7 **A,** Anterior (frontal) view of the skull. **B,** Posterior view of the skull. **C,** Detailed view of the base of the skull. The sphenoid, occipital, and temporal bones are presented as slightly separated to show that many of the important apertures traversing the floor of the skull are found within one of these bones or along their mutual borders. **D,** Basal view of the skull, showing several of the important foramina that convey nerves and vessels in and out of the cranial cavity. (From Mathers LH et al: Clinical anatomy principles, St. Louis, 1996, Mosby.)

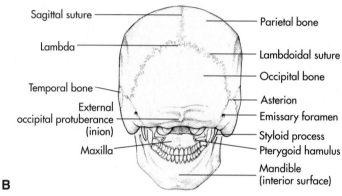

B

Sagittal suture
Lambda
Temporal bone
External occipital protuberance (inion)
Maxilla

Parietal bone
Lambdoidal suture
Occipital bone
Asterion
Emissary foramen
Styloid process
Pterygoid hamulus
Mandible (interior surface)

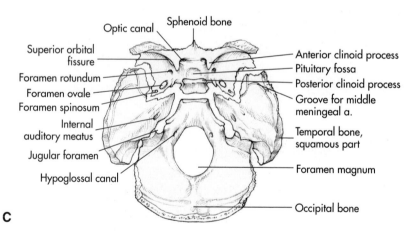

C

Optic canal
Sphenoid bone
Superior orbital fissure
Foramen rotundum
Foramen ovale
Foramen spinosum
Internal auditory meatus
Jugular foramen
Hypoglossal canal

Anterior clinoid process
Pituitary fossa
Posterior clinoid process
Groove for middle meningeal a.
Temporal bone, squamous part
Foramen magnum
Occipital bone

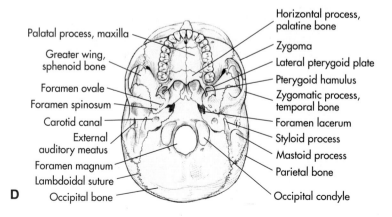

D

Palatal process, maxilla
Greater wing, sphenoid bone
Foramen ovale
Foramen spinosum
Carotid canal
External auditory meatus
Foramen magnum
Lambdoidal suture
Occipital bone

Horizontal process, palatine bone
Zygoma
Lateral pterygoid plate
Pterygoid hamulus
Zygomatic process, temporal bone
Foramen lacerum
Styloid process
Mastoid process
Parietal bone
Occipital condyle

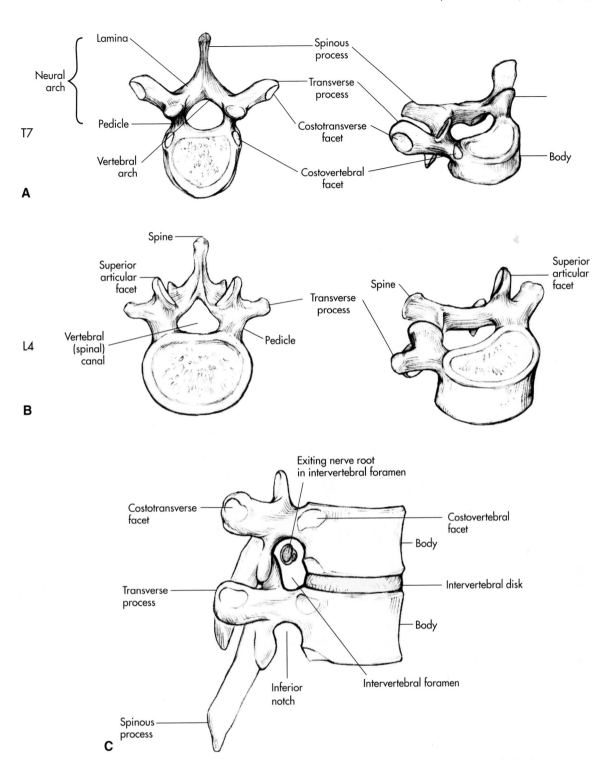

Figure 17-8   Common types of vertebrae (two views of T7 and L4 vertebrae). **A,** Superoinferior views. **B,** Right anterior oblique views. **C,** Intervertebral foramen. Vertebrae T5 and T6 have been articulated, showing the resulting intervertebral foramen with a segmental nerve in place. Blood vessels (not shown) enter and leave the interior of the vertebral canal through the intervertebral foramen. (From Mathers LH et al: Clinical anatomy principles, St. Louis, 1996, Mosby.)

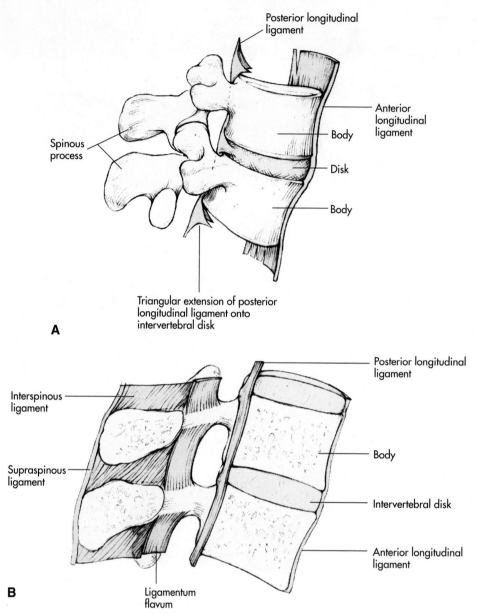

Posterior longitudinal ligament

Anterior longitudinal ligament

Body

Disk

Body

Spinous process

Triangular extension of posterior longitudinal ligament onto intervertebral disk

A

Posterior longitudinal ligament

Interspinous ligament

Supraspinous ligament

Body

Intervertebral disk

Anterior longitudinal ligament

Ligamentum flavum

B

Figure 17-9 Vertebral ligament. (From Mathers LH et al: Clinical anatomy principles, St. Louis, 1996, Mosby.)

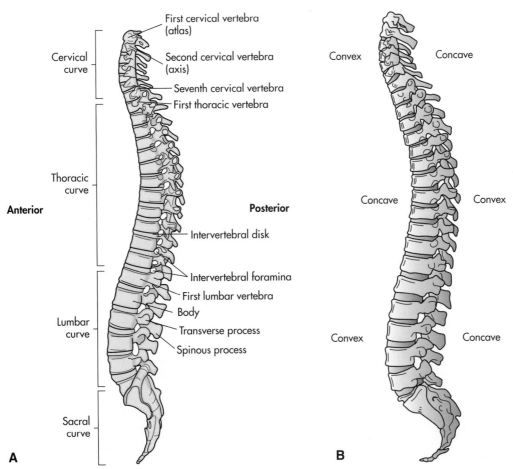

Cervical curve

First cervical vertebra (atlas)

Second cervical vertebra (axis)

Seventh cervical vertebra

First thoracic vertebra

Thoracic curve

Anterior

Posterior

Intervertebral disk

Intervertebral foramina

First lumbar vertebra

Body

Transverse process

Spinous process

Lumbar curve

Sacral curve

A

Convex   Concave

Concave   Convex

Convex   Concave

B

Figure 17-10   **A,** Vertebral column. **B,** The convex and concave curves of the vertebral column.

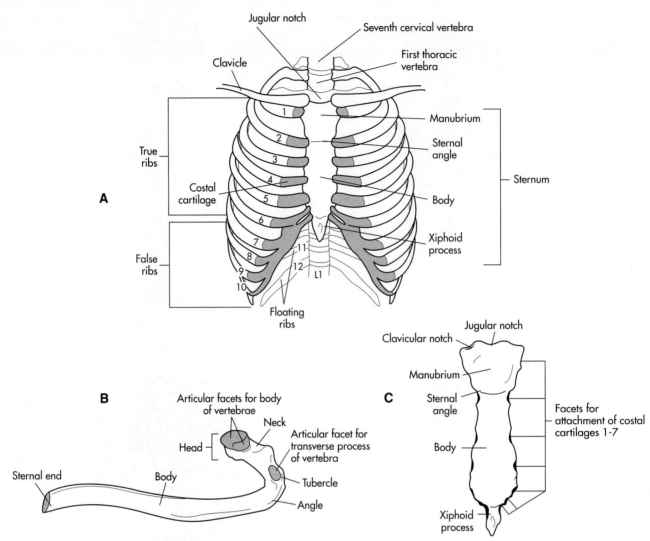

Figure 17-11 **A,** Rib cage. **B,** Typical rib. **C,** Sternum.

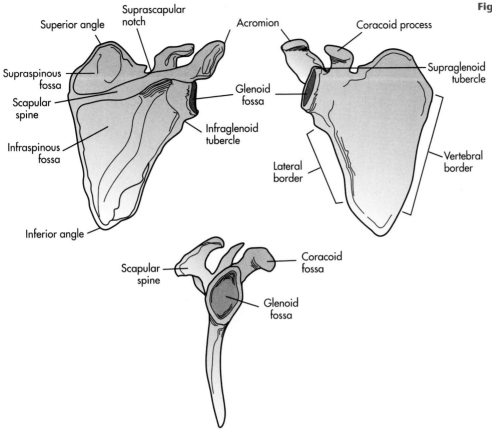

Figure 17-12   Scapula (three views).

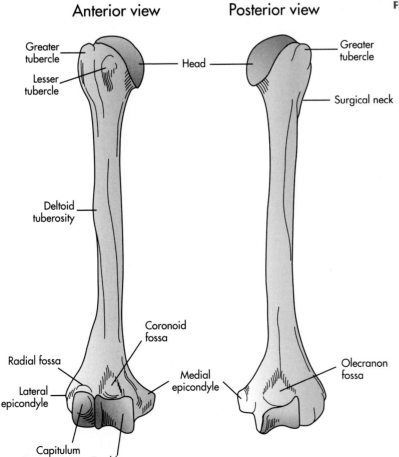

Anterior view   Posterior view

Figure 17-13   Humerus (anterior and posterior views).

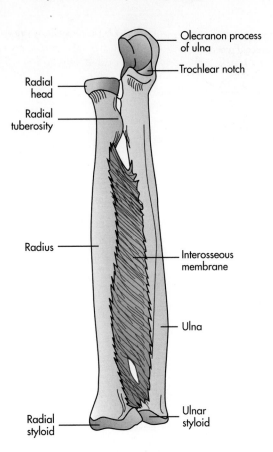

Olecranon process of ulna
Trochlear notch
Radial head
Radial tuberosity
Radius
Interosseous membrane
Ulna
Ulnar styloid
Radial styloid

Figure 17-14   Forearm bones.

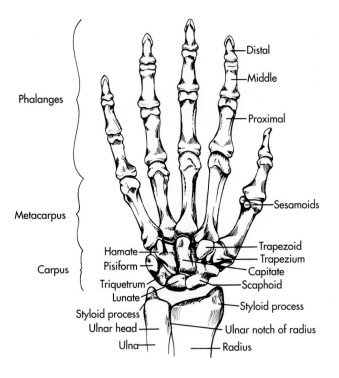

Distal
Middle
Proximal
Phalanges
Sesamoids
Metacarpus
Hamate
Trapezoid
Pisiform
Trapezium
Capitate
Triquetrum
Scaphoid
Lunate
Styloid process
Carpus
Styloid process
Ulnar head
Ulnar notch of radius
Ulna
Radius

Figure 17-15   Volar view of the bones of the hand. (From Malone TR, McPoil T, Nitz AJ: Orthopedic and sports physical therapy, ed 3, St Louis, 1996, Mosby.)

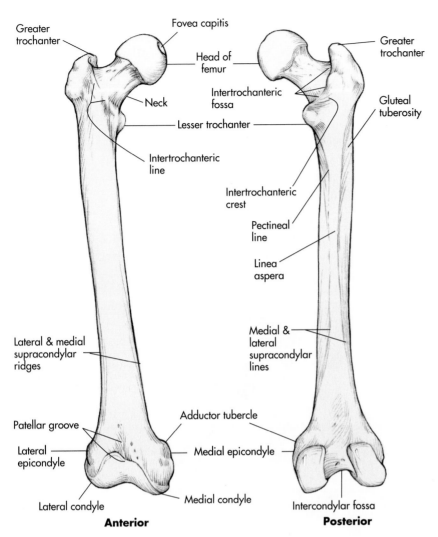

Greater trochanter

Fovea capitis

Head of femur

Neck

Lesser trochanter

Intertrochanteric line

Intertrochanteric fossa

Lateral & medial supracondylar ridges

Patellar groove

Lateral epicondyle

Lateral condyle

Adductor tubercle

Medial epicondyle

Medial condyle

Anterior

Greater trochanter

Gluteal tuberosity

Intertrochanteric crest

Pectineal line

Linea aspera

Medial & lateral supracondylar lines

Intercondylar fossa

Posterior

Figure 17-16   Femur (anterior and posterior views of the right femur). (From Mathers LH et al: Clinical anatomy principles, St. Louis, 1996, Mosby.)

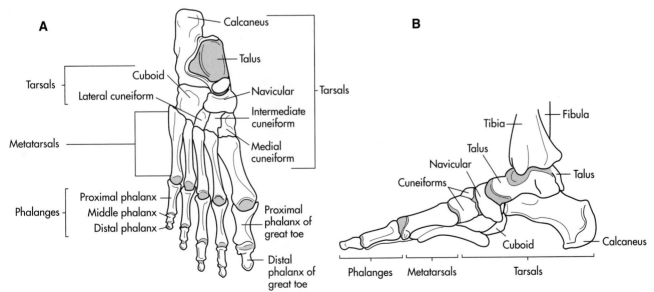

A

Tarsals

Metatarsals

Phalanges

Calcaneus

Talus

Cuboid

Lateral cuneiform

Navicular

Intermediate cuneiform

Medial cuneiform

Tarsals

Proximal phalanx

Middle phalanx

Distal phalanx

Proximal phalanx of great toe

Distal phalanx of great toe

B

Tibia

Fibula

Talus

Navicular

Cuneiforms

Talus

Cuboid

Calcaneus

Phalanges   Metatarsals   Tarsals

Figure 17-17   **A,** Dorsal view of the bones of the foot. **B,** Medial view of the bones of the foot and ankle.

MUSCULAR FIGURE

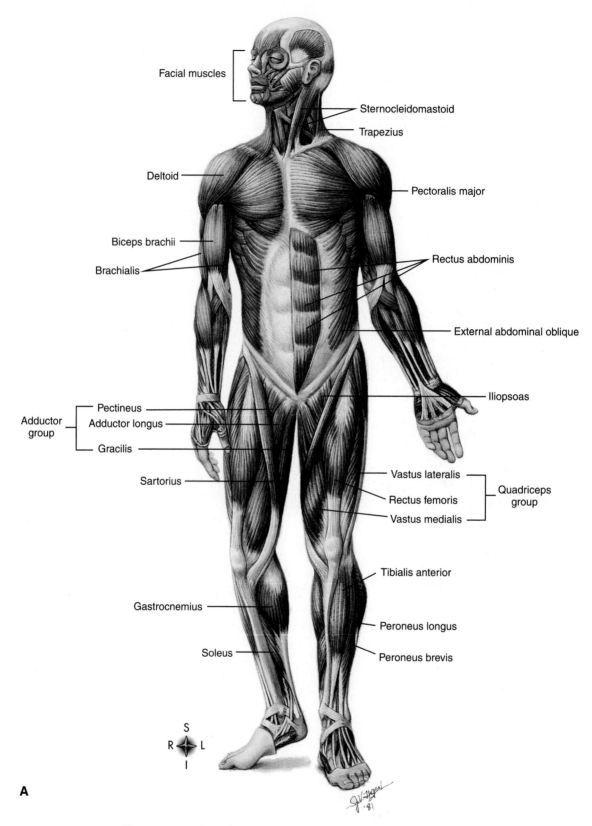

Figure 17-18   General overview of the body musculature. **A,** Anterior view.

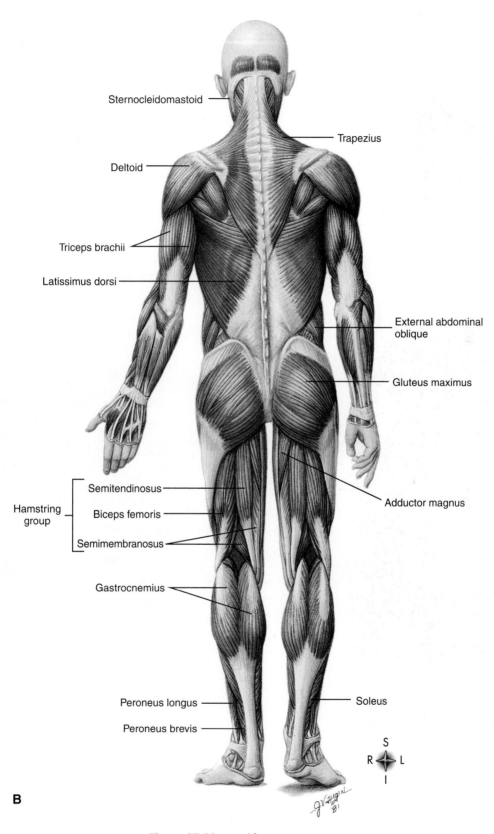

Sternocleidomastoid

Deltoid

Triceps brachii

Latissimus dorsi

Trapezius

External abdominal oblique

Gluteus maximus

Adductor magnus

Hamstring group
- Semitendinosus
- Biceps femoris
- Semimembranosus

Gastrocnemius

Peroneus longus

Peroneus brevis

Soleus

S
R ← → L
I

B

Figure 17-18, cont'd   B, Posterior view.

Chapter 18

Massage Therapy Procedures

TABLE HEIGHT

Figure 18-1 A typical portable massage table.

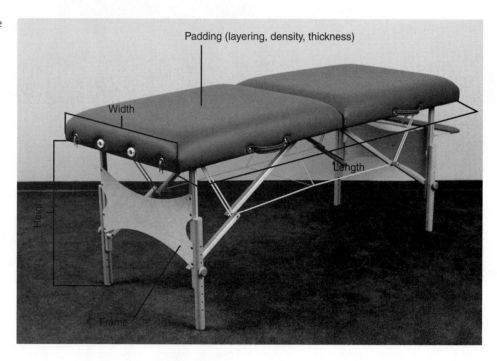

Padding (layering, density, thickness)

Width

Length

Height

Frame

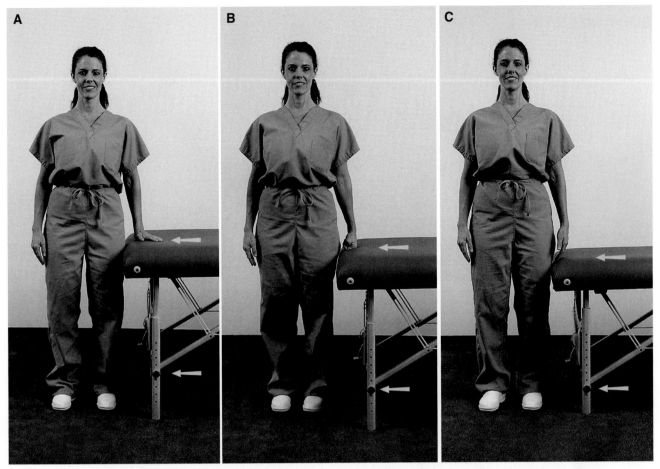

Figure 18-2   Three methods of determining the correct height for a massage table. **A,** Wrist extended 90 degrees with palm touching tabletop. **B,** Hand in a fist touching tabletop. **C,** Hand relaxed with fingertips touching tabletop.

BODY MECHANICS

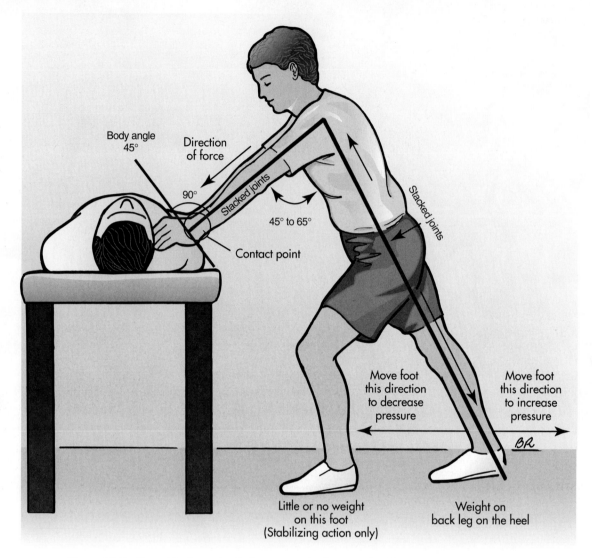

Figure 18-3 Correct body mechanics for compressive force required for massage.

Figure 18-4 Comparison of correct and incorrect body mechanics in two positions. **A,** Correct position using the hand. **B,** Incorrect position using the hand. **C,** Correct position using the forearm. **D,** Incorrect position using the forearm. Note the equilateral triangle formed by the hip, the axilla, and the client contact point in the correct positions.

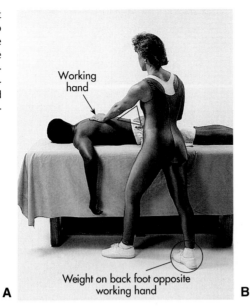

Working hand

Weight on back foot opposite working hand

A

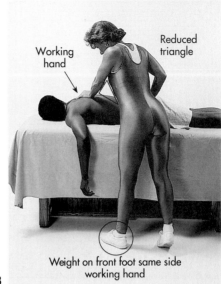

Working hand

Reduced triangle

Weight on front foot same side working hand

B

Working hand

Weight on front foot same side working hand

C

Working arm

Weight on back foot opposite working arm

D

Figure 18-5 Comparison of correct leaning position to apply compressive force to exert pressure. Exaggerated leaning position for emphasis in two positions: **A,** forearm and **B,** hand. When leaning correctly, the massage practitioner should be able to lift the front supportive leg from the floor and raise the opposite arm.

A

B

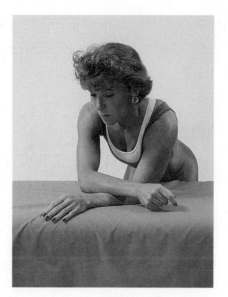

Figure 18-6   Self-massage.

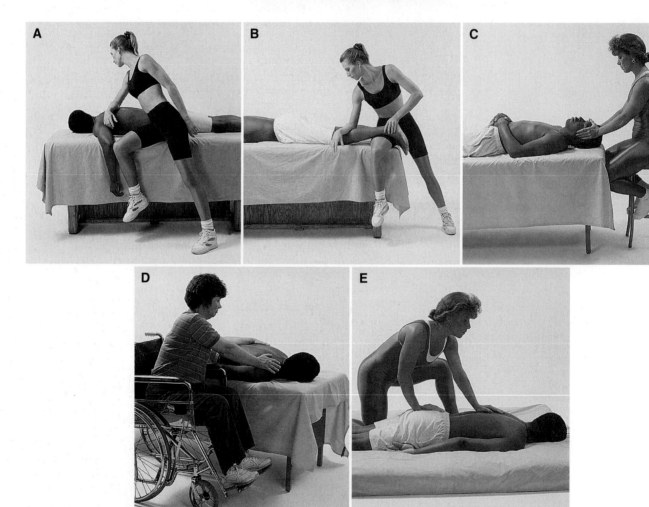

Figure 18-7   Various positions for use of tall tables, short tables, and massage mats. **A**, Tall table. **B**, Tall table with practitioner sitting on the end of the table. (Note: For **A** and **B** appropriate use of draping material is required for sanitary purposes when sitting on the massage table.) **C**, Short table with stool. **D**, Short table with practitioner using a chair. **E**, Massage mat.

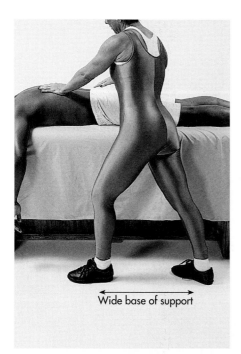

Figure 18-8 Practitioner's feet positioned to provide a wide base of support.

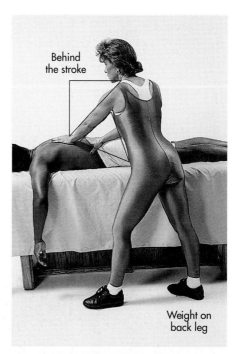

Figure 18-9 Correct position—weight on back leg. Wide base of support in asymmetric stance; equilateral triangles are maintained so that the practitioner stays behind the stroke.

Figure 18-10 Incorrect position—weight on front leg, moving the practitioner on top of the stroke and losing the triangles.

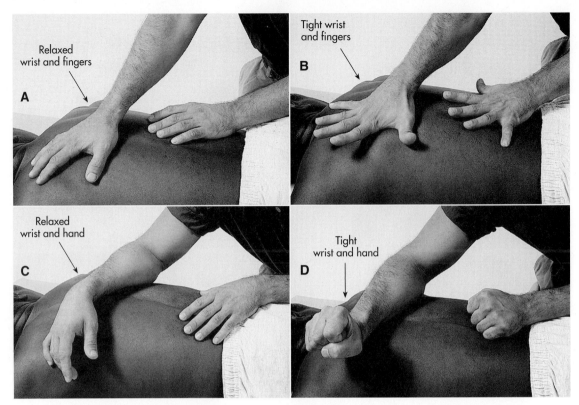

Figure 18-11   Comparison of correct and incorrect wrist and hand positions. **A,** Correct hand positions. **B,** Incorrect hand positions. **C,** Correct forearm position. **D,** Incorrect forearm position.

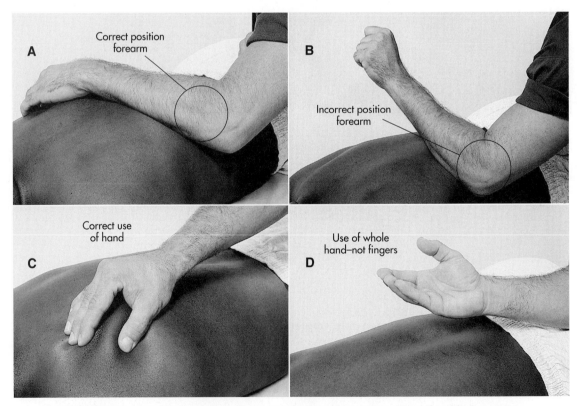

Figure 18-12   **A** and **B,** Comparison of correct and incorrect forearm positions. **C** and **D,** Demonstration of effective use of the whole hand to apply massage.

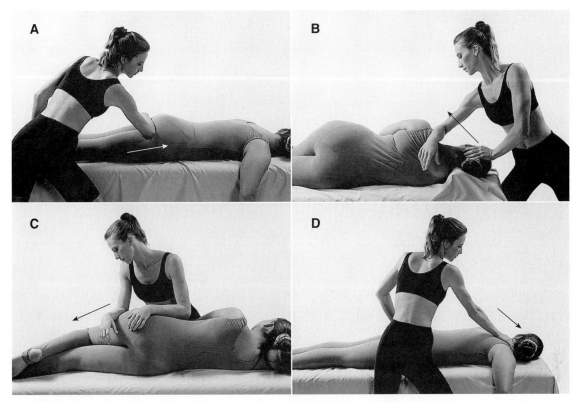

Figure 18-13 Examples of leaning uphill and sliding downhill. **A** and **B,** Correct leaning uphill to apply pressure. **C** and **D,** Correct sliding downhill without pressure as a focus to move to a different location on the body and maintain the flow of the massage.

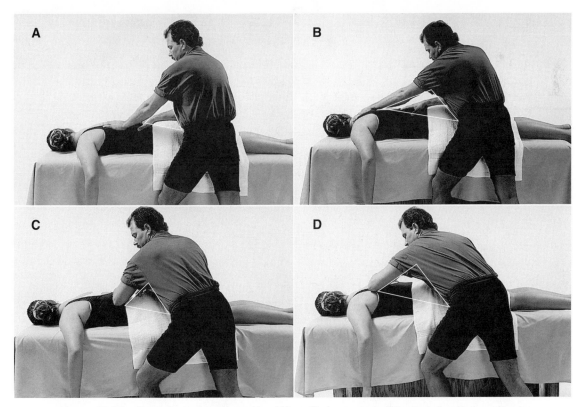

Figure 18-14 Comparison of correct position (45- to 60-degree angle of the stroke) and incorrect position (reaching for the stroke) in two positions—hand and forearm. **A,** Correct hand position. **B,** Incorrect hand position (reaching). **C,** Correct forearm position. **D,** Incorrect forearm position (reaching).

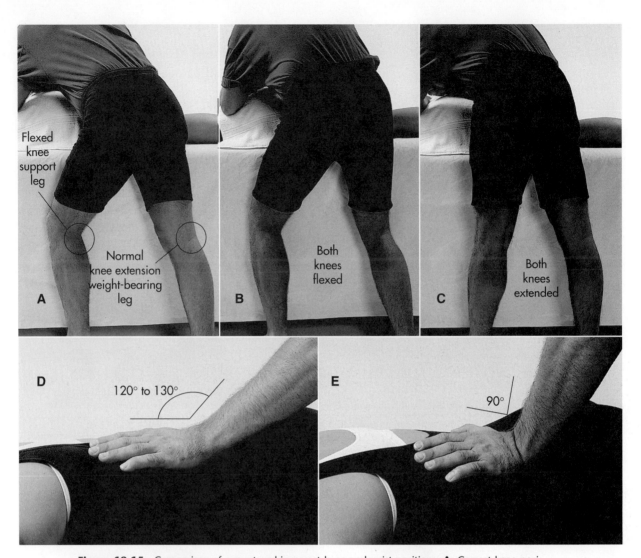

Figure 18-15 Comparison of correct and incorrect knee and wrist positions. **A,** Correct knee position. **B,** Incorrect knee position, both knees flexed. **C,** Incorrect knee position, both knees extended. **D,** Correct wrist position. **E,** Incorrect wrist position.

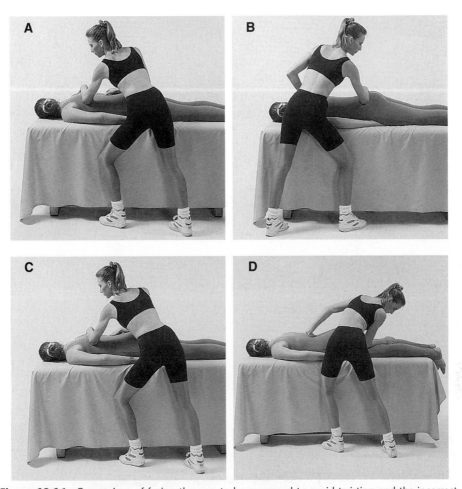

Figure 18-16 Comparison of facing the area to be massaged to avoid twisting and the incorrect, twisted position. **A,** Correct starting position. **B,** Correct shifted position. Turn entire body; shift weight-bearing leg. **C,** Correct starting position. **D,** Incorrect (twisted) position. Feet did not move; torso becomes twisted.

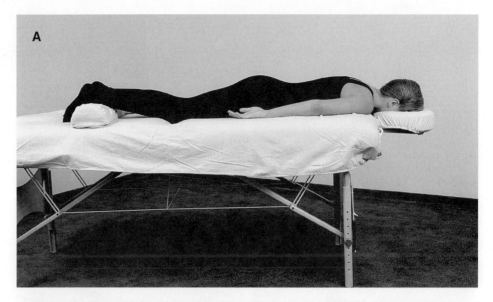

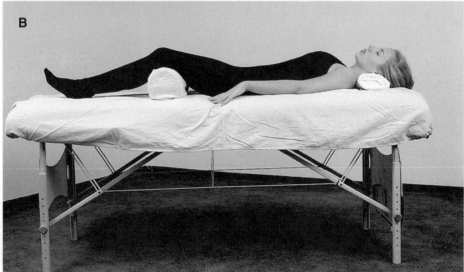

Figure 18-17 Bolsters are used to support the client's neck, ankles, and knees. **A,** Prone. **B,** Supine.

DRAPING PROCEDURES

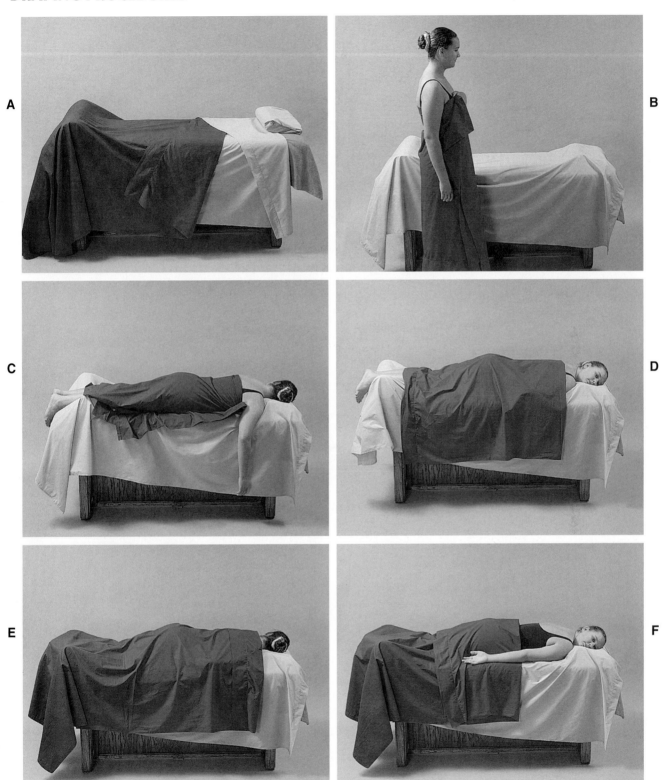

Figure 18-18 Draping sequences using sheets and towels. **A,** Basic table setup for draping. **B,** Client wrapped in top sheet. Top sheet is folded in half with fold at the top and end held in the front. **C,** Client lies in prone position, and the sides of the drape are moved to the side of the table. **D,** Drape is spread to cover client. **E,** Client fully draped in prone position. **F,** Drape is folded back to provide access to the back.

Continued

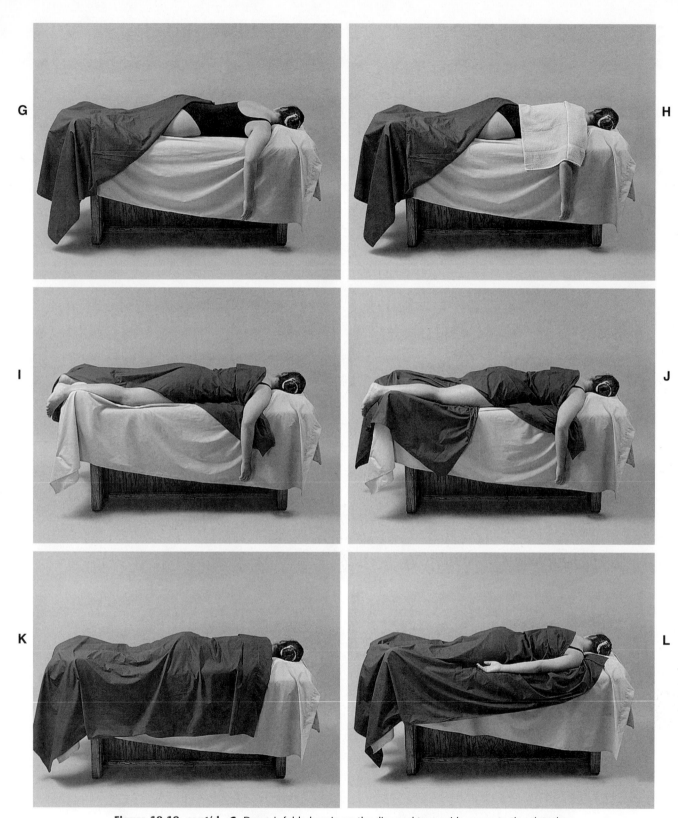

Figure 18-18, cont'd G, Drape is folded again on the diagonal to provide access to the gluteal region. **H,** Towel is used to drape the back while the gluteal region is massaged. **I,** Drape is repositioned to cover client, and towel is removed. The end of the drape is folded on the diagonal to provide access to the leg. **J,** Drape is positioned under the leg to be massaged to secure it. **K,** Client is redraped. **L,** Arm is positioned over the drape, which is held secure by the arm.

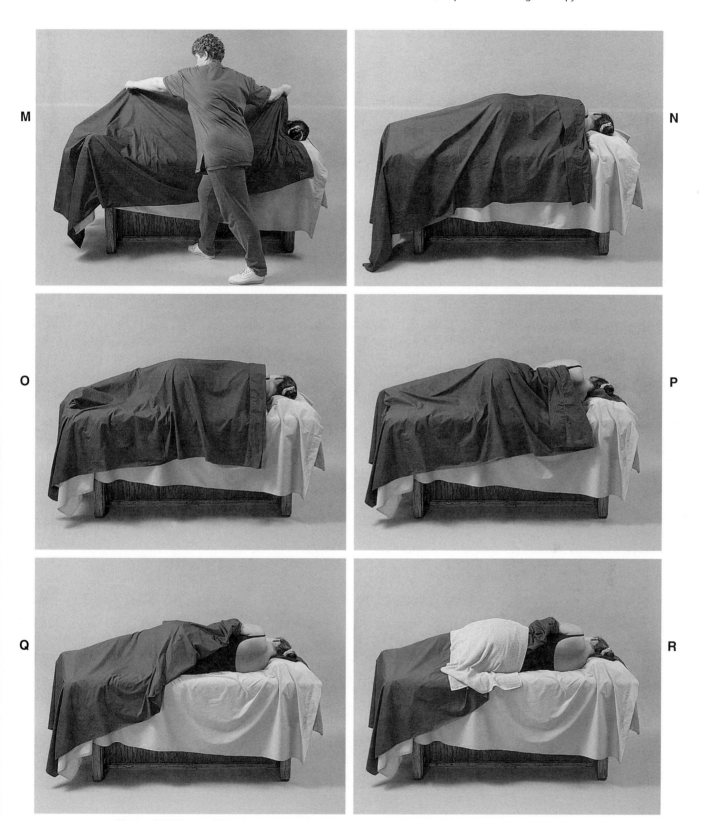

Figure 18-18, cont'd **M,** Position for holding the drape while the client turns to the side position. Drape is held in the middle in a tent fashion; massage practitioner's knee secures the drape against the table. **N,** Client in side-lying position with full draping. **O,** Client with top leg drawn up and supported with body support. **P,** Drape folded under top arm to provide access to arm, with opposite corner of drape under client's head to secure it (see Figure 14-36, W). **Q,** Top corner of drape folded diagonally to provide access to the back. **R,** Towel positioned to drape the gluteal area.

Continued

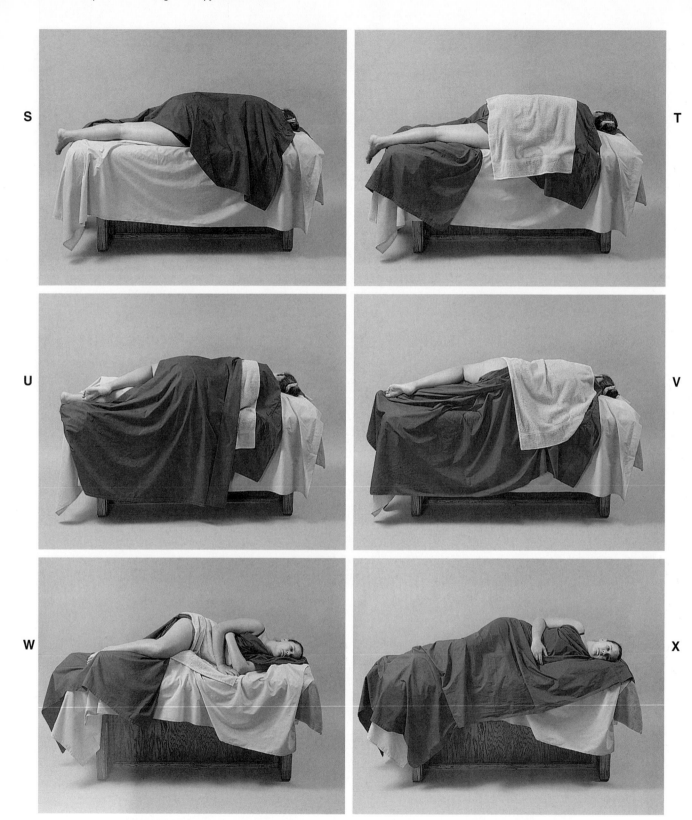

Figure 18-18, cont'd **S,** Client with back redraped and end corner of drape folded diagonally to provide access to the leg. **T,** Drape moved under exposed lower leg and towel used to drape the gluteal area. Drape is secured under the lower leg. **U,** Lower leg is redraped, and the opposite end corner of the drape is folded diagonally to provide access to the upper leg. **V,** Folded corner of drape is brought through the legs and secured under the upper leg. Towel is used to drape the gluteal and abdominal area. **W,** Front view of this position. Note that the drape across the chest is secured under the client's head. **X,** Client is redraped, and towels are removed.

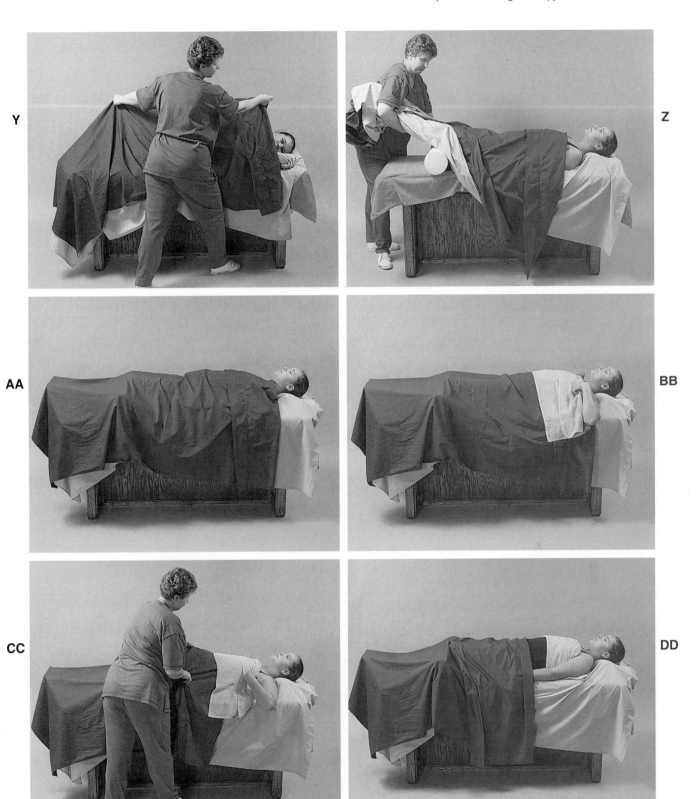

Figure 18-18, cont'd   Y, Drape is held in tent fashion and secured against the table with the practitioner's knee as the client turns to supine position. **Z,** Both top and bottom drapes are folded over client's legs to provide access to body support; the body support is placed under the client's knees. **AA,** Client is fully draped in supine position. **BB,** Towel is placed on the client's chest over the top drape. Client holds the towel in place. **CC,** The practitioner pulls the top of the drape from under the towel to provide access to the abdomen. **DD,** Drape is repositioned over the towel.

Continued

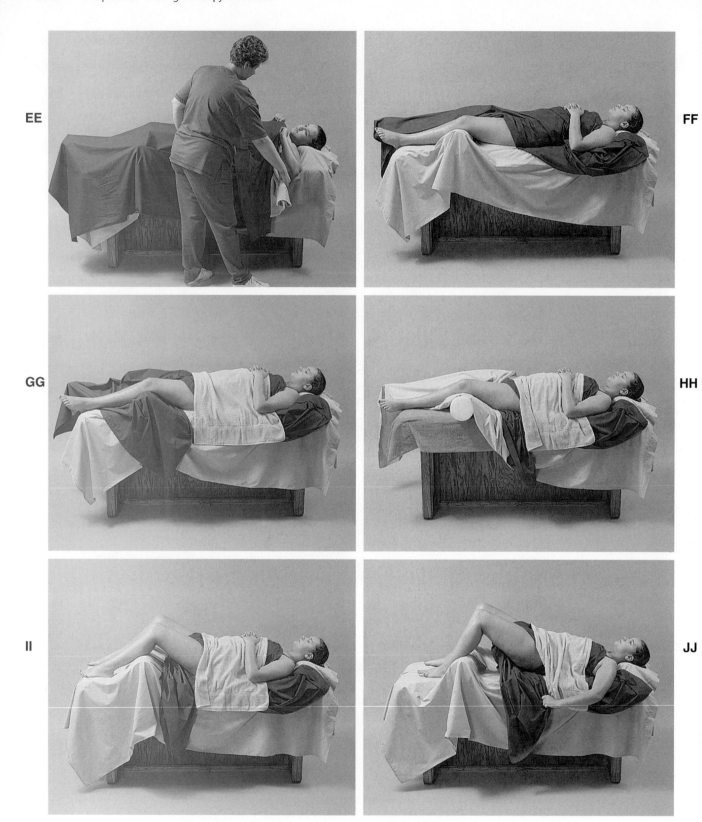

Figure 18-18, cont'd EE, Towel is removed from underneath the drape. **FF,** Lower corner of the top drape is folded diagonally to provide access to the client's leg. **GG,** Top drape is positioned under the client's leg and secured by the leg. Towel is placed over the client's abdomen and groin. **HH,** Lower corner of bottom drape is brought under the leg diagonally and draped over the opposite leg; this exposes the secondary sanitary bottom drape. Note that the client's leg does not touch the body support. This draping provides a secure groin covering during massaging, stretching, or providing range of motion to the leg. **II,** Alternate leg draping to allow access to both legs and provide groin draping. Client bends knees, and both end corners of the drape are folded diagonally and positioned between the knees. The corners are spread at either side of the table. **JJ,** Client grasps each corner, lifts buttocks, and pulls drape under them.

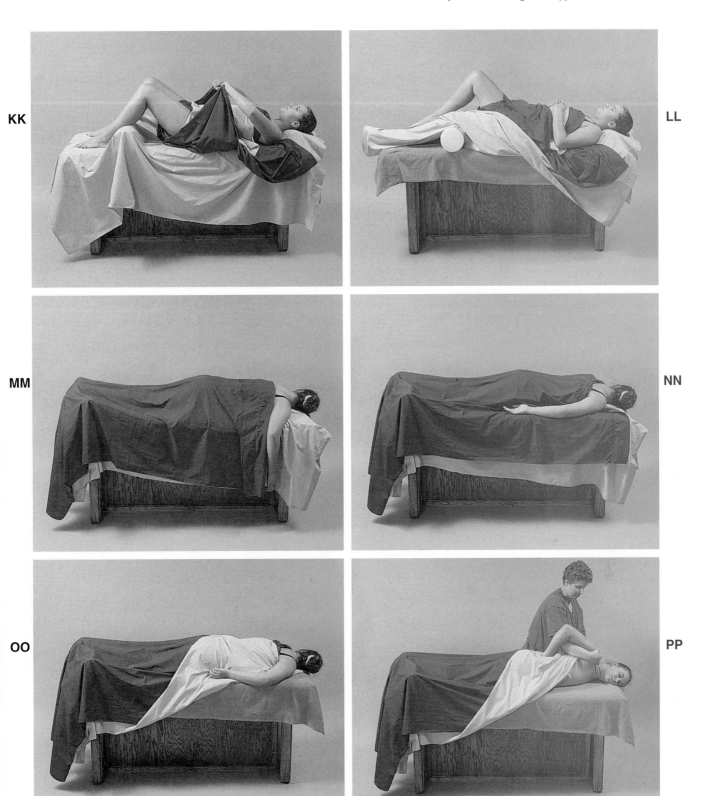

Figure 18-18, cont'd   KK, Client or practitioner can then tie the ends together to secure the drape. **LL,** One leg is lowered, and the bottom drape is used to cover it, leaving only the area to be massaged exposed. **MM,** Client prone and fully draped. Additional example of using bottom sheet for draping. **NN,** Client's arm is positioned outside the drape. **OO,** Corners of both the top and bottom drapes are folded diagonally under the arm and over the back. **PP,** Practitioner secures the bottom drape while moving the shoulder and arm.

Continued

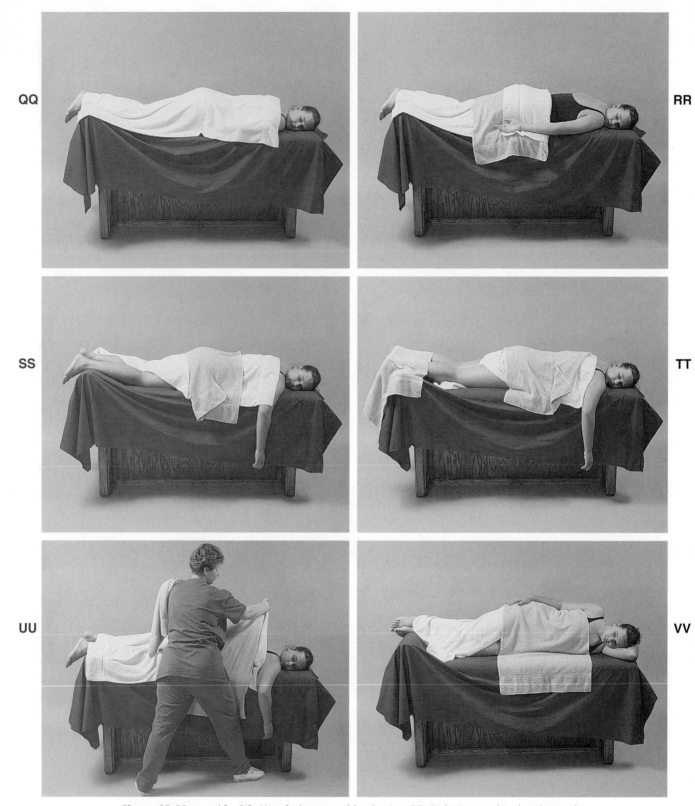

Figure 18-18, cont'd   QQ, Use of a large towel for draping. **RR,** Bath-size towel is placed over gluteal area for additional drape while top of the towel is folded back to provide access to client's back.
SS, Back is redraped, and end corners of towel are folded diagonally to provide access to the legs.
TT, Folded towel ends are placed between the client's knees, and an additional towel is used to cover
the feet. **UU,** Foot towel is removed, and large and small towels are secured against the table by the
practitioner's knee and lifted to allow the client to turn to side position. **VV,** Large towel and bath-size
towel are repositioned over client.

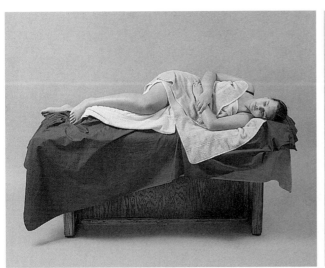 **WW**

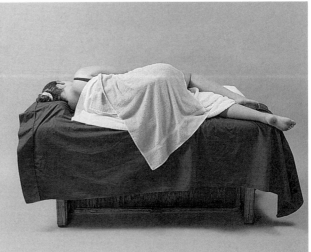 **XX**

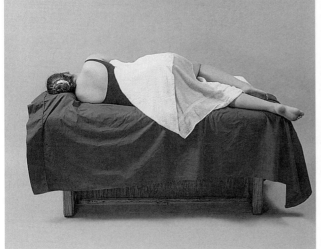 **YY**

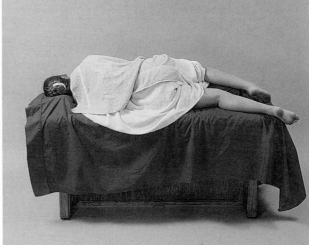 **ZZ**

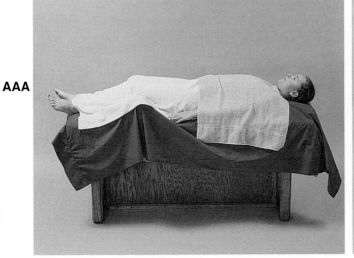 **AAA**

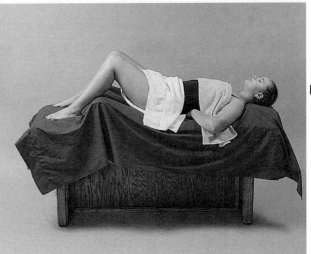 **BBB**

Figure 18-18, cont'd **WW,** Large towel end corner is folded diagonally to provide access to top leg and brought under top leg to be secured between leg and support under bent knee. Additional bath towel is placed over gluteal region. **XX,** Back view. **YY,** Top end of drape is folded diagonally to provide access to the back. **ZZ,** Drape over gluteal area and bottom lower leg is folded up to provide access to the bottom leg. **AAA,** Client draped with towels in supine position. **BBB,** Client draped to provide access to the abdomen and legs. Bath towel is used over large towel and held in place by the client as the practitioner pulls the large towel under and folds it back to expose the abdomen. Bottom ends of large towel are diagonally folded in and placed between the client's knees with the ends at the side of the table, so that the client is able to grasp the ends of the towel and pull it under her, providing secure draping of the groin.

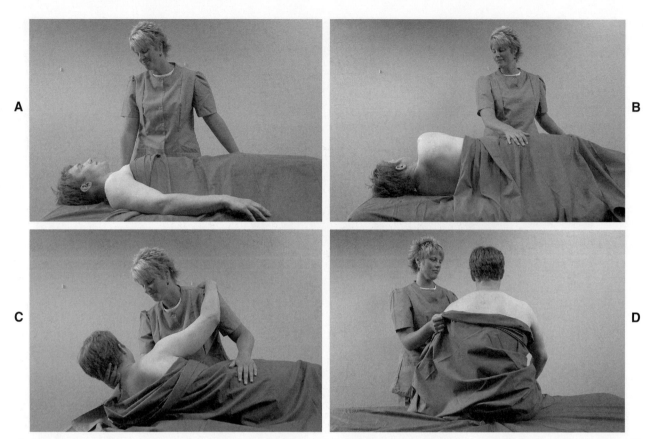

Figure 18-19   Assisting a client off the massage table. **A,** The procedure begins with the client prone. **B,** The client rolls to the side and bends the knees. **C,** The client wraps his arm around the practitioner's shoulder. The practitioner brings the sheet under the client's head and holds the front and back portions together while using the other hand behind the client's hip to provide support. **D,** The practitioner lifts the client by standing up and leaning back while swinging the client's knees over the table to the seated position. The practitioner then adjusts the drape and assists the client from the table. The use of a foot stool for the client is helpful.

TABLE 18-1   Massage Strokes and Their Variations

Massage Stroke	Variations
Effleurage (*gliding*)	One-handed (*raking, ironing, circular*) Two-handed (*heart, circular*) Alternate hand (*raking, circular*) Nerve stroke
Pétrissage (*kneading*)	One-handed Two-handed (*praying hands, ocean waves*) Alternate hand Fulling Skin rolling
Friction	Superficial warming (sawing) Rolling Wringing Cross fiber Chucking Circular
Tapotement (*percussion*)	Tapping (*punctuation, pulsing, raindrops*) Pincement Hacking (*quacking*) Cupping Pounding (*rapping*) Clapping Diffused
Vibration (*shaking*)	Fine Jostling Rocking

**Flowchart for a
Massage Therapy Session**

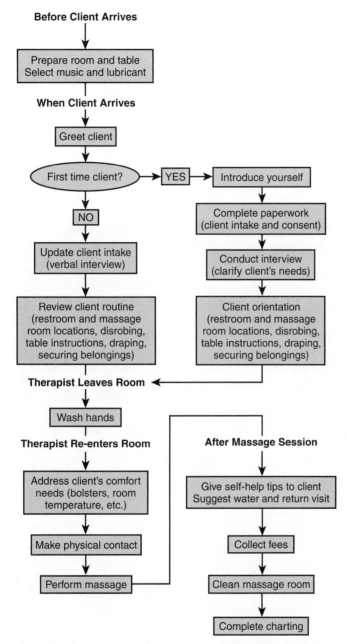

Figure 18-20 Flowchart for a massage therapy session. © Copyright 2001 Louisiana Institute of Massage Therapy.

Chapter 19

The Client Consultation

Informed Consent Process

A new client arrives for a massage.

The massage professional shows the client an informational brochure explaining massage, why it works, the procedures and process of massage, the benefits of massage, and the general contraindications. The client is asked to read the information. The massage professional then discusses the information with the client. In general terms the massage professional explains alternatives to massage, such as exercise and self-hypnosis, that provide benefits similar to massage.

The massage professional then tells the client about his or her professional background: that he or she graduated from a state-licensed massage therapy school 2 years ago, after a training program of 1000 hours; that he or she has been nationally certified by the National Certification Board for Therapeutic Massage and Bodywork; that he or she has been in professional practice part time for 2 years and averages eight massages a week; and that he or she has taken additional training in myofascial approaches and massage for elderly persons (approximately 100 hours for each). The client also is given information on methods of reporting misconduct of the massage therapist to state agencies, national professional organizations, and the police.

The client is given the policy and procedures booklet or statement and asked to read it. After he or she has done so, the massage professional goes over the booklet with the client, point by point, so that he or she understands the rules and requirements of the massage therapist. The massage professional makes sure that the requirements to report abuse and threat of deadly harm, as well as the release of files by court order, are discussed.

The massage professional hands the client a form that states the following:

I, (client's name) _____ , have received a copy of the rules and regulations for Massage Works operated by Sue and John Grey. I have read the rules and regulations, and I understand them. The massage procedures, information about massage in general, general benefits of massage, contraindications for massage, and possible alternatives have been explained to me. The qualifications of the massage professional and reporting measures for misconduct have been disclosed to me.

I understand that the massage I receive is for the purpose of stress reduction and relief from muscular tension, spasm, or pain and to increase circulation. If I experience any pain or discomfort, I will immediately inform the massage practitioner so that the pressure or methods can be adjusted to my comfort level. I understand that massage professionals do not diagnose illness or disease or perform any spinal manipulations, nor do they prescribe any medical treatments, and nothing said or done during the session should be construed as such. I acknowledge that massage is not a substitute for medical examination or diagnosis and that I should see a health care provider for those services. Because massage should not be performed under certain circumstances, I agree to keep the massage practitioner updated as to any changes in my health profile, and I release the massage professional from any liability if I fail to do so.

Client's signature _____

Date _____

Therapist's signature _____

Date _____

Consent to Treat a Minor

By my signature I authorize _____ to provide therapeutic massage to my child or dependent.

Informed Consent Process—cont'd

Signature of Parent
or Guardian _____

Date _____

For clients who will have several sessions, the next step is completion of the needs assessment and initial treatment plan.

Modified Informed Consent Form for Single Session

For clients who will be seen only once (such as might occur if the professional is working on a cruise ship, doing sports massage at an event, or doing promotional chair massage at a health fair), the following modification in informed consent can be made.

I, (client's name) _____ , have received a copy of the rules and regulations for

(name of business) _____ , operated by (owner) . I have read the rules and regulations, and I understand them. The general benefits of massage and contraindications for massage have been explained to me. I have disclosed to the therapist any condition I have that would contraindicate massage. Other than to determine contraindications, I understand that no specific needs assessment has been performed. The qualifications of the massage professional and reporting measures for misconduct have been disclosed to me.

I understand that the massage I receive is for the purpose of stress reduction and relief from muscular tension, spasm, or pain and to increase circulation. If I experience any pain or discomfort, I will immediately inform the massage practitioner so that the pressure or methods can be adjusted to my comfort level. I understand that massage professionals do not diagnose illness or disease or perform any spinal manipulations, nor do they prescribe any medical treatments. I acknowledge that massage is not a substitute for medical examination or diagnosis and that I should see a health care provider for those services.

I understand that a single massage session or massage used on a random basis is limited to providing a general, nonspecific massage approach using standard massage methods and does not include any methods to address soft tissue structure or function specifically.

Client's signature _____

Date _____

Therapist's signature _____

Date _____

Consent to Treat a Minor

By my signature I authorize _____ to provide massage work to my child or dependent.

Signature of Parent
or Guardian _____

Date _____

MASSAGE ASSESSMENT/PHYSICAL OBSERVATION/PALPATION AND GAIT

PRE

POST

Client Name: _____   **Date:** _____

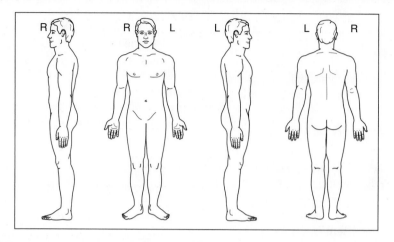

OBSERVATION & PALPATION	OBSERVATION & PALPATION	GAIT ASSESSMENT
ALIGNMENT	**RIBS**	
chin in line with nose, sternal notch, navel	Even	**HEAD**
Other:	Springy	Remains steady/eyes forward
HEAD	Other:	Other:
Tilted (L)	**ABDOMEN**	**TRUNK**
Tilted (R)	Firm and Pliable	Remains vertical
Rotated (L)	Hard areas	Other:
Rotated (R)	Other:	**SHOULDERS**
EYES	**WAIST**	Remain level
Level	Level	Rotate during walking
Equally set in socket	Other:	Other:
Other:	**SPINE CURVES**	**ARMS**
EARS	Normal	Motion is opposite leg swing
Level	Other:	Motion is even (L) and (R)
Other:	**GLUTEAL MUSCLE MASS**	Other:
SHOULDERS	Even	(L) swings freely
Level	Other:	(R) swings freely
(R) high / (L) low	**ILIAC CREST**	Other:
(L) high / (R) low	Level	**HIPS**
(L) rounded forward	Other:	Remain level
(R) rounded forward	**KNEES**	Other:
Muscle development even	Even/Symmetrical	Rotate during walking
Other:	Other:	Other:

Figure 19-1 Sample physical assessment form.

SCAPULA	PATELLA	LEGS
Even	(L)　☐　movable　☐　rigid	Swing freely at hip
Move freely	(R)　☐　movable　☐　rigid	Other:
Other:	**ANKLES**	**KNEES**
CLAVICLES	Even	Flex and extend freely through stance and swing phase
Level	Other:	Other:
Other:	**FEET**	**FEET**
ARMS	Mobile	Heel strikes first at start of stance
Hang evenly (internal)　　(external)	Other:	Plantar flexed at push-off
(L) rotated ☐ medial ☐ lateral	**ARCHES**	Foot clears floor during swing phase
(R) rotated ☐ medial ☐ lateral	Even	Other:
ELBOWS ☐	Other:	**STEP**
Even	**TOES**	Length is even
Other:	Straight	Timing is even
WRISTS	Other:	Other:
Even	**SKIN**	**OVERALL**
Other:	Moves freely and resilient	Rhythmic
FINGERTIPS	Pulls/restricted	Other:
Even	Puffy/baggy	
Other:	Other:	

Figure 19-1, cont'd.　Sample physical assessment form.

TREATMENT PLAN

Client Name:_____

Choose One: ☐ Original plan   ☐ Reassessment date_____

Short-term client goals:
_____
_____

Long-term client goals:
_____
_____

Therapist Objectives:
_____
_____

1) Frequency, 2) length, and 3) duration of visits:
1) _____   2) _____   3) _____

Progress "measurements" to be used: (Ex.— pain scale, range of motion, increased ability to perform function)
_____
_____

Dates of reassessment:
_____

Categories of massage methods to be used: (Ex.— relaxation, stress reduction, circulatory, lymphatic, neuromuscular, connective tissue, neurochemical, etc.)
_____
_____

Additional notes:
_____
_____
_____

Client Signature:_____   Date:_____

Therapist Signature:_____   Date:_____

Figure 19-2   Sample care/treatment plan form.

SESSION NOTES
SOAP CHARTING FORM

Client Name: _____ Date: _____
Practitioner Name: _____

Subjective

CLIENT STATUS
- **Information from client, referral source or reference books:**

1) Current conditions/changes from last session: _____
_____
_____
_____

Objective

2) Information from <u>assessment</u> (physical, gait, palpation, muscle testing): _____
_____
_____

CONTENT OF SESSION
- **Generate goal (possibilities) from analysis of information in <u>client status</u>.**

1) Goals worked on this session. (Base information on client status this session and goals previously established in Treatment Plan):
_____
_____

What was <u>done</u> this session:
_____
_____

Analysis

RESULTS
- **Analyze results of session in relationship to what was done and how this relates to the session goals. (This is based on <u>cause</u> and <u>effect</u> of methods used and the effects on the persons involved).**

1) What worked/what didn't: (Based on measureable and objective Post Assessment)
_____
_____
_____

Plan

PLAN: Plans for next session, what client will work on, what next massage will reassess and continue to assess: _____
_____
_____

CLIENT COMMENTS:
_____

Time In: _____ Time Out: _____

Therapist signature: _____

Figure 19-3 SOAP charting form.

Summary

Massage has a powerful impact on the health and functioning of the body and has beneficial effects on virtually every body system. Yet it is not the preeminent answer for all problems and ills. The massage therapist who has studied and learned the indications and contraindications inspires confidence in his clients by demonstrating a strong grasp of anatomy, physiology, and pathology. This includes the science of how massage provides pain relief through such mechanisms as the gate theory. No greater gift can be given to a client than the attention to and caution against contraindicated conditions and vascular, nervous, osseous, and other miscellaneous endangerment sites. In this way the therapist also demonstrates an appreciation for his own abilities, an awareness of his own limitations, and an unflagging reputation for acting in the best interest of his clients.

PART III

Appendices

Appendix A

HIPAA Compliance and Privacy

Adapted from Fordney: *Insurance Handbook for the Medical Office,* **10th Edition, Chapter 2***

HEALTH INSURANCE PORTABILITY AND ACCOUNTABILITY ACT (HIPAA)

Compliance Deadlines

- ☐ Transactions and Code Set Standards: October 16, 2003
- ☐ Privacy: April 14, 2003
- ☐ Security Standards: April 21, 2005

COMPLIANCE DEFINED

Compliance in the health care industry is the process of meeting regulations, recommendations, and expectations of federal and state agencies that pay for health care services and regulate the industry. Health care compliance encompasses the claims reimbursement processes, managed care procedures, Occupational Safety and Health Administration (OSHA), Clinical Laboratory Improvement Amendments (CLIA), licensure, and due diligence in obeying the law.

Any business that is involved with the health care industry must conform its practices to follow the principles and practices as identified by state and federal agencies. The professional elements of the principles and practices include:

- ❏ Regulations and recommendations to protect individuals
- ❏ Streamline processes
- ❏ Supporting system-wide stability

A compliance strategy provides a standardized process for handling business functions, much like a "user's manual." This will enable consistent and effective management and staff performance. Fail-

ure to comply with mandates leads to sanctions and fines from state and federal agencies. Failure to follow guidelines potentially results in more fraud and abuse in the claims reimbursement cycle.

HEALTH INFORMATION USING ELECTRONIC TECHNOLOGIES

Over the past decade, the United States health care system has undergone rapid change with regard to the separate issues of privacy, security, and claims processing. A number of organizations have participated to help standardize and improve the delivery and quality of health care.

Some code systems and additional terminology have been created by the adoption of the many federal statutes. In this appendix, you will learn some important key terms related to health information as it pertains to compliance and its role in electronic technology. You will also get acquainted with important initiatives that control the use of health information.

e-Health Information Management

e-Health information management, more commonly seen as eHIM, is a term coined by the American Health Information Management Association's eHealth Task Force to describe any and all transactions in which health care information is accessed, processed, stored, and transferred using electronic technologies.

National Health Information Infrastructure

The National Health Information Infrastructure (NHII) is an initiative set forth to improve patient

---

*This paper is intended to promote awareness. It is not all-encompassing in regard to HIPAA and OIG compliance. It is not intended to replace policy and procedures manuals and similar policy documents.
Definitions from the *Federal Register* are excerpts, used for ease of understanding.

safety and the quality of health care as well as to better inform individuals regarding their own health information and to help them understand health care costs. It has also encouraged the use of computers and standardized electronic financial transactions.

NHII is overseen by the Department of Health and Human Services with the National Committee on Vital and Health Statistics (NCVHS) serving as a public advisory committee.

HEALTH INSURANCE PORTABILITY AND ACCOUNTABILITY ACT (HIPAA)

The Health Insurance Portability and Accountability Act of 1996 (HIPAA), Public Law 104-191, has significant impact on both individuals and health care providers. There are five titles but two provisions of HIPAA relate most to health care, Title I: Insurance Reform and Title II: Administrative Simplification. HIPAA projects long-term benefits that include lowered administrative costs, increased accuracy of data, increased patient and customer satisfaction, and reduced revenue cycle time, ultimately improving financial management.

Title I: Health Insurance Reform

The primary purpose of HIPAA Title I: Insurance Reform is to provide continuous insurance coverage for workers and their insured dependents when they change or lose jobs. This aspect of HIPAA affects individuals as consumers, not particularly as patients. Previously, when an employee left or lost a job and changed insurance coverage, a "preexisting" clause prevented or limited coverage for certain medical conditions. HIPAA now limits the use of preexisting condition exclusions, prohibits discrimination for past or present poor health, and guarantees certain employers and individuals the right to purchase new health insurance coverage after losing a job. Additionally, HIPAA allows renewal of health insurance coverage regardless of an individual's health condition that is covered under the particular policy.

Title II: Administrative Simplification

The goals of HIPAA Title II: Administrative Simplification focus on the health care practice setting and aim to reduce administrative costs and burdens. Standardizing electronic transmissions of administrative and financial information will reduce the number of forms and methods used in the claims processing cycle and reduce the non-

productive effort that goes into processing paper or nonstandard electronic claims. Additional provisions are meant to ensure the privacy and security of an individual's health data.

Two parts of the Administrative Simplification provisions are as follows:

1. Development and implementation of standardized electronic transactions using common sets of descriptors (i.e., standard code sets). These must be used to represent health care concepts and procedures when performing health-related financial and administrative activities electronically (i.e., standard transactions). HIPAA has been part of a great shift in processing electronic data. Transaction standards apply to the following, which are called covered entities under HIPAA: health care third-party payers, health care providers, and health care clearinghouses. A clearinghouse is an independent organization that receives insurance claims from the physician's office, performs software edits, and redistributes the claims electronically to various third-party payers.

2. Implementation of privacy and security procedures to prevent the misuse of health information by ensuring:
❏ Privacy and confidentiality
❏ Security of health information

Administrative simplification has created uniform sets of standards that protect and place limits on how confidential health information can be used. For years, health care providers have locked medical records in file cabinets and refused to share patient health information. Patients now have specific rights regarding how their health information is used and disclosed because federal and state laws regulate the protection of an individual's privacy. Knowledge and attention to the rights of patients are important to the compliance endeavor in a health care practice. Providers are entrusted with health information and are expected to recognize when certain health information can be used or disclosed.

Patients have the legal right to request (1) access and amendments to their health records, (2) an accounting of those who have received their health information, and (3) restrictions on who can access their health records. Understanding the parameters concerning these rights is crucial to complying with HIPAA.

Health care providers and their employees can be held accountable for using or disclosing patient health information inappropriately. HIPAA regulations will be enforced, as clearly stated by the U.S. government. The revolution of HIPAA will take time to understand and implement correctly, but as the standards are put into action, both within the practice setting and across the many different fields comprising the health industry, greater benefits will be appreciated by the health care provider, staff, and patients.

Defining Roles and Relationships: Key Terms

HIPAA legislation required the U.S. Department of Health and Human Services (HHS) to establish national standards and identifiers for electronic transactions as well as implement privacy and security standards. In regard to HIPAA, Secretary refers to the HHS Secretary or any officer or employee of HHS to whom the authority involved has been delegated.

The Centers for Medicare and Medicaid Services (CMS), previously known as the Health Care Financing Administration (HCFA), will enforce the insurance portability and transaction and code set requirements of HIPAA for Medicare and Medicaid programs.

The Office for Civil Rights (OCR) will enforce privacy standards.

Electronic media refers to the mode of electronic transmission, including the following:
❑ Internet (online mode—wide open)
❑ Extranet or private network using Internet technology to link business parties
❑ Leased telephone or dial-up telephone lines, including fax modems (speaking over telephone is not considered an electronic transmission)
❑ Transmissions that are physically moved from one location to another using magnetic tape, disk, or compact disk media

A transaction refers to the transmission of information between two parties to carry out financial or administrative activities related to health care.

Refer to Box A.1 for titles of additional entities that oversee the HIPAA-related functions.

HIPAA in the Practice Setting

The individuals mentioned in Box A.1 create relationships that guide the health care provider and the practice. A health care provider can be a physician's assistant, nurse practitioner, social worker, chiropractor, radiologist, or dentist; HIPAA does not only affect medical physicians. The health care provider is designated as an HIPAA-mandated covered entity under certain conditions. It is important to remember that health care providers who transmit any health information in electronic form in connection with an HIPAA transaction are covered entities. Electronic form or media can include floppy disk, compact disk (CD), or file transfer protocol (FTP) over the Internet. Voice-over-modem faxes, meaning a telephone line, are not considered electronic media, although a fax from a computer (e.g., WinFax program) is considered an electronic medium.

HIPAA requires the designation of a privacy officer or privacy official (PO) to develop and implement the organization's policies and procedures (P&P). The PO for an organization may hold another position within the practice or may not be an employee of the practice at all. Often, the PO is a contracted professional and available to the practice through established means of contact.

The business associate often is considered an extension of the provider practice. If an office function is outsourced with use or disclosure of individually identifiable health information, the organization that is acting on behalf of the health care provider is considered a business associate. For example, if the office's medical transcription is performed by an outside service, the transcription service is a business associate of the covered entity (the health care provider/practice).

HIPAA privacy regulations as a federal mandate will apply unless the state laws are contrary or more stringent with regard to privacy. A state law is contrary if it is impossible to comply with the state law while complying with federal requirements or if the state law stands as an obstacle to the purposes of the federal law. State preemption, a complex technical issue not within the scope of the health care provider's role, refers to instances when state law takes precedence over federal law. The PO determines when the need for preemption arises.

THE PRIVACY RULE: CONFIDENTIALITY AND PROTECTED HEALTH INFORMATION

What I may see or hear in the course of the treatment or even outside of the treatment in regard to the life of men, which on no account one must spread abroad, I will keep to myself holding such things shameful to be spoken about.
HIPPOCRATES, 400 BC

The Hippocratic Oath, federal and state regulations, professional standards, and ethics all address patient privacy. Because current technology

Box A-1   Overseers of HIPAA Functions

A covered entity transmits health information in electronic form in connection with a transaction covered by HIPAA. The covered entity may be (1) a health care coverage carrier such as Blue Cross/Blue Shield, (2) a health care clearinghouse through which claims are submitted, or (3) a health care provider such as the primary care physician.

A business associate is a person who, on behalf of the covered entity, performs or assists in the performance of a function or activity involving the use or disclosure of individually identifiable health information, including claims processing or administration, data analysis, processing or administration, utilization review, quality assurance, billing, benefit management, practice management, and repricing. For example, if a provider practice contracts with an outside billing company to manage its claims and accounts receivable, the billing company would be a business associate of the provider (the covered entity).

A health care provider is a person trained and licensed to provide care to a patient, and also a place that is licensed to give health care, such as a hospital, skilled nursing facility, inpatient/outpatient rehabilitation facility, home health agency, hospice program, physician, diagnostic department, outpatient physical or occupational therapy, rural clinic, or home dialysis supplier.

Privacy and security officers oversee the HIPAA-related functions. These individuals may or may not be employees of a particular health care practice. A privacy officer or privacy official (PO) is designated to help the provider remain in compliance by setting policies and procedures (P&P) and by training and managing the staff regarding HIPAA and patient rights, and the PO is usually the contact person for questions and complaints.

A security officer protects the computer and networking systems within the practice and implements protocols such as password assignment, backup procedures, firewalls, virus protection, and contingency planning for emergencies.

allows easy access to health care information, HIPAA imposes new requirements for health care providers. Since computers have become indispensable for the health care office, confidential health data have been sent across networks, e-mailed over the Internet, and even exposed by hackers, with few safeguards taken to protect data and prevent information from being intercepted or lost. With the implementation of standardizing electronic transactions of health care information, the use of technologies will pose new risks for privacy and security. These concerns were addressed under HIPAA, and regulations now closely govern how the industry handles its electronic activities.

Privacy is the condition of being secluded from the presence or view of others. Confidentiality is using discretion in keeping secret information. Integrity plays an important part in the health care setting. Staff members of a health care organization need a good understanding of HIPAA's basic requirements and must be committed to protecting the privacy and rights of the practice's patients.

Disclosure means the release, transfer, provision of access to, or divulging in any other manner of information outside the entity holding the information. An example of a disclosure is giving information to the hospital's outpatient surgery center about a patient you are scheduling for a procedure.

Consent is the verbal or written agreement that gives approval to some action, situation, or statement. A consent form is not required before physicians use or disclose protected health information (PHI) for treatment, payment, or routine health care operations (TPO).

Treatment includes coordination or management of health care between providers or referral of a patient to another provider. PHI can be disclosed to obtain reimbursement. Other health care operations include performance reviews, audits, training programs, and certain types of fundraising (Figures A–1 through A–4).

Keep in mind that an HIPAA privacy consent is not the same as a consent to treat.

Exceptions may be based on specific state law requirements, on an emergency situation, on a language barrier that makes it impossible to obtain, or when treating prison inmates.

Under the HIPAA privacy rule, authorization is an individual's formal, written permission to use

**REQUIRED ELEMENTS
OF HIPAA AUTHORIZATION**

Identification of person (or class)
authorized to request

Identification of person (or class)
to whom covered entity is to
use/disclose

Description of information to be
released with specificity to allow
entity to know which information
the authorization references

Description of each purpose of the
requested use or disclosure

Expiration date, time period,
or event

Statement that is revocable by
written request

Individual's (patient's) signature
and date

Statement of representative's
authority

Authorization for Release of Information

PATIENT NAME: ___Levy_____ ___Chloe_____ ___E.___ _____
                      LAST   FIRST   MI   MAIDEN OR OTHER NAME
DATE OF BIRTH: _02_ - _12_ - _1950_ SS# _320_ - _21_ - _3408_ MEDICAL RECORD #: _____3075_____
                MO DAY   YR
ADDRESS: _____3298 East Main Street_____ CITY: __Woodland Hills__ STATE: _XY_ ZIP: _12345-0001_

DAY PHONE: _____013-340-9800_____ EVENING PHONE: _____013-549-8708_____

I hereby authorize _____Gerald Practon, MD_____ **(Print Name of Provider) to release information from my medical record
as indicated below to:**
NAME: _____Margaret L. Lee, MD_____
ADDRESS: _____328 Seward Street_____ CITY: _____Anytown_____ STATE: _XY_ ZIP: _45601-0731_

PHONE: _____013-219-7698_____ FAX: _____013-290-9877_____

INFORMATION TO BE RELEASED:
                     DATES:
☒ History and physical exam _____6-8-20XX_____
❑ Progress notes _____
❑ Lab reports _____
❑ X-ray reports _____
❑ Other:_____ _____
_____ _____

I specifically authorize the release of information relating to:
❑ Substance abuse (including alcohol/drug abuse)
❑ Mental health (including psychotherapy notes)
❑ HIV related information (AIDS related testing)
X _____
SIGNATURE OF PATIENT OR LEGAL GUARDIAN   DATE

PURPOSE OF DISCLOSURE: ❑ Changing physicians   ☒ Consultation/second opinion   ❑ Continuing care
❑ Legal   ❑ School   ❑ Insurance   ❑ Workers Compensation
❑ Other (please specify):_____

1. I understand that this authorization will expire on __09/01/20XX__ (Print the Date this Form Expires) days after I have signed
   the form.

2. I understand that I may revoke this authorization at any time by notifying the providing organization in writing, and it will be
   effective on the date notified except to the extent action has already been taken in reliance upon it.

3. I understand that information used or disclosed pursuant to this authorization may be subject to redisclosure by the recipient
   and no longer be protected by Federal privacy regulations.

4. I understand that if I am being requested to release this information by _____Gerald Practon, MD_____ (Print Name of
   Provider) for the purpose of:
   _____

   a. By authorizing this release of information, my health care and payment for my health care will not be affected if I do not
      sign this form.
   b. I understand I may see and copy the information described on this form if I ask for it, and that I will get a copy of this
      form after I sign it.
   c. I have been informed that _____Gerald Practon, MD_____ (Print Name of Provider) will/will not receive financial
      or in-kind compensation in exchange for using or disclosing the health information described above.

5. I understand that in compliance with _____XY_____ (Print the State Whose Laws Govern the Provider) statute, I will pay a
   fee of $ _5.00_ (Print the Fee Charged). There is no charge for medical records if copies are sent to facilities for ongoing
   care or follow up treament.

_____*Chloe E. Levy*_____ ___*6/1/XX*___ OR _____ _____
SIGNATURE OF PATIENT   DATE   PARENT/LEGAL GUARDIAN/AUTHORIZED PERSON DATE

                                                  ❑ _____
_____ _____ RELATIONSHIP TO PATIENT
RECORDS RECEIVED BY   DATE

                                  FOR OFFICE USE ONLY
DATE REQUEST FILLED _____ _____BY: _____
IDENTIFICATION PRESENTED_____ FEE COLLECTED $_____

Figure A-1 Completed authorization for release of information form for a patient relocating to another
city. The figure indicates the required elements for HIPAA authorization. Note: This form is used on a
one-time basis for reasons other than treatment, payment, or health care operations. When the patient
arrives at the new physician's office, a consent for treatment, payment, and health care operations form
will need to be signed. (From Federal Register, Vol. 64, No. 212, Appendix to Subpart E of Part 164:
Model Authorization Form, November 3, 1999.)

NAME OF FACILITY
Consent for Release of Information

Date May 16, 20XX

1. I hereby authorize College Hospital (Name of Institution) to release the following information from the health record(s) of Martha T. Jacobson (Patient name)

   52 East Rugby Street, Woodland Hills, XY 12345 (Address)

   covering the period(s) of hospitalization from:

   Date of Admission January 3, 20XX
   Date of Discharge January 5, 20XX
   Hospital # 278-1200 Birthdate June 27, 1960
2. Information to be released:
   - ☐ Copy of (complete) health record(s)
   - ☑ Discharge summary
   - ☐ History and physical
   - ☐ Operative report
   - ☐ Other ______
3. Information is to be released to: Michael Hotta, MD
   260 West Main Street, Woodland Hills, XY 12345
4. Purpose of disclosure June 14, 20XX consultation
5. I understand this consent can be revoked at any time except to the extent that disclosure made in good faith has already occurred in reliance to this consent.
6. Specification of the date, event, or condition upon which this consent expires:
   December 31, 20XX
7. The facility, its employees and officers, and attending physician are released from legal responsibility or liability for the release of the above information to the extent indicated and authorized herein.

Signed *Martha T. Jacobson*
(Patient or Representative)

______
(Relationship to Patient)

May 16, 20XX
(Date of Signature)

Figure A-2 Consent for Release of Information form to a hospital. (From the American Health Information Management Association, Chicago.)

or disclose his or her personally identifiable health information for purposes other than treatment, payment, or health care operations. For some "extra" activities, including marketing, research, and psychotherapy notes, an authorization form is needed for use and disclosure of PHI that is not included in any existing consent form agreements. Documentation pertaining to psychiatric counseling is kept with the patient's medical records but psychotherapy notes should be kept separate.

Individually identifiable health information (IIHI) is any part of an individual's health information, including demographic information (e.g., address, date of birth) collected from the individual, that is created or received by a covered entity. This information relates to the individual's past, present, or future physical or mental health or condition; the provision of health care to the individual; or the past, present, or future payment for the provision of health care. IIHI data identify the individual or establish a reasonable basis to believe the information can be used to identify the individual. For example, if you as a health care provider are talking to an insurance representative, you will likely give information such as the patient's date of birth and last name. These pieces of information would make it reasonably easy to identify the patient. If you are talking to a pharmaceutical representative about a drug assistance program that covers a new pill for heartburn and you only say that your practice has a patient living in your town who is indigent and has stomach problems, you are not divulging information that would identify the patient.

Protected health information (PHI) is any information that identifies an individual and describes his or her health status, age, sex, ethnicity, or other demographic characteristics, whether or

COLLEGE CLINIC
4567 Broad Avenue
Woodland Hills, XY 12345-0001
Phone: 555/486-9002
Fax: 555/487-8976

CONSENT TO THE USE AND DISCLOSURE OF HEALTH INFORMATION

I understand that this organization originates and maintains health records which describe my health history, symptoms, examination, test results, diagnoses, treatment, and any plans for future care or treatment. I understand that this information is used to:

- plan my care and treatment
- communicate among health professionals who contribute to my care
- apply my diagnosis and services, procedures, and surgical information to my bill
- verify services billed by third-party payers
- assess quality of care and review the competence of healthcare professionals in routine healthcare operations

I further understand that:

- a complete description of information uses and disclosures is included in a *Notice of Information Practices* which has been provided to me
- I have a right to review the notice prior to signing this consent
- the organization reserves the right to change their notice and practices
- any revised notice will be mailed to the address I have provided prior to implementation
- I have the right to object to the use of my health information for directory purposes
- I have the right to request restrictions as to how my health information may be used or disclosed to carry out treatment, payment, or health care operations
- the organization is not required to agree to the restrictions requested
- I may revoke this consent in writing, except to the extent that the organization has already taken action in reliance thereon.

☐ I request the following restrictions to the use or disclosure of my health information.

_____

_____ Date	_____ Notice Effective Date
_____ Signature of Patient or Legal Representative	_____ Witness
_____ Signature	_____ Title
Date _____	__ Accepted __ Rejected

Figure A-3   An example of a consent form used to disclose and use health information for treatment, payment, or health care operations. This is not required under HIPAA but you may find that some medical practices use it. (From Fordney MT, French L: Medical insurance billing and coding: a worktext. Philadelphia, 2003, Elsevier.)

not that information is stored or transmitted electronically. It refers to IIHI that is transmitted by electronic media, maintained in electronic form or transmitted, or maintained in any other form or medium. PHI does not include IHII in education records covered by the Family Educational Right and Privacy Act.

Traditionally, the focus was on protecting paper medical records and documentation that held patient's health information, such as laboratory results and radiology reports. HIPAA Privacy Regulation expands these protections to apply to PHI. The individual's health information is protected regardless of the type of medium in which it is maintained. This includes paper, the health care provider's computerized practice management and billing system, spoken words, and x-ray films.

Use means the sharing, employment, application, utilization, examination, or analysis of IHII within an organization that holds such information. When a patient's billing record is accessed to review the claim submission history, the individual's health information is in "use."

HIPAA imposes requirements to protect not only disclosure of PHI outside of the organization, but also for internal uses of health information. PHI may not be used or disclosed without permission of the patient or someone authorized to act on behalf of the patient, unless the use or disclosure is specifically required or permitted by the regulation (e.g., TPO). The two types of disclosure required by HIPAA Privacy Rule are to the individual who is the subject of the PHI and to the Secretary or DHHS to investigate compliance with the rule.

Confidential Information

Medical professionals must be responsible for maintaining confidentiality of patients' health information when working with patients and their medical records. Example A.1 lists some of the PHI that is typical in a medical office that falls under HIPAA compliance regulations.

The patient record and any photographs obtained are confidential documents and require an authorization form that must be signed by the patient to release information (see Figures A–1 through A–4). If the form is a photocopy, it is necessary to state that the photocopy is approved by the patient, or write to the patient and obtain an original signed document.

Exceptions to HIPAA

Unauthorized release of information is called breach of confidential communication and is considered an HIPAA violation, which may lead to fines.

Confidentiality between the physician and patient is automatically waived in the following situations:

1. When the patient is a member of a managed care organization (MCO) and the physician has signed a contract with the MCO that has a clause that says "for quality care purposes, the MCO has a right to access the medical records of their patients, and for utilization management purposes," the MCO has a right to audit those patients' financial records. Other managed care providers need to know about the patients if involved in the care and treatment of members of the MCO.

Figure A-4 Patient signing a consent form.

2. When patients have certain communicable diseases that are highly contagious or infectious and state health agencies require providers to report, even if the patient does not want the information reported.
3. When a medical device breaks or malfunctions, the Food and Drug Administration requires providers to report certain information.
4. When a patient is suspect in a criminal investigation or to assist in locating a missing person, material witness, or suspect, police have the right to request certain information.
5. When the patient's records are subpoenaed or there is a search warrant. The courts have the right to order providers to release patient information.
6. When the patient is suing someone, such as an employer, and wishes to protect herself or himself.
7. When there is a suspicious death or suspected crime victim, providers must report cases.
8. When the physician examines a patient at the request of a third party who is paying the bill, as in workers' compensation cases.
9. When state law requires the release of information to police that is for the good of society, such as reporting cases of child abuse, elder abuse, domestic violence, or gunshot wounds.

The purpose of the privacy rule is to ensure that patients who receive medical treatment may have control in the manner in which specific information is used and to whom it is disclosed. Confidential communication is a privileged communication that may be disclosed only with the patient's permission. Everything you see, hear, or read about patients remains confidential and does not leave the office. Never talk about patients or data contained in medical records where others may overhear. Some employers require employees to sign a confidentiality agreement. Such agreements should be updated periodically to address issues raised by the use of new technologies.

Privileged Information

Privileged information is related to the treatment and progress of the patient. The patient must sign an authorization to release this information or selected facts from the medical record. Some states have passed laws allowing certain test results (e.g., disclosure of the presence of the human immunodeficiency virus [HIV] or alcohol or substance abuse) and other information to be placed separate from the patient's medical record. A special authorization form is used to release this information.

Nonprivileged Information

Nonprivileged information consists of ordinary facts unrelated to treatment of the patient, including the patient's name, city of residence, and dates of admission or discharge. This information must be sensitized against unauthorized disclosure under the Privacy section of the HIPAA. The patient's authorization is not needed for the purposes of treatment, payment, or health care operations, unless the record is in a specialty hospital (e.g., alcohol treatment) or a special service unit of a general hospital (e.g., psychiatric unit). Professional judgment is required. The information is disclosed on a legitimate need-to-know basis, meaning that the medical data should be revealed to the attending physician because the information may have some effect on the treatment of the patient.

Patients' Rights
Right to Privacy

All patients have a right to privacy. It is important never to discuss patient information other than with the physician, an insurance company, or individual who has been authorized by the patient. If a telephone inquiry is made and you need to verify that callers are who they say they are:

❑ Ask for one or more of the following items: patient's full name, home address, date of birth, Social Security number, mother's maiden name, or dates of service.

❑ Ask for a call-back number and compare it to the number on file.

❑ Ask the patient to fax a sheet with his or her signature on it so you can compare it to one on file.

❑ Some hospitals may assign a code word or number that may be a middle name or date that is easy for patients to remember. If a patient does not know the code word, then ask for personal identifying information as mentioned.

If a telephone inquiry is made about a patient, ask the caller to put the request in writing and include the patient's signed authorization. If the caller refuses, have the physician return the call. If a relative telephones asking about a patient, have the physician return the call. When you telephone a patient about an insurance matter and reach voice mail, use care in the choice of words when leaving the message in the event the call was inadvertently received at the wrong number. Leave your name, the office name, and the return telephone number. Never attempt to interpret a report or provide information about the outcome of laboratory or other diagnostic tests to the patient. Let the physician do it.

Do's and Don'ts of Confidentiality

Don't: Discuss a patient with acquaintances, yours or the patient's.

Don't: Leave patients' records or appointment books exposed on your desk. If confidential documents are on your desk that patients can easily see as they walk by, either turn the documents over or lock them in a secure drawer when you leave your desk, even if you are gone for only a few moments.

Don't: Leave a computer screen with patient information visible, even for a moment, if another patient may see the data. If patient information is on your computer, either turn the screen off or save it on disk, lock the disk in a secure place, and clear the information from the screen.

DO: Properly dispose of notes, papers, and memos by using a shredding device.

DO: Be careful when using the copying machine because it is easy to forget to remove the original insurance claim or medical record from the document glass.

DO: Use common sense and follow the guidelines mentioned in this appendix to help you keep your professional credibility and integrity.

Privacy Rules: Patient Rights under HIPAA

Patients are granted the following federal rights that allow them to be informed about PHI and to control how their PHI is used and disclosed:

1. Right to Notice of Privacy Practices
2. Right to request restrictions on certain uses and disclosures of PHI
3. Right to request confidential communications
4. Right to access (inspect and obtain a copy of) PHI
5. Right to request an amendment of PHI
6. Right to receive an accounting of disclosures of PHI

Right to Notice of Privacy Practices

Under HIPAA, patients are entitled to receive the written Notice of Privacy Practices (NPP) of their provider, such as at the first visit or at enrollment.

The NPP is a document that outlines the individual's rights and covered entity's legal duties in regard to PHI. The NPP must be provided and written in "plain language" and the staff must make a reasonable "best effort" to obtain a signature from the patient acknowledging receipt. If it is an emergency treatment situation, get the acknowledgment signed at the earliest time practicable following the emergency. Getting the patient acknowledgment or documenting that an attempt was made to do so must be done once only. This can be recorded simply as signing a label on the inside cover of the chart. The front desk reception area is an ideal location for distribution of the NPP to the patient with the registration sheet and other required forms. If the patient cannot or will not sign, a staff member should document this in the patient's health record. An NPP will be tailored to each organization and must explain the following:

❑ How PHI may be used and disclosed by the organization
❑ Health provider duties to protect PHI
❑ Patient's rights regarding PHI
❑ How complaints may be filed with the office and HHS if the patient believes his or her privacy rights have been violated
❑ Who to contact for further information (usually the PO)
❑ Effective date of the NPP

You may have already seen these notices posted at a local pharmacy or had to sign an acknowledgment that you read a copy of the NPP at your personal physician's office. The health care provider's patients must have ready access to your organization's NPP. This notice must be posted prominently in the office (e.g., on the wall by the reception desk) and must be available in paper form for patients who request it. If the office has a website, the notice must be posted prominently there as well. HIPAA states that covered entities may not require individuals to waive their rights "as a condition of the provision of treatment or payment." A provider with a website that provides information about customer services or benefits must have the NPP placed on the site and must deliver a copy electronically on request.

Right to Request Restrictions on Certain Uses and Disclosures of PHI

Patients do have the right to ask for restrictions on how your office uses and discloses PHI for TPO. The patient may have items in his or her previous medical history that are not applicable to the current disclosure and may even cause the patient embarrassment; the patient may request that this PHI not be disclosed. (e.g., a patient had a successfully treated sexually transmitted disease many years before and requests that, whenever possible, this material not be disclosed). The covered entity is not required to agree to these requests but must have a process to review the requests, accept and review any appeal, and give a sound reason for not agreeing to the request. If agreed upon, however, the restrictions must be documented and followed. Such restrictions may be tracked by flagging the patient's medical chart that indicates a restriction applies or by using a pop-up note in the practice management software. There must be an implemented procedure in place to check for any restrictions before PHI is disclosed. See Box A.2, which details the regulations for disclosing the minimum necessary PHI, de-identification of PHI, marketing related to the patient, and fundraising activities related to patients.

You can ask your PO or refer to the medical practice's policy and procedure manual for clarification when disclosures are permissible.

In addition, unless a patient has requested that such disclosures not occur and the provider has agreed, health information may be disclosed to a family member, relative, close friend, or any other person identified by the patient.

Right to Request Confidential Communications

A patient can request to receive confidential communications by alternative means or at an alter-

Box A-2   HIPAA Help

You will find key terms addressed in the NPP that apply to the patient's right to request restrictions on certain uses and disclosures of PHI.

- Minimum Necessary. Privacy regulations require that use or disclosure of only the minimum amount of information necessary to fulfill the intended purpose be permitted. There are some exceptions to this rule. You do not need to limit PHI for disclosures in regard to health care providers for treatment, the patient, HHS for investigations of compliance with HIPAA, or as required by law.

Minimum Necessary determinations for uses of PHI must be determined within each organization, and reasonable efforts must be made to limit access to only the minimum amount of information needed by identified staff members. In smaller offices, employees may have multiple job functions. If a medical assistant helps with the patient examination, documents vital signs, and then collects the patient's copayment at the reception area, the assistant will likely access clinical and billing records. Simple procedure and policy (P&P) about appropriate access to PHI may be sufficient to satisfy the Minimum Necessary requirement. Larger organizations may have specific restrictions on who should have access to different types of PHI, because staff members tend to have a more targeted job role. Remain knowledgeable about your office's policy regarding Minimum Necessary. If you are strictly scheduling appointments, you may not need access to the clinical record. An x-ray technician will likely not need to access the patient billing records.

Minimum Necessary determinations for disclosures of PHI are distinguished by two categories within the Privacy Rule:

1. For disclosures made on a routine and recurring basis, you may implement policies and procedures, or standard protocols, for what will be disclosed. These disclosures would be common in your practice. Examples may include disclosures for workers' compensation claims or school physical forms.
2. For other disclosures that would be considered nonroutine, criteria should be established for determining the Minimum Necessary amount of PHI and to review each request for disclosure on an individual basis. A staff member (e.g., PO, medical records supervisor) will likely be assigned to determine this situation when the need arises.

As a general rule, remember that you must limit your requests to access PHI to the Minimum Necessary to accomplish the task for which you will need the information.

- De-identification of Confidential Information. Other requirement relating to uses and disclosures of PHI include health information that does not identify an individual or leaves no reasonable basis to believe that the information can be used to identify an individual. This "de-identified" information is no longer individually identifiable health information (IIHI). Most providers will never have the need to de-identify patient information, and the requirements for de-identifying PHI are lengthy. The regulations give specific directions on how to ensure all pieces of necessary information are removed to fit the definition. De-identified information is not subject to the privacy regulations because it does not specifically identify an individual.
- Marketing. When communicating about a product or service, the goal is to encourage patients to purchase or use the product or service. For instance, a dermatologist may advertise for a discount on facial cream when you schedule a dermabrasion treatment. You will likely not be involved in marketing, but keep in mind the general rule that PHI (including names and addresses) cannot be used for marketing purposes without specific authorization of the patient. Sending appointment reminders and general news updates about your organization and the services you provide would not be considered marketing and would not require patient authorization.
- Fundraising. Again, you will likely not be involved in fundraising activities, but HIPAA allows demographic information and dates of care to be used for fundraising purposes without patient authorization. The disclosure of any additional information requires patient authorization. Your organization's NPP will state that patients may receive fundraising materials and are given the opportunity to opt out of receiving future solicitations.

native location. For example, a patient may ask that the health care provider call the patient at work rather than at the residence, or patients may request that their test results be sent to them in writing rather than by telephone. It is the patient's right to request such alternative methods of communication, and the health care office must accommodate reasonable requests. This can become a serious issue, especially in cases of domestic violence when the individual is at risk for physical harm within the home environment. The patient does not need to explain the reason for the request. The health care office must have a process in place both to evaluate requests and appeals and to respond to the patient.

Patients may be required by the office to make their request in writing. Documenting such requests in writing with the patient's signature is an effective way to protect the practice's compliance endeavors. The office may even condition the agreement by arranging for payment of any additional costs from the patient that the request has created. For example, the patient asks that all correspondence be sent by registered mail; this request may be able to be honored without significant additional staff time but the patient should expect to incur the actual additional mailing costs.

Right to Access, Inspect, and Obtain PHI

A patient has the right to access, inspect, and obtain a copy of his or her confidential health information. Privacy regulations allow the provider to require the patient make the request for access in writing. Generally, a request must be acted on within 30 days. A reasonable, cost-based fee for copies of PHI may only include the costs for the following:

❏ Supplies and labor for copying
❏ Postage when mailed
❏ Preparing a summary of the PHI if the patient has agreed to this instead of complete access

This "fee" for copying varies widely by state and each provider should be aware of the state allowances and conform their fee to that which gives most relief to the patient. The HIPAA-determined fee applies only to fees for copies to patients and not copies for other required or allowed disclosures, such as subpoenas. The fee structures for other disclosures are often set by state law. If you are a staff member involved in applying fees for copying, you should seek guidance from your PO.

Under HIPAA Privacy Regulation, patients do not have the right to access the following:

❏ Psychotherapy notes
❏ Information compiled in reasonable anticipation of, or for use in, legal proceedings
❏ Information exempted from disclosure under the Clinical Laboratory Improvements Amendment (CLIA)

The office may deny patient access for the above reasons without giving the patient the right to review the denial. Also, if the PHI was obtained from an individual other than a health care provider under a promise of confidentiality, access may be denied if such access would likely reveal the identity of the source. Other circumstances in which an individual may be denied access will be detailed in the practice's policy manual.

If the health care provider has determined that the patient would be endangered (or cause danger to another person) from accessing the confidential health information, access may be denied. In this case, the patient has the right to have the denial reviewed by another licensed professional who did not participate in the initial denial decision.

Regarding psychotherapy notes, HIPAA gives special protection to PHI. Disclosure of a patient's mental health records requires specific patient permission. This means that when an insurance payer requests the health records to review the claim, a patient authorization is required.

Certain clinical data are excluded from the definition of psychotherapy notes. In other words, when an individual is utilizing the services of a mental health professional, not all information gathered and recorded in the health record of the mental health provider is considered psychotherapy notes. The law lists specific items that are excluded from such notes:

❏ Medication prescription and monitoring
❏ Counseling session start and stop times
❏ Modalities and frequencies of treatment furnished
❏ Results of clinical tests
❏ Any summary of the following items: diagnosis, functional status, treatment plan, symptoms, prognosis, and progress to date

In general, the major difference between what are and what are not considered psychotherapy notes is the information that is the recorded (in any manner) documentation and/or analysis of conversation. This information should also be kept separate from the medical section of the patient health record to be distinguished as psychotherapy notes. For example, Jane Doe tells her psychologist the details of her childhood trauma. The documented conversation specific to her trauma (e.g., what occurred, how she felt) is considered the psychotherapy notes and cannot be released without specific permission from Jane Doe.

It is important also to understand that patients do not have the right to obtain a copy of psychotherapy notes under HIPAA. However, the treating mental health provider may decide when a patient may obtain access to this health information.

State law must always be considered. Some states allow patients access to their psychotherapy notes; therefore state law would take precedence over HIPAA as a result of the state preemption allowance.

Right to Request Amendment of PHI

Patients have the right to request that their PHI be amended. As with the other requests, the provider may require the request be in writing. The provider must have a process to accept and review both the request and any appeal in a timely fashion. The health care provider may deny this request in the following circumstances:

❏ The provider who is being requested to change the PHI is not the creator of the information (e.g., office has records sent by referring physician).
❏ The PHI is believed to be accurate and complete as it stands in the provider's records.
❏ The information is not required to be accessible to the patient (see Right to Access, Inspect, and Obtain PHI).

Generally, the office must respond to a patient's request for amendment within 60 days. If a request is denied, the patient must be informed in writing of the reason for the denial. The patient must also be given the opportunity to file a statement of disagreement. These rules are complex in regard to steps of appeal, rebuttal, and documentation that must be provided if a request for amendment is denied. The PO will instruct providers on additional responsibilities if they are directly involved in this process.

Right to Receive an Accounting of Disclosures of PHI

Providers should maintain a log of disclosures of PHI, either on paper or within the organization's computer system, of all disclosures other than those made for TPO, facility directories, and some national security and law enforcement agencies.

The process for providing an accounting should be outlined in the practice's policy manual. Patients may request an accounting (or tracking) of disclosures of their confidential information and are granted the right to receive this accounting once a year without charge. Additional accountings may be assessed a cost-based fee.

These accountings were required to start on April 14, 2003, when privacy regulations became enforceable. Items to be documented must include the following:

❏ Date of disclosure
❏ Name of the entity or person who received the PHI, including their address, if known
❏ Brief description of the PHI disclosed
❏ Brief statement of the purpose of the disclosure

The patient is entitled to one accounting per year free of charge. Additional accountings may be assessed a cost-based fee.

Verification of Identity and Authority

Before any disclosure, you must verify the identity of persons requesting PHI if they are unknown to you. You may request identifying information such as date of birth, Social Security number, or even a code word stored in your practice management system that is unique to each patient. Public officials may show you badges, credentials, official letterheads, and other legal documents of authority for identification purposes.

Additionally, you must verify that the requestor has the right and the need to have the PHI.

Exercising professional judgment will fulfill your verification requirements for most disclosures because you are acting on "good faith" in believing the identity of the individual requesting PHI. It is good practice, when making any disclosure to note, to note the "authority" of the person receiving the PHI and how this was determined. This evidence of due diligence on your part would enforce a needed structure on your staff and dampen any complaints that might arise.

Validating Patient Permission

Before making any uses or disclosures of confidential health information other than for the purposes of TPO, your office must have appropriate patient permission. Always check for conflicts between various permissions your office may have on file for a given patient. This information should be maintained either in your practice management system or in the medical chart, where it can be easily identified and retrieved.

For example, if a covered entity has agreed to a patient's request to limit how much of the PHI is sent to a consulting physician for treatment, but then received the patient's authorization to disclose the entire medical record to that physician, this would be a conflict. In general, the more restrictive permission would be the deciding factor. Privacy regulations allow resolving conflicting permissions by either obtaining new permission from the patient or by communicating orally or in writing with the patient to determine the patient's preference. Be sure to document any form of communication in writing.

Guidelines for HIPAA Privacy Compliance

As a medical professional, you will likely answer the telephone and speak during the course of your business, and there will be questions about what you can and cannot say. Reasonable and appropriate safeguards must be taken to ensure that all confidential health information in your office is protected from unauthorized and inappropriate access, including both verbal and written forms.

Some of the following situations may be referred to as incidental disclosures, and this topic is discussed in further detail with additional examples later in this appendix.

1. Consider that conversations occurring throughout the office could be overheard. The reception area and waiting room are often linked, and it is easy to hear the scheduling of appointments and exchange of confidential information. It is necessary to observe areas and maximize efforts to avoid unauthorized disclosures. Simple and affordable precautions include using privacy glass at the front desk and having conversations away from settings where other patients or visitors are present. Health care providers can move their dictation stations away from patient areas or wait until no patients are present before dictating. Telephone conversations by providers in front of patients, even in emergency situations, should be avoided. Providers and staff must use their best professional judgment.

2. Be sure to check in the patient medical record and in your computer system to determine whether there are any special instructions for contacting the patient regarding scheduling or reporting test results. Follow these requests as agreed by the office.

3. Patient sign-in sheets are permissible, but limit the information you request when a patient signs in, and change it periodically during the day. A sign-in sheet must not contain information such as reason for visit or the patient's medical condition because some providers specialize in treating patients with sensitive issues. Thus showing that a particular individual has an appointment with your practice may pose a breach of patient confidentiality.

4. Make sure you have patients sign a form acknowledging receipt of the NPP. The NPP allows you to release the patient's confidential information for billing and other purposes. If your practice has other confidentiality statements and policies besides HIPAA mandates, these must be reviewed to ensure they meet HIPAA requirements.

5. Formal policies for transferring and accepting outside PHI must address how your office keeps this information confidential. When using courier services, billing services, transcription services, or e-mail, you must ensure that transferring PHI is done in a secure and compliant manner.

6. Computers are used for a variety of administrative functions, including scheduling, billing, and managing medical records. Computers typically are present at the reception area. Keep the computer screen turned so that viewing is restricted to authorized staff. Screen savers should be used to prevent unauthorized viewing or access. The computer should automatically log off the user after a period of being idle, requiring the staff member to reenter his or her password.

7. Keep your user name and password confidential, and change them often. Do not share this information. An authorized staff member such as the PO will have administrative access to reset your password if you lose it or if someone discovers it. Also, practice management software can track users and follow their activity. Do not set yourself up by giving out your password. Safeguards include password protection for electronic data and storing paper records securely.

8. Safeguard your work area; do not place notes with confidential information in areas that are easy to view by nonstaff. Cleaning services will access your building, usually after

Appendix B

OSHA/Bloodborne Pathogens

Student Objectives:

Upon completion of the lecture presentation, students will be able to:

- ☐ Understand the scope and purpose of OSHA regulations
- ☐ Identify required personal protective equipment
- ☐ Understand how to prevent needlestick injury
- ☐ Understand how to document occupational exposure
- ☐ Identify potentially infectious materials
- ☐ Identify bloodborne diseases and the symptoms they produce
- ☐ Understand what constitutes regulated waste
- ☐ Understand an exposure control plan
- ☐ Identify work practice controls
- ☐ Identify engineering practice controls
- ☐ Understand what is required for post-exposure incidents

Introduction

OSHA is the branch of the U.S. Department of Labor that protects employees in the health care field. The primary purpose of OSHA is to enforce procedures that limit the employees who are at risk for exposure to bloodborne pathogens. The standards are clearly written and the rules apply to all health care facilities where the risk of occupational exposure to bloodborne pathogens or other potentially infectious materials exists.

Lecture

I. OSHA—Occupational Safety and Health Administration

A. A federal agency that regulates occupational exposure to bloodborne pathogens and other potentially infectious materials
B. OSHA sets standards that are designed to reduce or eliminate the risk of exposure, and are required by law to be followed.
C. Also regulates safety for other fields of employment, such as construction

II. Definitions
A. Bloodborne pathogens—pathogenic microorganisms that are present in human blood and can cause disease in humans. These pathogens include, but are not limited to, HBV (hepatitis B virus) and HIV (human immunodeficiency virus).
B. Contaminated—the presence or the reasonable anticipated presence of blood or other potentially infectious materials on an item or surface
C. Contaminated laundry—laundry that has been soiled with blood or other potentially infectious materials or that may contain sharps
D. Decontamination—the use of physical or chemical means to remove, inactivate, or destroy bloodborne pathogens on a surface or item to the point where they are no longer capable of transmitting infectious particles and the surface or item is rendered safe for handling, use, or disposal
E. Engineering controls—means of eliminating or minimizing exposure in the workplace. Structural or mechanical devices that are designed to isolate or remove bloodborne pathogen hazards from the workplace. Examples are handwashing facilities, eye wash stations, sharps containers, and biohazard signs.

F. Exposure incident—specific eye, mouth, mucous membrane, non-intact skin, or parenteral contact with blood or other infectious materials that results from the performance of an employee's duties

G. Occupational exposure—skin, eye, mucous membrane, or parenteral contact with blood or other potentially infectious materials that results from the performance of an employee's duties

H. Other potentially infectious materials—these are defined by OSHA as being the following:
   1. Human body fluids including:
      a. Urine
      b. Stool
      c. Saliva or sputum
      d. Semen
      e. Vaginal secretions
      f. Cerebrospinal fluid
      g. Synovial fluid
      h. Pleural fluid
      i. Pericardial fluid
      j. Amniotic fluid
      k. Any body fluid that is visibly contaminated with blood
      l. All body fluids that are difficult or impossible to differentiate
   2. Any unfixed tissue or organ from a human (living or deceased)

III. Bloodborne pathogens—disease-producing microorganisms present in the blood that can cause disease in humans. The following are the most prevalent pathogens:
A. Hepatitis B virus (HBV)—major cause of viral hepatitis
   1. Preventable with immunization
   2. Symptoms include swelling, soreness, loss of liver function, and jaundice of skin and mucous membranes.
   3. May cause no symptoms and therefore not be diagnosed
   4. Infected person's blood will test positive for HBV within 2 to 6 weeks after symptoms appear.
   5. 85% of infected persons recover in 6 to 8 weeks, but their blood will always be positive for the HBV surface antibody, and they are often chronic carriers and can still transmit the disease to others.
   6. Approximately 12,000 health care workers contract HBV each year, and at least 220 per year will die.
   7. Rate of infection after a needlestick exposure is an average of 18%.

B. Human immunodeficiency virus (HIV)—virus infects the T4 white blood cells of the immune system, which become ineffective
   1. There is no immunization available for HIV.
   2. Symptoms include night sweats, weight loss, fever, fatigue, glandular pain or swelling, muscular pain, or joint pain. Patients frequently acquire secondary respiratory infection.
   3. Infected persons may carry the virus for 8 to 10 years before symptoms begin to develop. However, such persons are still able to spread the disease.
   4. May take up to 1 year for HIV antibodies to test positive; therefore, a test for HIV may be negative even if the patient is actually HIV positive
   5. 1 in 250 people in the United States is infected.
   6. Of exposed health care workers, 145 in 1,000 will become seropositive.
   7. Needlestick is the #1 source of occupationally acquired HIV in hospitals.

C. Other bloodborne pathogens include hepatitis A virus, hepatitis C virus, human T-cell lymphotropic virus types I and II, syphilis, malaria, babesiosis, and Colorado tick fever.

D. Portals of entry—the following are possible routes of infection with bloodborne pathogens and other potentially infectious materials
   1. Direct contact
      a. Percutaneous incidences such as needlesticks, scalpel cuts, and other sharps injuries
      b. Non-intact skin contact such as wounds, scratches, abrasions, burns, and hangnails
      c. Nasal mucous membranes from splashing or rubbing
      d. Conjunctiva from being rubbed or sprayed into the eye
   2. Indirect contact
      a. Telephones, test tubes, lab instruments
      b. Nail biting, smoking, eating, and contact lens manipulation
      c. Airborne transmission

3. Viral survival is much longer than previously believed.
   a. HBV may be stable in dried blood and blood products for at least 7 days.
   b. HIV has been detected for 1 to 3 days after drying—longer if frozen.
   c. HIV has been detected in tissue culture fluid at room temperature for up to 15 days.
   d. Beware of quality control products manufactured from human products.

IV. Prevention techniques—to prevent and reduce occupational exposure, use precautions, engineering practice controls, work practice controls, and personal protective equipment (PPE).

1. Universal Precautions—OSHA requires Universal Precautions be observed to prevent contact with blood of OPIM.
   a. Under circumstances in which differentiation between body fluid types is difficult or impossible, all body fluids are to be considered potentially infectious materials.

2. Engineering and work practice controls must be used to eliminate or minimize employee exposure. Where occupational exposure remains after the institution of these controls, personal protective equipment must also be used.
   a. Engineering controls are structural and mechanical devices such as handwashing facilities, eyewash stations, safe medical devices, sharps containers, and biohazard signs.
   b. Work practice controls are behaviors intended to make engineering controls effective, such as using sharps containers, handwashing, waste removal, and Universal Precautions.
   c. Employers must provide handwashing facilities which are readily accessible to employees. When handwashing facilities are not feasible, the employer must provide antiseptic towelettes or an appropriate hand cleanser in conjunction with clean cloths/paper towels. When hand cleansers or towelettes are used, hands need to be washed as soon as possible with soap and running water.
   d. Handwashing must be done with soap and water immediately in the following situations:
      i. Visible contamination
      ii. Before putting gloves on and after removing them
      iii. Between each patient
      iv. After handling and collecting lab specimens and collection containers
      v. Before leaving the immediate work area, such as lab or exam room
      vi. Whenever gloves or PPE are removed
      vii. Before and after eating, drinking, applying makeup, changing or manipulating contact lenses, and using the restroom
      viii. Before all other activities involving hand contact with mucous membranes, eyes, or breaks in the skin
   e. Do not bend, recap, or break needles. (Recapping is allowed only when the employer can demonstrate that there is no feasible alternative. In these instances, a mechanical device or a one-handed method must be used.) Do not remove needles from the syringe.
   f. Employers are required to provide "Sharps with Engineered Sharps Injury Protections," as of April 18, 2001. This phrase encompasses a broad array of medical devices that make injury involving a contaminated sharp less likely, and includes, but is not limited to, the following:
      i. Syringes with a sliding sheath that shields the attached needle after use
      ii. Needles that retract into a syringe after use
      iii. Shielded or retracting catheters used to access the bloodstream for intravenous administration of medication or fluids

iv. Intravenous medication delivery systems that administer medication or fluids through a catheter port or connector site using a needle that is housed in a protective covering

g. After use, contaminated needles and other sharps must be placed in an approved, puncture-resistant, leak-proof, disposable container bearing the appropriate color-coded biohazard label. Containers must be:
   i. Conveniently located
   ii. Discarded when they are two-thirds full, and not reopened after they have been closed
   iii. Maintained upright and replaced routinely

h. There is no national policy on waste removal, so state, city, and county ordinances must be followed. Biohazardous waste removal is usually arranged through contractual agreement with an outside agency.
   i. Full, closed sharps containers must be placed into a second container and properly sealed and clearly labeled "Biohazard" prior to being transported from the medical facility.

i. Eating, drinking, smoking, applying cosmetics or lip balm, and handling contact lenses are prohibited in work areas where there is a reasonable likelihood of occupational exposure.

j. Food and drink shall not be kept in refrigerators, freezers, shelves, cabinets, or on countertops where blood or OPIM are present.

k. Equipment which may become contaminated with blood or OPIM shall be examined prior to servicing or shipping and shall be decontaminated as necessary, unless an employer can demonstrate that decontamination of such equipment or portions of the equipment is not feasible.
   i. The employer must inform all affected employees, servicing representatives, and/or manufacturers as appropriate.

3. Personal Protective Equipment (PPE)—PPE must be worn in every situation in which contact with blood or OPIM may be reasonably anticipated to occur. PPE is considered appropriate only if it does not permit blood or other OPIMs to pass through to reach the employee's clothes, skin, mucous membranes, eyes, or mouth and is OSHA approved. Employers must provide, at no cost to the employee, all employees with appropriate PPE which includes, but is not limited to, the following:
   a. Gloves
      i Must be fresh and free from cracks, discolorations, punctures, or other defects
      ii. Must be made of vinyl or latex, fit snugly, and be placed over the sleeve cuff so that no skin is exposed
      iii. Disposable gloves are not to be washed or decontaminated for reuse.
      iv. Utility gloves may be washed and decontaminated for reuse if the integrity is not compromised.
   b. Gowns and laboratory coats
      i. Must be fluid-impervious and worn during any procedure or task in which contamination is possible
      ii. The type and characteristics of protective body clothing will depend upon the task and degree of anticipated exposure.
      iii. Surgical caps, hood, and/or shoe coverings must be worn when gross contamination is anticipated.
   c. Face shields or masks
      i. When face shields or masks are provided to avoid sprays and splashes, eye protection must also be worn.
      ii. Must be disposable, single-use products
   d. Eye protection
      i. Must protect from all directions, not just straight on
      ii. Goggles must be decontaminated after use.

iii. Prescription eye protection must be provided, when necessary, to an employee.

e. Mouthpieces and resuscitation devices

   i. Mechanical respiratory-assist devices and CPR face shields must be worn to minimize the transmission of OPIM that may be present in saliva.

   ii. Disposable mouthpieces should be available for use in areas in which the need for resuscitation is predictable.

   iii. Mouth pipetting of blood and other body fluids is prohibited.

V. Exposure Control Plan—Each employer having an employee(s) with occupational exposure to bloodborne pathogens and OPIM must establish a written Exposure Control Plan to design, eliminate, or minimize employee exposure. This plan must be reviewed annually and include the following:

A. Exposure determination

   1. A list of all job classifications in which all or some employees in those classifications have occupational exposure

   2. A list of all tasks and procedures in which occupational exposure occurs

B. Methods of compliance—The schedule and method of implementation for use of engineering and work practice controls by employees and:

   1. Dates of training for employee use of PPE

   2. Documentation that employees who have had a change in job tasks have been trained in their new classification

C. Hepatitis B vaccination and post-exposure evaluation and follow-up guidelines

D. Communication hazards to employees

E. Recordkeeping of all OSHA standards, and the implementation of them in the medical facility

VI. Vaccination

A. Hepatitis B vaccination must be made available to each employee, at no cost to the employee, who has occupational exposure to blood or OPIM.

B. The employee may refuse the vaccination series; however, he/she must sign a hepatitis B declination form. This form must be placed in the Exposure Control Plan. The employee may later change his/her mind and receive the vaccine at no charge.

C. HBV vaccination is a series of 3 injections over a 6-month period. Immunity should be verified after the series, as only 87% of those who receive the series become immune. Documentation of this immunity must be kept in the Exposure Control Plan.

VII. Post-exposure Evaluation and Follow-up

A. Occupational exposure by direct contact with blood or OPIM must be reported to the employer (e.g., needlestick, laceration, splash).

B. Following a report of the exposure incident, the employer shall make available to the employee a confidential medical evaluation (by physician or facility of the employee's choice) and follow up including the following elements:

   1. Documentation of the route(s) of exposure, and the circumstances under which the exposure incident occurred

   2. Identification of the source individual, unless the employer can establish that the identification is infeasible or prohibited by state or local law

      a. Source individual's blood will be tested as soon as possible and after consent is obtained to determine HBV and HIV status. If consent is not obtained, the employer shall establish that legally required consent cannot be obtained. When the source individual's consent is not required by law, the blood, if available, will be tested and results documented.

      b. When the source individual is already known to be infected with HBV or HIV, testing does not need to be repeated.

      c. Results of this testing must be made available to the exposed employee.

   3. Collection and testing of the exposed employee's blood for HBV and HIV status

      a. Blood shall be collected and tested as soon as possible, and after consent is obtained.

b. If the employee consents to baseline blood collection, and not to testing, the blood will be held for 90 days. The employee may decide to have testing during that time.

4. Post-exposure prophylaxis, when medically indicated
5. Counseling
6. Evaluation of a reported illness if obtained

VIII. Information and Training

A. Employers must ensure that all employees with occupational exposure participate in a training program for bloodborne pathogen standards, at no cost to the employee.

1. This training must be provided within 90 days of employment and repeated annually.
2. Training must include the following:
   a. An accessible copy of the OSHA Bloodborne Regulatory Text 1910.1030
   b. A general explanation of the epidemiology and symptoms of bloodborne diseases
   c. An explanation of the modes of transmission of bloodborne pathogens
   d. An explanation of the employer's Exposure Control Plan
   e. An explanation of the appropriate methods for recognizing tasks and other activities that may involve exposure to blood and OPIM
   f. An explanation of the use and limitations of methods that will prevent or reduce exposure, including engineering controls, work practices, and personal protective equipment
   g. Information on the types, proper use, location, removal, handling, decontamination and disposal of personal protective equipment
   h. Information on the HBV vaccine
   i. Information on the appropriate actions to take and the persons to contact in the event of an exposure incident
   j. An explanation of the procedure to follow in an exposure incident, and the medical follow-up that will be made available
   k. Information on post-exposure evaluation and follow-up that the employer is required to provide for the employee following occupational exposure

Review Questions

1. What are the most prevalent bloodborne pathogens among health care workers?
2. What is OPIM?
3. What is the survival time of HBV and HIV on surfaces?
4. What are Universal Precautions?
5. What are five common engineering practice controls used in a medical facility?
6. What are work practice controls?
7. What is PPE?
8. What is exposure determination?
9. What is an Exposure Control Plan?
10. Describe post-exposure follow-up.

Appendix C

Acknowledgments

CORINTHIAN
COLLEGES, INC.

Receipt of Handbook

Date: _____

To: All Allied Health Students

Subject: Acknowledgment

I have received a copy of the Student Handbook.

_____   _____
Print Name Here   Date

_____
Signature

Student Verification of HIPAA Training Curriculum Content

Student Name

_____

Last   First   Middle Initial

Date of Birth: _____   Social Security Number: _____

Profession for Which Student Is Training: _____

This form certifies that the above named participant has successfully completed the required HIPAA (Health Insurance Portability and Accountability Act) training. Additionally, the student has passed a HIPAA exam based on this material, with a score of 70% or higher. This test has been placed in the student's permanent academic file.

Date of HIPAA Training: _____

I certify that the above individual has been presented with the HIPAA handout. The student has read the handout and agrees to comply with all requirements.

Instructor Name: _____
Title: _____

![CCi CORINTHIAN COLLEGES, INC.]

School/Program: _____
Date of Verification: _____

OSHA Protective Practices

Date: _____

To: All Allied Health Students

Subject: OSHA Blood / Airborne Pathogens Protective Practices

The attached handout is required reading for all Allied Health students. If any student does not understand the material, he/she should ask the instructor for clarification.

The instructors have presented this material as well as shown the film.

I have received the OSHA Blood / Airborne Pathogens handout. I have read the handout and will comply with all requirements.

_____   _____

Print Name Here   Date

_____

Signature